The Crazy Mirror

DURGNAT, Raymond. **The crazy mirror; Hollywood comedy and the American image.** Horizon, 1970 (c1969). 280p il bibl filmography 76-114309. 7.50.   SBN 8180-0701-X

Studying the ways Hollywood comedy reflects and refracts images of American society, Durgnat discusses both major and minor film makers, ranging from Sennett through sophisticated directors like Lubitsch and Sturges all the way to Jerry Lewis. The result sheds new light on individual films, on the development of comic types and techniques, and on the always complex relations between art and society. For Durgnat is that rarity among film scholars who is able to intertwine film criticism and social history meaningfully, treating neither films as mere documentation nor history as mere backdrop. His book is the most comprehensive examination of American film comedy yet attempted. Prefaced by a lengthy essay in comic theory, strengthened by its annotated bibliography and careful index, it is necessary for libraries with even a minimal film collection.

CHOICE   *JAN. '71*
Speech, Theater & Dance

n d C
aiff pub
Faber 1969

by the same author

FILMS AND FEELINGS

*

NOUVELLE VAGUE, THE FIRST DECADE
(*Motion Publications*)

GRETA GARBO (with John Kobal)

LUIS BUNUEL

FRANJU
(*Studio-Vista*)

THE MARX BROTHERS
(*Osterreichisches Filmmuseum*)

EROS IN THE CINEMA
(*Calder and Boyars*)

The Crazy Mirror

Hollywood Comedy and the American Image

RAYMOND DURGNAT

HORIZON PRESS
New York

First American Edition 1970
Published by Horizon Press, New York
Library of Congress Catalog Card Number 76–114309
Printed in Great Britain
by Latimer Trend & Co Ltd Plymouth
All rights reserved

SBN 8180–0701–X

© *1969 by Raymond Durgnat*

Acknowledgements

Several sections are based on a Postgraduate research thesis prepared under the auspices of the Department of Film at the Slade School of Fine Art, University College, in 1960–1, and printed in *Films and Filming* between July 1965 and January 1966. The chapter on the Marx Brothers is a part of the monograph prepared at the request of the Austrian Film Museum and published for their Marx Brothers retrospective in 1966.

My thanks are due to Professor Thorold Dickinson, Sir William Coldstream and Peter Baker, editor of *Films and Filming*, for leaving me the reprint rights of material prepared in the first place for them.

Most of the photographs were very kindly provided by John Kobal from his collection, and credit is due to Universal, Paramount, Columbia, 20th-Century-Fox, United Artists, M.G.M. and Barrie Pattison. And I must particularly thank Miss Vivienne Ward for typing the manuscript.

The words of the song 'Well, Did You Ever?', from *High Society*, are published by and copyright of Chappell & Co. Inc., New York.

Contents

PART THREE—**Who's Afraid of the Big Bad Wolf?**

PART FOUR—**Kiss the Boys Good-bye**

PART FIVE—**And Therefore Take the Present Time**

Illustrations

11

Foreword

The Crazy Mirror offers, not so much a history of the Hollywood comedy, as an attempt to explain some of its crazy images.

Caliban raged when he saw his own face in the glass. The moviegoer just laughs as he strolls through the cinema's distorting mirrors. But as he laughs, he may also spot a familiar face.

People who have enjoyed the films mentioned may find some pleasant memories refreshed, and enjoy comparing the author's interpretations with their own. After seeing a film through one's own eyes, it's intriguing to see it again through someone else's. It's almost as refreshing as seeing a different film. But as it's the same film, a lively set of discrepancies can arise—those little discrepancies which turn a flat image into a three-dimensional one. Reading is discussing.

The book originated in an essay on slapstick, written to follow up the feeling that slapstick comedies weren't only comic, and poetic, but reflected some tensions in American society more accurately than one might expect. This essay was serialized in *Films and Filming*, and its final point was that the 50's saw a merger of slapstick, sophisticated comedy and satire. So there seemed something to be said for expanding the earlier chapters to take in the whole field of comedy.

This softened the knotty question of deciding just when a comedy ought to be classified as slapstick, although it introduced a new one, of when comedy becomes drama. Musicals have been excluded in favour of cartoons. It's true that the question of when a comedy with a few musical numbers becomes a musical comedy is more arbitrary than the question of when a photographed film becomes a cartoon; but cartoons go back through silent days and so afford a better continuity. I have also excluded such fantasies as *Alice In Wonderland*,

The Wizard Of Oz and, with particular regrets, *The 5000 Fingers Of Dr. T.*

Regrettable omissions are inevitable, and not all of them are due to pressure of space, though this has been considerable. Many omissions, possibly the most serious, are due to nothing other than the author's ignorance. Research problems, and consequent omissions, bulk largely in almost all movie writing; as, notably, Andrew Sarris, Kevin Brownlow and Philip Jenkinson have repeatedly demonstrated. It's now clear that movie history is as mysterious as any iceberg. Some of the major movies are currently visible; some exist in archives but to see them all would be a major research project involving university funds which are rarely made available for the insignificant mass media; many others were dismissed when they appeared, and have never been revalued since.

It would be pleasant to be in a position to answer some of the research problems indicated here; to have seen, for example, more of those cheap, hectic, cynical comedies of the early 30's. But even a map with white spaces clearly marked 'terra incognita' may be not altogether useless. In fact one's misgivings, that one shouldn't write this book yet, are soon countered by the reflection that even an incomplete one may stimulate, and offer an alternative set of guidelines for, what is really needed, a collective research effort, and a controversy, sustained over years. Meanwhile, one can at least hope that what this book points to is so interesting that its omissions are utterly infuriating. But half an *hors-d'œuvre* is better than no banquet. And each generation has its own perspectives into the past, as well as into the present and future.

So far as social history is concerned, this study restricts itself to the kind of general reference found in, notably, Lewis Jacob's *The Rise of the American Film* and Siegfried Kracauer's *From Caligari To Hitler*. As Hitchcock remarked, no film-maker expects his movie to fit exactly every one of America's infinite variety of subcultures and racial groups. He works to a kind of common denominator, to a relevant and effective average, artificial as it may be, and the critic is justified in working in the same way. Obviously our interest is in explaining trends in movies, and no claim is made that we do justice to the complexities of a cultural history of the U.S.A.

Not that it's easy for the cinema tourist to know when to trust Hollywood, when to denounce it. Indeed, intriguing cultural titbits are often presented so casually as to almost slide past notice. Many a European spectator might well raise his eyebrows when, in *Kiss Me Stupid*, husband and wife, deciding to make love, rush off, each into his own shower, while, in *Rally Round The Flag, Boys*, a wife ogles her husband with the proposition, 'Will you use the shower first, or shall I?' Not only are Europeans (a section of the middle classes apart) more tactile than our American cousins, we are also more olfactory, it would seem.

Hollywood is, in some ways, more accurate than it is often given credit for, particularly by critics in the old 'documentary' tradition, and by those critics, American as well as European, who forget that Americans don't always subscribe to British, or Bostonian, norms. Hollywood's moral, stylistic and cultural assumptions are really a kind of 'classicism', and its inaccuracies are a matter, not so much of carelessness or thoughtlessness, as of certain limitations, of decorum, of depth, of wish-fulfilment, which it has imposed on itself, or accepted from without. But, as a result of those limitations, 90 per cent of American movies are set within a 2 per cent income-group, and important subcultures hardly appear at all. After Hollywood, *cinéma-vérité*, and underground movies, aren't just new idioms; they're a new world.

This study attempts to find terms and a tone which get the best of two distinct attitudes to Hollywood (and indeed to movies generally). An older tradition, too drastically, dismisses too many Hollywood movies as insignificant, or, if significant, unconsciously so, and merely symptomatic. A younger generation (including some of the present writer's most gifted contemporaries, from the *Movie* circle) have suggested that movies ought to be judged only within their own terms, and that the accuracy or validity of those terms is no business of the movie critic's. The assumption behind this book is that a movie critic is anyone who says anything interesting about movies, including the validity or otherwise of the terms they set themselves. It's relevant to reveal myths as only myths—and to improve our myths about myths.

The analysis of individual films is more detailed than it can be in Jacobs's astute, but more general, history; and it's less preoccupied with depth psychology than Kracauer's brilliantly intuitive tome.

By throwing some light on the movies, we may also throw some light on the mass media generally—not only in demonstrating that their content is determined by the dialectic of, or compromise between, realism and daydream (so that it's never enough to see Hollywood as simply a dream factory), but also in exploring the constantly shifting balance-points between the two.

Our remarks on the escapist evasions of these comedies may seem at times to imply the belief that the only worthwhile function of art is to mirror social reality exactly—or at least to bring the book very close to this critical tradition. In fact the starting point for these criticisms is rather different; the concern being that movies should, where possible, sharpen, rather than blunt, people's awareness of their inner experiences, as of the world around. Nor do I assume that the tensions between art and entertainment are not real ones; only if we admit that they are can we find better ways of reconciling the two functions. But even if Hollywood comedy doesn't offer a shining example of artistic realism, it emerges well, on both artistic and realistic grounds, from comparison with, say, English drama, from Elizabethan times right down to the mid-50's.

Part One

JOKES AND HOW TO SPOT THEM

1 · Custard Pies with a Message

It's something of a paradox if words like 'mad' and 'crazy' have become critical terms of the highest praise. It's as if we feel that comedy's higher lunacy is a salutary kickback by that disreputable thing, human nature, against a too-well-ordered world. Indeed, its connections with childishness and irresponsibility highlight certain facets of human nature and experience more startlingly than drama.

This survey takes a closer look at the images of society offered in the crazy mirror of Hollywood comedy. Since it's human nature to deceive ourselves about society and our plight in it, comedy's distorting mirror, by a kind of double distortion, sometimes puts things right. At least it breaks the frames of reference, and many a King, including King Lear, would have done well to heed the words of his Fool. Our purpose isn't to solemnize humour, to explain it away, but, on the contrary, to enhance its excitement and spice, to sharpen its cutting edge. There's nothing like danger to multiply mirth by itself. The danger is that of spiritual self-liberation, and perhaps that's the most dangerous thing there is.

But what distinguishes the dramatic from the comic? How does one shade into the other?

2 · The Emotional Anatomy of a Gag

Comedy is drama with a kink. We speak of drama as 'straight', and so imply that comedy is crooked, a matter of hooks, crochets, zig-zags, feints, double-bluffs and double-crosses. Comedy feels like drama with little convulsions of incongruous surprise, little looping-the-loops of surprise, confusion, hysteria.

Timing is particularly important in comedy, which often depends on surprise. The characteristic response to a dramatic climax or a twist in suspense is suddenly indrawn breath—a gasp. In laughter, held breath is rowdily expelled in a de-gasp. Audacious jokes produce a little gasp followed by a sustained bellow. Others, though in them-selves inoffensive, seem to tap, or trigger, reservoirs of perplexity be-neath our minds, and we get confused between gasp and bellow, eventually capsizing into the happy hysteria of wheezing, weeping, hiccoughing and so on.

Comedy often employs exaggeration. The funny moustaches, the big boots with floppy toes, the bandy-legged gait, the comedian's paroxysms of fright, reassure us that it's all unreal, that it's not really happening, that if it were it could only happen to inconsiderable be-ings far inferior to us. So, instead of taking it seriously, we can relax and laugh instead.

Again, comedy is often described as depending on detachment, whereas drama depends on identification. And it's true that if I slip on a banana-skin, I consider that to be dramatic, even tragic, whereas if you slip on a banana-skin I find that highly comic, and criticize your sense of humour in not seeing the funny side. And you return the compliment when I slip up.

Often, too, comedy is connected with feelings of superiority, not infrequently screwed up to the pitch of cruelty. Comfortably seated in our cinema seats, we laugh with harsh complacency at the mishaps befalling the unfortunate comedians on the silver screen. We might spot the odd tinge of their inferiorities in ourselves but our trousers are never quite as baggy, our bowlers never quite as battered, our apprehensions never quite plunge us into their panicky paroxysms. So we can mock them. In fact, the argument runs, every laugh has a sadistic lining.

Yet, of these helpful explanations, none fits all the facts about our fits of mirth.

Comedy may use surprise, but surprise by itself explains little about mirth. Thrillers are full of surprises, which cause, not laughter, but disappointment, horror, or awe. And laughter can be doubled or tripled by expectation, suspense, and, afterwards, a kind of savouring, that is to say, by diluting the element of surprise. The entertainer's adage, 'Tell 'em you're going to do it, do it, tell 'em you've done it,' applies as much to comedy as to drama. As the veteran director Arthur Ripley commented: 'You can do wonders in a scene by letting the audience in on a secret the character doesn't know, like you show them an open manhole, and then you see Charlie Chaplin walking towards it, innocently swinging his stick.' Thus a typical gag 'shape' is:

1. Charlie approaches an open manhole.
2. Charlie is nearer the open manhole, and about to see it, but he turns to ogle a pretty girl instead.
3. Charlie, lifting his hat, takes a graceful step backward to bow, and falls down the manhole.
4. Dazed, Charlie sits on coke-heap.
5. Girl is mystified as to where he's gone.

Each stage has its laugh, none of which comes from our surprise.

It's certainly true that many jokes aren't funny at a second hearing, but equally, many dramatic films don't stand a second viewing, when novelty and suspense have gone. After all, the better jokes, witticisms and paradoxes, do stand 'savouring', while comedy films certainly stand repeated seeings as well as dramas. It's as if the comic surprise is one special arrangement of ingredients which can equally be arranged so as to be savoured and mulled over. *Alice in Wonderland* is quietly, richly comic over and over again. After uncountable viewings of Chaplin's *The Pawnshop* and *The Adventurer*, I still find them funny. For the profoundly comic is as durable as the beautiful, the true and the good.

The description of comedy as exaggeration fits aspects of farce, but it doesn't seem adequate for sophisticated comedy. Such George Cukor comedies as *Pat and Mike* and *The Marrying Kind* are undoubtedly comedies, but they're not particularly unconvincing or untrue. They're certainly more convincing and true than many dramas. In *The African Queen* and *Saturday Night and Sunday Morning*, we laugh at the characters one moment, and take them with dramatic seriousness the next, or both at once, as when Bogart panics at the leeches peppering his body. Similarly, in real life, we may laugh at our friends, but it's not because we think they're exaggerations of themselves or unreal in any way. We know that they're real people. Indeed satire depends on our knowing that what we're laughing at is typical of real and important people.

And isn't there more to comedy than detachment? We don't go to the cinema to be detached from the screen characters; we go to share their troubles and pleasures, to feel suspense, grief and relief. It may be true that the 'disconnection' between ourselves (in the cinema) from the characters (on the screen) enables us to share their unpleasant feelings pleasurably. Thus 'detachment', far from being peculiar to comedy, is also a condition of drama.

To approach the question from another angle: it's surely not because we're detached from the comic action that we laugh till we choke, or cry, or till our ribs ache, or our sides split, or we laugh ourselves sick, or roll in the aisles, or die laughing. We seem to relish comedy best when it makes us participate to the point of hysteria. Indeed, we have a faint suspicion that laughing constitutes a halfway stage to the laughing house. It's hysterical, crazy, mad, our intellectual stability is altogether fantangled. Indeed, the satirical humour of Swift is clearly steering us towards a whole network of very real and unfunny spiritual crises.

Nor is all laughter superior and cruel. Much of it is kindly and indulgent. We laugh for pleasure, we laugh when things go well or just because we're happy. We laugh *with* people as well as *at* them. When we're profoundly happy, we laugh out loud for no reason at all. A laugh is a vehement smile, and just as natural an expression of kindness as a smile. Certainly, comedy can be as cruel as human nature, and some of it is crueller than it's comfortable to notice. But it is often kindly, often kindly and cruel, together, or kindly precisely

22

because it can paint a scathing picture of man, yet, in the same breath (or gasp) accept and forgive.

So these theories illuminate various aspects and moods of comedy; but presumably something more evasive unites them. Though one cannot really speak of detachment, perhaps we can approach comedy by considering it as drama-with-a-kink, the kink being a particular kind of incongruity of mood. It also has to be a special kind of incongruity, for not all incongruities are comic. Some are romantic. For instance, in Albert Lewin's *Pandora and the Flying Dutchman*, a jazz band plays on a moonlit beach, while ancient statues of pagan Gods and Goddesses stand around—listening? Lovely statues and rasping trombones are incongruous enough, and perhaps we smile, but also it is a dramatic incongruity, creating beauty and longing— comedy in reverse. Incongruity may be sinister, as when in Bunuel's *Viridiana* a crucifix turns out to conceal a flick-knife. We may raise an uneasy titter, but this sort of incongruity is more likely to wipe any stray smile off our faces than to put one on, and we can all think of *tragic* incongruities.

The structures of jokes and anecdotes, of comedies and dramas, are identical—and indeed there is only a blurred frontier between taking things seriously and taking them comically. Reflection blunts some jokes or reveals new comic aspects to other jokes. We often mull over a joke before smiling at it anew. It may take time and thought before we see the funny side of things.

It does seem, though, that comedy operates within certain limits, not of subject-matter so much as of attitude. Every joke is half-serious, has a dramatic undertow, which is its emotional 'mainspring'. To vary our banana-skin saga. If a pompous-looking gent slips on a banana-skin in long-shot, that's a comedy. It's another laugh, if, after he's slipped, we cut in a close-up of his face showing pompous wrath (which also reassures that he's not too badly hurt). But if instead we cut in a close-up of his face showing severe and convincing pain, our laugh is cut off short. We may even feel indignant at the film, both for having given us a nasty shock, and for making us feel we have been thoughtless and heartless.

The differences seem to be on these lines. When the victim slipped in long-shot we didn't identify with him too closely. The event was remote, impersonal, half-way to abstraction. This distant pin-man suddenly lost his dignity and came a calligraphic tumble. The alteration in his method of locomotion, the abrupt loss of dignity, a not-too-strong empathy with his shock, create a little bundle of emotional contradictions. The laugh depends on there being a little shock, and on that being rapidly followed by a reassurance. If there's no reassurance, then we feel concern, and whatever is happening becomes a *dramatic* worry or anguish.

Sometimes, by a farcical unreality of style, the director keeps us reassured that whatever's happening is not to be taken dramatically. In a very schematic way, we can say that the broader the style, the more violent the mishaps that can befall the characters. All's fair in a Mack Sennett comedy, e.g. the Keystone Kops may catapult out of their Ford Model T as it rounds the bend, and fly through the air with the greatest of ease before cannonballing into, say, a pile of bricks. On the other hand, a more realistic comedy may raise laughs by taking something perfectly plausible, but trifling, like, say, the loss of a collar-stud, and showing its characters working themselves into a lather of hypersensitive emotion which in real life we would prefer not to stoop to feel (although, of course, we often have an impulse towards absurd excess). In many films the outrageous and the trifling may be combined, and indeed they set each other off very well—as when a character in a desperate situation is affected only by some very trivial matter. Of course we may laugh even when we are the butts of our own laughter. For example, a little girl may develop a fit of hiccoughing in church, and laugh at her own embarrassment, laugh in an effort to throw off her embarrassment, even though laughter, being incongruous too, only intensifies it, so sending her into the positive feedback of a giggling fit. She isn't being 'cruel' at her own expense. She is exploiting, in an effort to spare herself dramatic embarrassment, a certain balance of shock and reassurance ('perhaps they haven't heard, I can't help it, it's not really harmful, I'm really suffering'). This balance is not the joke's first cause (which is its serious mainspring of dramatic emotion). But it is the condition of the embarrassment being comic as well as dramatic. All the same, her embarrassment is both real and dramatic, she may blush scarlet. For comedy can bear the shock of real emotion—how much it can bear depends on the victim's spiritual resilience.[1]

Too little shock, and a joke is feeble or tame; too much, and it's

---

[1] In cases where hysterical laughter embarrasses the laugher, it's reasonable to suppose, with depth psychology, that her conscious embarrassment is being compensated for by some unconscious pleasure—some sort of triumph over those who embarrass her.

drama. If we sense that someone else is treating what we really feel is tragedy as comedy, then we may well be disgusted at their lack of feeling, experience an extra dramatic shock akin to hatred. Conversely, a sense of humour is often linked with a sense of proportion, with having an emotional resilience which prevents one from feeling too shattered by minor discomfitures. We can turn drama into comedy, even when we are the victims, by taking refuge in a position of *inner* self-assurance, or of wry indifference, as we may do when caught out or in situations of very real danger. The stronger the situation, the weaker the joke need be, to do its job.

In many ways the comic attitude is an acquired one. Lily Abegg recounts how 'in Peking I had to witness how an elderly man at the point of death, whose mouth was already flecked with foam, lay on the ground in violent convulsions, while the Chinese standing around shook with laughter at his every movement'. The guards in German concentration camps frequently showed an equally lively sense of humour at their guests' expense. To most of us such reactions are abhorrent and incomprehensible, because in the presence of genuine suffering we have been trained, and have trained ourselves, to feel either compassion or guilt, or both, and, even in apathy, respect. So we can't laugh at suffering except in the absurd-mild forms of slipping-on-a-banana-skin or of sick jokes. The merry Chinese, less schooled to compassion, were more detached, could ignore the suffering, and laugh at the 'banana-skin' type indignity of uncontrolled behaviour.

But human nature is double-edged in this, as in other ways. Even our relatively compassionate culture has to encourage its more sensitive children to treat brutality as funny. It's not rare for children to feel quite sorry for the circus clowns. It's their parents who reassure them that 'they're only pretending', that it's a game, that laughter is the right, robust reaction. 'The first film I saw was a silent film, I remember feeling a wee bit sorry for the poor man who had fallen head first into a barrel of flour,' reminisces a civil servant clerk quoted by J. P. Mayer, and a teenage girl writes: 'At first I liked every film I was taken to . . . save for a few slapstick and Laurel and Hardy efforts where physical discomfort was the cause of laughter. Now I can look on somebody being bopped on the head without wincing, although such scenes do not produce the appropriate "belly laugh", but merely a slight cracking of the face where I am concerned.' Tom and Jerry cartoons are many, many stages away from dramatic straightness, as cartoon cats and mice batter one another with golf-clubs, flat-irons, piano-lids and sticks of dynamite. Yet the ideas and style are rough and tough enough to shock and alarm many adults, sparking off many a shrill squeal for the still stricter censorship of our amusements. They're an acquired taste, like strong curries.

Conversely, it needs only slight lingering on a comic gesture of Chaplin's, a subtle flash of eloquent sadness in his mask-like countenance; and suddenly our eyes are welling with tears so prompt that they cannot have been very far from the surface of our feelings. It's as if they were already, secretly, activated beneath our noisy guffaws. We were already responding to the dramatic, even tragic, undertow, paraphrased by the comedy. It needed only a twist of the artist's wrist for our feelings to turn turtle and show their tragic keel.

3· The Mechanics of Comic Criticism

Philosophers occasionally attempt to define the 'spirit of comedy'. It has been defined as a moral spirit because it shows us our vices; or a cruel one, because it shows us other people's weaknesses; or a mellow and tolerant one because it arouses laughter rather than anger; and so on and so forth. But perhaps it's as misleading to seek 'the spirit of comedy' as to seek 'the spirit of drama'. Comedy is a dislocation of drama, and what the spirit of the comedy is depends on which dramatic values make the incongruity. It has as many topics, attitudes, moods and morals as straight drama, i.e. as human nature. *Candide, Alice in Wonderland* and *Gulliver's Travels* (in its unexpurgated version) may all be comic masterpieces, but their moods and morals are very different indeed.

Often all that's needed to turn drama (for the characters) into comedy (for the audience) is to present reality absolutely straight. One simply withholds those compassionate emphases and tactful idealizations which lead an audience to sympathize fully with the screen character.

To extract from its packed audiences a big, prompt, sustained sonic boom of hilarity, *Saturday Night and Sunday Morning* needed just one 'straight', uncaricatured, neo-realistic shot of old Ma Bull the local busybody standing at her front gate, arms toughly folded, ready for battle. There was no need at all to exaggerate reality, to add satire or comment. The audience did all that for itself, in a split second, just as it does when characteristic faces appear in newsreel shot of football crowds.

In Mark Sandrich's *Top Hat* the main plot concerns an (idealized) romantic couple, Ginger Rogers and Fred Astaire. The subplot features Edward Everett Horton as a middle-aged tycoon terrified of

27

his formidable wife. The main, straight plot is too good to be true, while what is all too often true and depressing is treated, by the audience, as ridiculous. In the same way, in Shakespeare's plays, the subplot is often a low burlesque of the theme of the main plot. When, if ever, such parallelism is deliberate is a matter for discussion. But one would expect it to happen automatically, partly through the artist's search for a neat form, partly through his association of ideas.

In Delbert Mann's *Marty*, the main romantic plot, involving Ernest Borgnine and Betsy Blair, is taken straight, and ends happily. But a subplot about Marty's sister and brother-in-law shows ugly marital quarrellings with a vehement exactness. The dramatic impact is sufficient for us to understand why this unfortunate example seriously scares Marty off marriage. The audience treats it—though very gingerly, and with many twinges—as comic relief. In a similar way, Marty's street-corner buddies, with their misogynistic Mickey Spillane fixation, are cases of tragic loneliness and emotional perversity, none too thinly disguised as comic relief.

Joshua Logan's *Picnic* is worth analysing at a little more length. The plot concerns the impact on three small-town middle-class females of a handsome, likeable, hobo (William Holden). He himself falls in love with Kim Novak, his friend's fiancée. Her adolescent sister (Susan Strasberg) falls in love with him in a starry-eyed, 'poetical' way, to the chagrin of her teenage boyfriend. His presence further upsets the emotional equilibrium of a lonely, middle-aged schoolmarm (Rosalind Russell), whose primness conceals a case of sex-starvation (though a fatal perfectionism will drive her to nag any man she finds into being the down-trodden creature, the 'perfect hubby').

The film is a protest against the enemies of erotic love in American small-town middle-class culture. Logan handles the principal romance (Holden–Novak) in a lush style, with sensual-romantic daydream elements. The younger sister's love is treated with a tender humour. But the portraits of the schoolmarm and the teenage boy are more scathing.

She is discreetly glamourized (i.e. played by Rosalind Russell). She is treated sufficiently seriously for us to feel the anguish of her loneliness (so that the criticisms of her can be felt as cruel). She has some excuses for her objectionable behaviour (she was lonely, she had drunk too much, hell hath no fury, etc.). But she is embarrassing (mauling Holden who doesn't love her), spiteful (trying to turn the townsfolk against him) and grossly selfish (bulldozing a placid bachelor into matrimony).

The streak of laboured cruelty in the film's heavy presentation of her sins, which turns our easy laughter back into embarrassment or disapproval, is analogous to the heavily moral 'humours' of Ben Jonson's plays, and has much the same purpose. The comedy too is didactic, aimed at exposing the schoolmarm's follies as such. Unless the schoolmarm's defects are made plain, schoolmarms and others in the audience won't recognize them as defects. But at the same time, the humour arouses less resentment and resistance than a direct denunciation.

A similar psychology determines the caricature of the teenage boy who tries to fight William Holden over Kim Novak. He's obviously too young for her, but we assume that when he's quietened down a little he'll settle down happily with Susan Strasberg, when she's got her romantic poetry out of her system. He feels utterly humiliated when Holden just pushes him away, but Holden and Kim both feel quite sympathetic towards him in his 'comic error', of self-centred toughness embarrassment. For the grown-ups in the audience he represents teenage males, who will probably feel a certain relevance to their own immaturity, and take the hint.

With its distaste for unredeemingly depressing entertainment, the general public doesn't always welcome 'straight' presentations of its own indignities and vices (which is why it tries to turn the subplot of *Marty* into comic relief). Hence certain kinds of semi-caricature, like schoolmarm and teenager in *Picnic*, play a more important role than one might expect from simple considerations of realism, as do satirical films like the Boulting Brothers comedies (*Private's Progress, I'm All Right Jack, Heavens Above*). They are a characteristic popular form, not only of satire, but of serious self-criticism, and there is satire and self-satire, of a rather amiable, naïve variety, even in the Crazy Gang and in their spiritual heirs, the *Carry On* squad.

That the popular audience had a taste for stinging and sophisticated satire was demonstrated to all when the original David Frost, Alf Garnett and other of their ilk burst in upon us. More traditional in screen satire is the blend of criticism and tolerance (even acquiescence?) typified, in unusually clear form, in Preston Sturges's *Sullivan's Travels*. Sullivan (Joel McCrea) is a sympathetic, but too idealistic, Hollywood director. He wants to make films which will inspire the common man. He suspects, however, that before he can inspire him, he ought to meet him. His travels lead him from one misfortune to another (the world being what it is, for common men). Having become a prisoner in a chain-gang, he realizes that what the convicts enjoy is neither 'the mirror up to nature', nor uplift of the 'Brother, where art thou?' variety, but—Mickey Mouse cartoons. Dissolve from the convict audience, laughing, to the audience in a neighbourhood cinema, laughing. Many a spectator will get the hint —and laugh at his own laughter, more uneasily than hitherto.

TW3 satire is hardly of the 'Brother, where art thou?' variety, but earthy and normally unidealistic; which is why the public accepted it, where every kind of idealistic attempt at social realism, political entertainment, and so on, had been decisively, and very properly, repudiated.

We don't want, do we, to dwell unduly on the 'bad taste' ingredients of comedy, but they are there, and, being touchier than more innocuous aspects of our topic, require appropriately laboured discussion. Most comedies, it should perhaps be repeated, are innocuous and unobjectionable from any reasonable point of view. Class snobbery (and its inversions), do-gooders, authority, bureaucracy, and various other Aunt Sallys are traditionally fair game for ridicule—at least in the context of entertainment.

Comedy, having an aura of irresponsibility, and being 'tactfully tactless', if it is to exist at all, can often claim a freedom in some ways greater than that of 'serious' drama. The Court Jester has his licence to insult the King. Robertson Hare's vicars have long been saying things about the Church of England which our censors would never have permitted to be said straight. But—how far is too far? when does humour imply serious criticism? when does such implied criticism become *lèse-majesté*? when does comic irresponsibility begin to seem disgusting or sick?

In mass media, jokes about 'sacred' subjects—principally religion, the government and sexuality—had to be few, mild or disguised (by ambiguity). But in convivial conversation, most people permit themselves rather more disrespectful attitudes. And serious art is often in hot water because, by definition, it often has to bring informal oral culture into the semi-official spheres of print and celluloid.

The boundaries of permissiveness have been changing, though in complex ways. In real life, adults no longer normally find physical deformity funny, or even bearable to contemplate (whereas their grandparents would have laughed at circus freaks). But in comedy

30

nothing's sacred. Ben Turpin's squint, Chaplin's bandy legs, Oliver Hardy's paunch and Stan Laurel's scraggy neck, are all hilarious. The more our culture insists that human life is instinctively sacred to us, the more intrigued and amused we are by comedies which invite us to share the glee of the killer and chuckle at the terrors of the victim (in Capra's *Arsenic and Old Lace*, in Hamer's *K nd Hearts and Coronets*, in Chaplin's *Monsieur Verdoux*). Nothing is jollier than people desperately trying to dispose of corpses (Zampi's *The Naked Truth*, Hitchcock's *The Trouble With Harry*). Funerals and bereavements can trigger volleys of chuckles (in Tati's *Jour de Fete*). Cannibalism is a feast of mirth (in Autant-Lara's *L'Auberge Rouge*, in Chaplin's *The Gold Rush*).

The connection between cruelty, laughter and satire is self-evident. It's often said that a sense of humour is a masculine prerogative, and, in so far as this is true, humour may constitute a sort of auto-defence against the masculine protest (anger). Not that women are entirely passive, helpless creatures. Martha Raye, notably, is a sort of pre- and proto-Jerry Lewis, incarnation of the American woman's aggressiveness. It does seem to be true that England and America, whose cultures tend to erect masculine standards of behaviour for women, provide most of the celebrated comediennes.

From the 30's to the 50's Anglo-Saxon film critics show a progressive hardening of the arteries, where questions of good and bad taste are concerned. The underlying reason is probably that movies are being taken more seriously, that expectations are higher, just when middle-class decorum is being more openly and insistently challenged (by a more affluent working-class, by foreign and cosmopolitan attitudes), and so becomes more touchy and defensive. The more compassionate attitude towards mental illness is an undoubted gain, but there is a real loss when it is accompanied by a distinctly hypochondriac susceptibility. Thus the Bob Hope–Fernandel comedy *Paris Holiday* raised cries of protest for showing the inmates of a mental home doing ludicrous things, whereas, in the 30's, no one would have dreamed of protesting at similar scenes in the Will Hay comedy, *My Learned Friend*. Insanity undoubtedly makes us uneasy, and one response is to turn uneasiness into laughter. In the same way, Londoners laughed about their own dangers in the blitz, but that didn't mean they were callous or heartless.

The new solemnity was evidenced in many ways, as when two Cambridge undergraduate critics worried about audience reaction to the climax of John Guillermin's *Never Let Go,* a savage fight in a garage between Richard Todd and Peter Sellers. This 'straightforward and well-made film about violence was received, at any rate in country cinemas, with laughter . . . the savage beatings which human beings received were funny. When violence is a joke, the public's sense of humour has been depraved; and for that the film industry is largely responsible'. The last proposition seems to me highly improbable, not to say crackpot, but in any case the writers seem to have misinterpreted audience reaction. Laughter, including mine, greeted the same sequence at the film's London trade show, but for different reasons. After receiving a punch massive enough to fell an ox, the recipient blinks briefly, or staggers back a couple of paces, before retaliating with undiminished zest, so that the fight was mildly incredible. Further, the villain was well-known goon Peter Sellers, doing his honest best to be a 'heavy' but never quite making it. Reassured on both counts, the audience settled down to enjoy a nice noisy brawl, like the statutory saloon fight in a Western. Two sorts of laughter predominated: the laughter of tension-incredulity, and the laughter of exuberant pleasure at a fine fight. It was akin to the laughter at the massive slugging-matches in so many John Ford films—*The Informer, What Price Glory, The Quiet Man,* and so on. It isn't laughter at pain at all; I've never known an audience to laugh at pain. It often feels intense moral sadism when a villain comes to a well-merited comeuppance; but it doesn't laugh, and its sadism is at least moral.

A mixed bag of pseudo-liberal fainthearts even had the gall to protest at the pale blue humour of *Carry On Nurse* (e.g. when a tough boxer is too embarrassed to undress in front of the sumptuous young nurses, who in a brisk no-nonsense way tug off his underpants and chuckle, 'What a lot of fuss about such a tichy little thing!'). Anyone who thinks such jokes are corrupting the whiter-than-whiteness of the general public must be Just Visiting from a Small Planet. Jokes like this were a staple of lowbrow show business back in the Victorian music hall, are hardly unknown in every day conviviality, and have the venerability of cultural age.

Against the solemnity of the period TW3 introduced a new mutation out of sophisticated revue, shedding its twee tone and picking on topics of general interest, and a more robustly polemical attack.

4 · Comedy as Sweet and Sour

The nub of comic incongruity (as opposed to dramatic incongruity) is a deflation of tension. The viewpoints, values or experiences so react that, after implying the greater tension, the lesser tension prevails.

Comedy is distinguished from mere reassurance in that in the deflation itself there must be a quality of shock. Shock does not imply surprise so much as an unresolved contradiction—unresolved either because the form is eccentric or odd (as in jokes which depend on wordplay) or elliptic or perhaps because an overt or covert paradox is involved. This formal quality gives many jokes their quality of riddle.

In the mixture of shock and reassurance, the latter must, eventually, prevail (for the purposes of deflation; as we've seen, a laugh is a reverse gasp). This may seem odd, since the form of a joke often suggests the opposite, i.e. the punch-line seems to aggravate the situation. But in such cases, the reassurance is already present in the context (the tone of voice, the nudge in the ribs, the curiously rigid solemnity). It may be implied by the implausibility of the anecdote ('this isn't really real, only an abstraction-with-emotional-resonance'), or often by the sheer fact of sharply opposed emotional evaluation co-existing ('therefore the serious one can't be conclusive'). A joke's logical incongruity is of secondary importance, merely a means to this emotional incongruity. The phrase 'a general in long underpants' is a little joke, though there's no logical incongruity in it. An airman on crutches' is incongruous too, but not funny (unless the context alters its import). The first phrase is funny because the prepared tensions (respect, authority, etc.) are subverted by the associations of underpants (vulnerability, unpreparedness, fear of the cold, near-nudity). A mere contradiction of the general's authority ('a general in confusion') would not, in itself, be funny, for such a contradiction could sustain and increase, rather than deflate, the overall tension.

In the same way, a man in woman's clothes may be funny whereas a handsome woman in man's clothes is—attractive? Whatever our logical mind thinks about the equal dignity of the sexes, our emotional mind sees the first transvestite as neither male nor female, as an abdication of sexual and personal dignity, the second as an audacious claim to double sexuality. The first deflates, the second does not. It may tickle us, but what it tickles is our fancy rather than our funny-bone.

The order of presentation may or may not be important. The idea of a general in long underpants doesn't depend on which idea comes first. Even where order is structural, a joke may first establish its comic context, and then introduce a dramatic tension. Or it may start as a drama, only to reveal its true colours by the twist. Such a twist, apparently an inflation, actually deflates by the incongruity between the aggravation itself and the elliptic nonchalance that deflates it. This nonchalance may be that of the victim himself, or of a commenting character in the story, or of the person listening to the story (as when you laugh at my combined slip, slide, skate and somersault on a banana-skin). But in each case the nonchalance produces a sudden swerve away from compassionate participation—this needn't disappear altogether, simply be scaled down sufficiently for the 'deflating' incongruity to prevail over it.

More important than order of presentation is the role of order in implying an evaluation. (The same is true of non-humorous statements: 'He's very slow, but a very steady chap' has a different meaning from 'He's a very steady chap, but very slow'.) So with jokes. Thus, 'not waving but drowning' may seem to be an anti-joke, a dramatic crescendo rather than a deflation. But it's a (grimmish) joke because the terse, deadpan play on verbal form asserts a kind of indifference. Since drama and the deflation don't abolish each other, it's a better (tenser) joke than the much more reassuring joke-idea 'not drowning but waving'; there the reassurance is too straightforward to provide much of a shock.[1]

---

[1] A side-effect is that in the first phase the joke is (mainly) on the drowning person (though a reassuringly abstract one), with a secondary joke about complacency. In the second phase, it's on the bystanders. A mere reversal of form does more than turn a crescendo into a deflation; it also slackens the tension and shifts the subject of the joke.

An important ingredient in many jokes is the 'riddle' atmosphere. Many jokes, not only those of the 'when-is-a-door-not-a-door' form, but also many plays on words and ideas, carry the tension of riddles. With their odd or far-fetched associations, they are a little puzzle for the listener, and some of his laughter comes from a pleased relief at solving the riddle, that is, 'seeing the point'. Again, the mystery is a mock mystery, quite different from a quiz, and less devious than the riddle. The point is meant to be seen with little ado, and to provide, when seen, a conflict-of-attitudes-in-reassurances. (If riddles aren't quite jokes, it's perhaps because their form retains something of the test of wit.)

The riddle's ellipse often distracts attention from the full implications of a joke (aiding the jester's licence). It also has the effect of striking our assumptions in a sidelong way, causing a little mobilization (tension) but only a little (reassurance).

Because so much of a joke takes place in the listener's mind, its apparent structure is more often than not opposed to the real, affective structure. One may take as example G. K. Chesterton's 'I like a dog when he isn't spelt backward'. The 'dog-spelt-backwards' presentation (as diffusive as an ellipse) gives the joke more than a little riddle tension. The contrast 'spelt-backwards = God' provides the dramatic crescendo: 'merely rearranged spelling = grave blasphemy', which reinforces the joke's main crescendo: from animal to pet to super-human to Supreme Being. But this isn't quite the joke's highest point of tension, for it leads to the (tacit) meta-tension, 'Is the remark irreverent in forcing on us (even though it contradicts) the incongruity dog-God, which we promptly toy with as possibly being God = dog?' In the end we decide that it isn't, and we do so mainly on considerations of tact. For the sentiment is that of a pro-God moral homily, and no homilist would be so blasphemous simply to warn us against dogolatry. Therefore it isn't blasphemous (reassurance). But it's still daringly near blasphemy, a kind of tonic fighting-fire-with-fire, and gives us the little pleasure of having a little tickle at a tabu.

Much of the remark's spirit comes from this tension. It strengthens the implied contract between the gooey indulgence of dog-lovers and the sprightliness of the tabu-tickler, that is, it also takes as butt the idea that real Christianity is gooily sentimental. It blends tolerance ('I like dogs and people who like them') with a certain severity ('senti-mentality is as heinous as blasphemy') which is itself a joke in that we don't take it too seriously either. The inflations and deflations are

35

held in a very nice tension. It's obviously a tenser joke for dog-lovers who hitherto thought that kindness to animals was next to Godliness, than for non dog-lovers.

But suppose that in the course of a theological discussion on the validity of man's direct awareness of the nature of the Most High, a speaker said, 'Yes, and the dog of the Gods wags its tail.' This riddle, solved, infringes a tabu, even though, logically it may only be directed at man's limited idea of God rather than at God himself. Thus it will only amuse people who allow themselves to play with disrespectful notions of God. This group will, of course, include open-minded Christians, but it will exclude many agnostics for whom the idea of God, even if wrong, is to be treated with respect, either as a noble moral idea, or for the sake of other people's feelings. In the same way many Catholic jokes shock non-Catholics more than Catholics.

This joke also hits another butt. Its verbal uncouthness has a derisory implication. It's an outrage to social conventions. It suggests, 'Uncouth as I am, I can still run rings round your highest thoughts.' It's in this respect that it goes beyond a joke, and its mongrelly disrespect for theological reverence might be relished among, for example, the *Private Eye* public. Thus a joke's intrinsic, and logical, incongruities are only a rough guide to the catchment areas of its emotional resonance.

Similarly, a variant form, 'Yes, and the dogs' God wags its tail' is, particularly when spoken, too curt and cryptic, the apostrophe is too short for the hearer's mind to work out the riddle, which becomes a headache, and it's hard to imagine it arousing any laughter in any circles.

Theodore Reik formulates the comic challenge of paradoxes very clearly. 'Whoever coins paradoxes unconsciously anticipates the impressions of his listeners, their opposition to his assertions, maybe even their mockery, and this very anticipation leads him into a specific formation. Thus the paradox contains an attack on generally accepted ideas; however, in a sense it enjoys the attack of the others, even of the future listeners, by anticipation, and by this very anticipation assumes a character of intentional absurdity. One has the impression that the speaker makes mock at himself, yet, knowing exactly how and why, remains in command. What he really mocks at is the anticipated argument of his enemies.'

5 · Comic Attack

Laughter is aggressive in the sense that it is directed against others (but we may also feel them to resemble ourselves), in that it is directed against assumptions (but then aren't all new thoughts aggressive?), in that it is irresponsible (but then this also diminishes its aggressive seriousness), and in that it comports a dramatic deflation (which also minimizes the damage done). In other words, what turns aggression into comedy is what turns a blow into a tickle; it feints an attack, but it is also a mock attack. A tickle is an apparent prod (or a little prod that threatens worse) that's really only a gentle little stroke but still a very jerky, withdrawn stroke that might turn into an attack at any moment. . . .

Thus, in a sense, aggressiveness is the catalyst of humour rather than its content. Even where aggressiveness is the mainspring, it is, usually perhaps, only a means to an end, the end of sudden pleasure, and a relief of one's own tension. The victim may relish it, if it's kindly, for then its aggression is deflated into a reassurance—a bewildering reassurance—a little relief from a little fear. Laughter is not, simply, derisive, towards other human beings, or one's own values; it is also a gurgle of relief, of triumph, at breaking a tabu (but with the approbation of others—that is, not breaking a tabu), at finding one's weaknesses, humiliations and indignities (the point of so many jokes), shared. Even the most aggressive form of laughter, open derision, is actually a pretext for, in Hobbes's phrase, a 'sudden glory', that is, relief and triumph. Smile and laughter at even the most cutting and sophisticated jokes are in essence just what they are in the little baby; a sensation of well-being, sometimes bubbling up out of sheer uncomplicated contentment or high spirits, sometimes—and more often in the adult, whose memories and fears complicate him—sprung by the mild discomfort of uncertainty, by the memory of tension. The wise man smiles even at real discomforts, for he has detachment; he is not in his sufferings but, incongruously, and reassuringly, in his contemplation of them, above them.

Direct, earnest mockery appeals not to the victim, but to others around. A more subtle variety of mocking attack is the real attack which feigns to be a mock attack. The victim's laughter, rarely sincere, is a defensive device, 'I'm not there where you're attacking me, I'm here, laughing too—ha—you missed!' Ridicule and morally didactic mockery may even 'cure folly', by forcing on the butt conduct, or thoughts, compatible with the new position to which he has, evasively, shifted.

The adoption of laughter for purposes of mockery (whether aggressive or defensive) implies, 'We're not seriously disturbed, because we're so immune from your puny antics.' The mocker's feelings of immune superiority often provoke a deeper resentment than an honest angry protest, and engender the special anger one reserves for smiling treachery. But the immune superiority may arise from another attitude, 'We're only gently attacking you because you're a dear friend whose weaknesses are relatively trivial, and only make us a little fonder of you.' There the laughter, instead of sharpening in the attack, blunts it. It is an anti-aggressive sign (whence the famous Western threat, 'Next time you say that—smile!').

The role of bluff-and-counter-bluff in comic aggression affords a reminder, useful when wondering what makes jokes tick, that much laughter is hypocritical or habitual or deferential or polite, and that, without any insincerity, we may laugh at jokes which in themselves aren't very funny, perhaps to escape the mockery in them, or perhaps to show goodwill, or perhaps as a pretext for letting off some high spirits. A study of the jokes people laugh at doesn't reveal what makes people laugh! Often the content of the joke is purely 'formalistic', the real source of the laughter is its context. Thus 'I'll tell you a joke' means 'let's relax', and 'I'm laughing at your joke' means 'I'm jettisoning my superiority and adopting complicity', and it's this little friendship which is the real source of the merriment. The aggression in the joke (tabu-tickling) is thus the opposite of aggression towards one's boon companion.

A good joke is like the ball on a pintable machine. It doesn't hit just one bulb, it zigzags its way around to ricochet off every bulb on the table. This complexity has its obverse in deviousness, which leads many satirists to overestimate the effect of their mockery (i.e. to underestimate the complexity of the spectator's defence-in-depth). The most common form of satire is satire-by-caricature, i.e. behaviour is demolished by reduction to its extreme, or by an aggregation of traits, which, until aggravated or isolated by the satirist, seemed to the audience quite justifiable or respectworthy. But these very processes, aggravation and isolation, are intuitively countered by the spectator's refusal to link them with non-extreme and non-isolated attitudes. He laughs at the absurd characters with a perfectly good conscience, and sincerely never connects them with the same traits in respectworthy situations. Such satire is sarcasm which has set up a straw man and attacked that.

There may indeed be a ricochet effect (from the straw man to the real man). And the more deadly satirist, like Voltaire, or a tragic satirist, like Swift, uses caricature as a front for sarcasm. His attack, initially directed at some straw man or other, gradually, as it develops, multiplies the similarities between the straw man and the reader, until they become so inescapable and disturbing that the reader realizes he has been laughing at his own profoundly held assumptions. Such attacks often arouse the resentment, not only of their victims, but of those whose viewpoint is nearer the satirist's; for the deeply human processes he satirizes have their sympathy too. With Swift one feels not so much, 'There, but for the grace of God, go I,' but, so deep is the level at which he attacks human nature, so widespread and grave are the follies he reveals, that one feels, rightly, that no human being is safe from criticisms which one hardly knows how to repudiate, and can only accept. Hence, Swift's satire is tragic, as *King Lear* is tragic. 'There, despite the grace of God, goes all mankind.'

Honest and self-critical sarcasm is the tragic form of wit. Yet, even irresponsible and inoffensive jokes, built as they are on clashes of serious attitude, can make the listener uncomfortably conscious of his own contradictions. Jokes are an important channel of cultural influence (a few dirty jokes at work rapidly undo years of Sunday School indoctrination), and the comic author can of course exploit innumerable interactions between the comic and the serious so as to be overtly or covertly serious as well as amusing.

But it is because comedy on certain issues can reassure only by omitting so many of our 'serious' feelings that, loud as is our laugh (partly a laugh of relief at the clever but friendly circumvention of our scruples), we don't take comedy seriously, we dismiss it as just emotional *trompe-coeur*, which it very often is. But we can make a rough but useful distinction between nervous comedy (full of tricks which dodge involvement) and tragic or mellow comedy (the smile *after* involvement). Mellow comedy often seems sad, frightening or sinister, to those who haven't yet been through it to say, 'Look—we have come through.'

Most jokes settle for a kind of compromise between affirmation and subversion, nervousness and mellowness (the compromise being the condition of shock reassurance). Thus comedy is never a pure upthrust of aggressive or subversive impulses. Much humour is moralistic, in its concern with deflating or ridiculing angry, erotic, or other anti-social and authentic feelings. Further, much humour exists in order to kathart such feelings, that is, to diminish their intensity by a brief, non-committal, scarcely understood, indulgence. Frequently, perhaps generally, humour is conformist, confusionist, masochistic, and a disturbingly acquiescent surrender to destructive forces outside the individual. Humour *per se* is neither on the side of the angels nor the devils. It can do you good or harm, or both at once.

It is ambivalent also in that, by challenging one of the listener's assumptions, it may indulge a contrary assumption. Though apparently a challenge, it is in fact tautologous, appealing to another assumption which is already implanted. From another angle, this is why so much apparently aggressive humour is really friendly, and vice versa. The real point of blue jokes is usually to get men to sin a little together, and so feel friendlier towards one another. Jokes about our inadequacies, real or assumed, help us shrug off feelings of shame, celebrate our spiritual resilience, and reassure our mates as to our complicity. Jokes about the infra dig reassure us that we are never infra dig! But, in its turn, the comic snub to our dignity works at the expense of omitting much that drama reminds us is relevant and respectworthy. We often accept an anecdote as a joke simply because we are reassured by its failure to fit so many of our feelings.

Even so, the joke is on us. We are *also*, on a sometimes conscious, sometimes repressed, level, as callous, saturnine and base as our jokes suggest we are. The generosity and resilience asserted by jokes may also be repressed by our social norms. An existential philosophy might do well to base its view of human nature on low comedy as well as on high tragedy, to alarm us all by taking jokes seriously.

Beyond that state of alarm lies the possibility of the tragicomic negation of humour adumbrated by Marcel Schwab. 'To laugh is suddenly to find oneself disregarding laws; did we then really believe in the world-order and a magnificent hierarchy of final causes? And when all anomalies have been linked up with some cosmic mechanism, men will laugh no longer. . . . To laugh is to feel superior. When we come to kneeling and making public confessions at cross-roads and humbling ourselves the better to love, we shall then have no understanding of the grotesque. . . .

'Laughter is probably destined to disappear. With so many animal species extinct, why should a tic peculiar to one of them persist? This coarse physical proof of our sense of a certain disharmony in the world will have to go by the board in the face of complete scepticism, absolute knowledge, universal pity and respect for all things. . . .

'I know that men will be astonished by our convulsed mouths and tear-filled eyes, our shaking shoulders and twitching bellies. . . .

'. . . those who wish to laugh now should make haste to do so. We are not yet at the stage of seeking out the pedestal of the Laughter God among the ruins. . . . When our statues have fallen and our customs have been swept away, when men number the years in some new era, they will tell each other this simple little legend of him who gave us so much joy:

'He was a charming little divinity of subtle wit and kind heart, who dwelt in Montmartre. He wrote with such grace that coarse words, seeking an indestructible sanctuary, found it in his work.'

Let the modern reader be reassured à propos such eerie serenity; the comic mask won't fade until the dramatic face has withered too.

6 · The Comic Underworld of the Infra Dig

In some ways comedy is more easily realistic than drama. Drama traditionally tends to the slightly exalted, idealized, superior. It tends to leave out many of the undignified topics and reactions which we like to feel don't concern us (although we secretly know they do, and allow that they concern others). When a comedy shows us these trivialities, then we feel an obscure affinity, which we don't always forget, but, reassured by comic exaggeration or inflation, we enjoy the antics of 'those' screen characters.

Comedy thrives on the petty, niggling, unworthy and humiliating aspects of things; the little things which we are ashamed to admit affect us but which, in reality, so often contribute to 'cut us down to size' without giving us (as dramatic things do) a consolatory sense of our own solid suffering, significance and dignity. The denizens of comedy include those intolerable mothers-in-law, those nagging wives with curlers, those men who stammer and simper in the presence of gorgeous females, and those pompous bluffers. We laugh at these things not because they're not real, but for the opposite reason; they strike a chord despite ourselves. And even if we aren't or don't have a grim mother-in-law and a nagging wife, we recognize in the situations a possibility, a certain range of emotional pettiness, we share the hero's reactions even while we're feeling 'above' him.

It's even arguable that people today are often too quick to laugh at themselves, laugh in a way presupposing an automatically derisive attitude to emotion.

Be that as it may, the comedy-drama antithesis still reflects a tendency even more marked in the Greek and Elizabethan theatre. The difference in dignity often takes the form of a social differentiation. Drama deals weightily with weighty characters—princes, governors,

42

rich merchants—while the comic relief centres on decayed gentlemen, peasants and 'base mechanicals'. In his *Poetics*, Aristotle says, 'This is the difference that marks tragedy out from comedy; comedy tends to deal with persons below the level of our world, tragedy persons above it.' Maybe these social layers are metaphors for a psychological factor: comedy deals with people below the level of our conscious images of ourselves.

The Aristotelian polarity is still observable, despite the levelling effect of democratic thought and of twentieth-century realism. Because comic inferiority is related to our conscious idea of ourselves, it frequently happens that the feeling of unreality associated with comedy persists even when, objectively considered, the screen characters are exceptionally faithful to everyday realism.

Of course films often facilitate our efforts to reassure ourselves by turning drama-without-dignity into comedy. The comic characters are generally kept inferior to our actual responses and behaviour. They overact (whereas we have the strength of character, not only to hide our feelings, but to dismiss them from our minds). Comic reality is our inner reality with bells on—like the Court Jester—or the soft pedal off. Frequently, the screen comics let rip on their immediate reactions during a scene—but begin the next scene completely undismayed by their previous experiences. The prompt exaggeration avoids too disturbing an identification, but it also reassures that no real harm is done. When, in Jacques Becker's relatively realistic comedy, *Edouard et Caroline*, the young married couple quarrel, Caroline forthwith takes it into her head to smash everything breakable in their household. No sooner thought than done. Considered as an act, in itself, it expresses a hysteria of Strindbergian violence. But it's devalued first because her decision was so quick and easy, and because so, afterwards, was her recovery. Moods flow through her as inconsequentially as through a child (i.e. through our childish self). So our pleasure (as often, wherever humour is involved) comes from two sources. There is the delight at seeing, and sharing, her devastating and excessive response. Our laughter is partly a gurgle of de-inhibited pleasure. But its improbability creates a feeling of unreality, which helps to reassure us. But it does so at the expense of making us feel that the screen characters are exaggerated, that we're detached from them (though not so detached that the film ceases to have a real dramatic-realistic quality which we recognize; hence we feel comedy as a form of expressionism). For dramatic and comic attitudes can be

43

maintained in the spectator simultaneously. Hollywood sophisticated comedy offers the spectator a variety of pleasures, mingling wish-fulfilment (physical beauty, luxury, nonchalance, *savoir-vivre* and so on) with an absurdity of response which is sometimes flattering, sometimes unflattering, to the characters.

Thus we can draw a schematic contrast between crazy and straight comedy. In crazy comedy, whether a Mack Sennett farce or a Tom-and-Jerry cartoon, a general oddity of appearance and gesture, precedes, and provides a comic context for, action in which the melodramatic tussles with the derisive and makes the most of a highly implausible immunity from consequences. In a more sophisticated comedy, the general appearance is dramatic, so is the action, and the comedy is introduced by a stream of reaction details. In the relatively dramatic context (and the constant possibility of non-immunity) subtle details which in crazy comedy would be dramatic (relative to the absurd context) carry a devaluating effect. Chaplin is very dramatic in a very absurd context, Cary Grant is lightly comic in a semi-dramatic one.

Thus Becker's Caroline isn't at all unreal in the sense that slapstick is. She's just as convincing as the heroines of many dramas, and a great deal more convincing than the heroines in unconvincing dramas which may bore us but don't make us laugh. For her unrealities are all of a particular sort—all in the way of deflating, devaluing the solid meaning, the tragi-dramatic importance of her reactions. So we cease taking her protestations seriously. Our decision to do so is purely intuitive—such-and-such a reaction is too volatile to be weighty and too frothy to be true. (It is because comedy depends on such nuances —fast timing is such a nuance—that comic acting is a notoriously difficult genre.) It is also a source of the special wish-fulfilment lift given by sophisticated comedy. Its whimsicality is also emotional freedom, freedom to treat tragedy as a tiff, to live with unstoppable control and style. Thus the very joke which deflates tragedy into something derisory can also elevate the characters into aristocrats of nonchalance whom we would dearly love to be. Our laughter is not so much *at*, but more, *with* them, as they avoid depression—much as, on the fairground roller-coaster, we laugh because we haven't fallen off, yet. Crazy comedy also exploits the twin aspects of the comedian's being both derisive and immune. Thus Harold Lloyd and Buster Keaton are in quick alternation exceptionally clumsy and exceptionally agile. The agility helps us to admire and care about them as deserving cases; sometimes, more of a gift from the Gods, sometimes it expresses the absurdity of a pleasantly unjust world. All these overtones can be combined, and when they do, they characteristically combine rather than cancel out. Thus both the infra dig and the wish-fulfilment, both the catastrophe and the immunity, combine to deflate the dramatic tension, and intensify the comic one.

Often we are half-aware, for all the comic unreality, that we have traits in common with the screen characters, that their weakness, rather than their immunity, is ours. But the humorous tone, the audience laughter, reassures us that we're forgiven, that everybody's in the same boat. Since weaknesses are inevitable and universal, let's relax and enjoy them.

The mixture may be tarter than that. The film may allow us to feel a definite shock between the comedy and the dramatic. Thus a director might show us A's response, which makes us laugh, and then switch to B's, whose convincing suffering sobers us.

Many comedy films become heavier, more sober, just around their climax, before a final, reassuring release.

In the midst of a bevy of 'dramatic' characters, the writer may introduce a jester whose job it is to periodically relax the immediate tension, while *also* introducing a deeper note of tragic 'cutting down to size'. Or, amongst sentimentally comic characters, he may introduce a sort of anti-jester whose cutting, realistic comments induce us to see the link between the absurd characters and ourselves, or between their comedy and its tragic potentialities, thus actualized. We smile on one side of our faces and wince on the other.

Thus, comedy can work on a sort of double-bluff. First we laugh at the comic characters, and then we're reminded we are them, we are the butts of our own mockery. We're not being forgiven, we're being condemned. We're hoist by our own petard. The satirist (if he hopes to improve the world, and isn't content with just sardonically showing us ourselves) hopes we will learn from our own laughter, and repent. More often, we don't make the connection between the screen characters and ourselves (or only dimly, or with all sorts of reservations and extenuations). We apply our laughter to the human race as an abstraction rather than to ourselves, and instead identify with the satirist, feeling very superior to all those other people who aren't in on the satire. If the satirist does ram the connection between his stooges and ourselves home, then we may feel angry and counter-attack; calling him bitter, sarcastic, misanthropic and so on. It isn't rare for satirists to have a saturnine streak, but often the rage which we attribute to the satirist really comes from ourselves. The author was mocking people in a sharp but still affectionate way, and it is the spectators who feel that the faults he depicts are too serious to be forgiven.

Conversely, satire-by-parody may be more apparent than real. It has often been pointed out that Chaplin's hat, cane and supercilious mannerisms give an impression of would-be gentility, which is constantly betrayed by his baggy trousers, big boots, clumsy gait and guttersnipe strategies in the face of life's challenges. Yet this isn't really satire, whether of gentility, affected gentility, or The Little Man. Our laughing at him is only a prelude to laughing with him. His absurdities are felt as expressionism for our bluffs and shifts, and our superior laugh coexist with our enthusiastic awareness that he is the underdog in us all. He's everything that's inferior about us, and we root for him with all our hearts. Even when he plays a social topdog —like the aristocrat in *The Idle Class*—we know he must be a psychological or spiritual underdog at heart. The satirical effect is very secondary to a kind of social levelling by complicity; 'why pretend to be superior when absolutely everybody is essentially and lovably inferior?' (Even: 'why bother about the rich when they're no happier than we are?' What is meant as social protest can be taken as the reverse!)

Comic heroes usually sport the obviously engaging vices, like being lazy, clumsy, stupid and absurdly romantic, but they often display many of the less respectable ones, like cowardice, pederasty, treachery, sadism and so on, and on, and on. The 'pathetic' Chaplin will happily boot inoffensive matrons up the backside. In *The Cure* he gratuitously and grievously maltreats a pathetic, old, stooping, trusting messenger-boy: terrified by a burly masseur, he tries to pacify him by making coy, feminine, mincing advances, eventually posing as a young lady in a fashion parade. It's a homosexual gag, of course, but plunges even deeper than that, into instinctual strata of fantastic depth. Among certain species of monkey, a weak or defeated animal will placate or confuse its adversary by adopting the posture of the female when on heat. Which is exactly what Charlie Chaplin does here. It's one of those reactions which sound far-fetched and incomprehensible when psychologists explain it, but which everybody understands without even noticing when it's slipped over in a comic context.

Comedy, like art generally, depends, not only on nuance, but on tact. For a spectator who is out of tune with, or stiffly self-conscious

46

about, the weaknesses to which a comic hero confesses, comedy may be a nightmare experience. Bernard Davidson writes, 'Jerry Lewis exercises a strange and really disquieting fascination over the patrons of the cinema's darkened halls. . . . If Lewis enjoys universal approval, the reason is simple: he is the incarnation of all the average man's repressions (eroticism, sadism, masochism, hysteria, homosexuality, destructive violence). . . . Lewis is the symbol of bad taste considered as one of the fine arts. . . . This monster named Jerry fascinates us by the double game of attraction-repulsion. . . . We are even more uneasy when we see women in his company. The introverted side of his personality harbours astounding reactions whereby timidity becomes aggressiveness. This repression and dissimulation are a virtual castration . . . and wherever Jerry discovers Woman, the effect is of startling bestiality. . . . Jerry reminds us of those madmen with strangler's hands. . . . That is why I constantly expect him to strangle each and every one of all the glamorous dolls placed within his reach.' In contrast to what one may expect from this description, Jerry has yet to play a malicious personality; when he damages things (which he does frequently) it is through his very eagerness to please. It's ironical that Davidson should be preoccupied by that aggressiveness which is conspicuously missing from the screen; ironic, but understandable, and good criticism, for what actually happens on the screen is only a stimulus to the spectator's reactions, which aren't limited to a passive tautology. And J. P. Coursodon concurs: 'Jerry Lewis is a pathological case . . . let us say no more than that Lewis seems to us to represent the lowest degree of physical, moral and intellectual abasement to which a comic actor can descend. The majority of his films are almost unbearable physically, even the least atrocious of them, such as *Artists and Models*.'

After testimonies like these (matched by Anglo-Saxon censure to the effect that Jerry Lewis is disgusting because he seems to think mental defectives amusing) it's hardly surprising to find this anti-hero listed as one of Hollywood's most popular stars through most of the 50's. For the anti-hero has been the kingpin of comedy from the year dot, from Plautus through the picaro to Mr. Polly. All that's newish about the anti-hero is his transposition from a semi-comic context to a serious, even a tragi-absurd one.

Ideas of just what is infra dig aren't invariable, but they do observe a certain consistency. One spectator finds Falstaff derisory and Henry V noble, another finds Falstaff realistically unheroic and Henry V a

Fascist, another may find both excessive. But Henry is *either* noble *or* a threat *or* both. He doesn't lack dignity as a man, and his speeches are not self-burlesquing. Whereas Falstaff's language is either derisory or self-burlesquing (even if his cowardice is the most sensible attitude, it is expressed in the language of flippant self-derision). Thus, Henry, whether hero, villain or hero-villain, never loses his dignity, whereas Falstaff never has any. Both characters are 'real' and felt by the spectator to be; but Falstaff's infra dig attitude is divorced from the motivations or objections that would give it Henry's dramatic 'strength'. It's not that the infra dig can't be handled in a dramatic or tragic way; modern psychological realism demands that it be, and Euripides's *The Bacchae*, with its humiliating transvestite episode, is already a tragedy of the derisory.

7 · How many Laughs can Dance on the Point of a Gag?

Much theorizing about comedy is simplistic because the aesthetician is looking for *the* meaning of a joke. This is as true of the screen's visual jokes as of verbal ones.

The hero of Tex Avery's extraordinary cartoon, *Slap Happy Lion*, is king of the jungle because his mighty roar is itself sufficient to browbeat all the other jungle animals. His authority is challenged by a huge and horrendous gorilla, who not only squares up to him, but towers over him menacingly. Leo performs a virtuoso roar so devastating that he twists himself in knots, from which he emerges with a blink to see if the simian colossus is still with him. Yes indeed. More suspense, as the gorilla glares back and we expect a king-sized counter-roar. But, instead, the challenger abruptly shrivels to postage-stamp size, turns tail and runs off. This delay in his reactions is repeated when, in the act of running off, he retains his old bulging-chested stance, as if he'd forgotten to get rid of it. (It also gives him a strange earnestness in flight). Each of these incongruous nuances is a joke in itself. There are incongruities within incongruities (though a kind of logic links them; his absent-minded retention of the muscle-man pose is 'like' his delay in reacting; apparent strength is revealed as panic paralysis).

Eventually, the lion comes up against a cheeky mouse whose guerrilla tactics reduce him to a nervous wreck. In these assaults the terrifying and the ludicrous splendidly alternate. One second the audience is shocked into a sort of incredulous quasi-seriousness as the midget mouse rapidly batters the poor lion literally flat with a colossal mallet about ten times larger than its wielder. The next second the mouse is giving his victim convulsions by blowing a squeaker into his ear from an unexpected quarter. Thus the incongruity 'mouse terrifies lion' envelops another series of incongruities. People often find this cartoon emotionally upsetting, not because it isn't funny, but because it's vivid too, and they are mesmerized with horror even as they laugh.

Almost by definition: all the best jokes are a collection of little jokes.[1] To take a simple example. When Groucho sidles in to tackle Margaret Dumont and to alternate outrageous insults and outrageous flatteries *a la mallet*-and-squeaker, we are tickled to see, as he glides on, (*a*) his sleek hunchbacked lope, a contradiction in itself, (*b*) his sidelong glance at the audience, a contradiction of the film, (*c*) the contrast between his shape and hers, (*d*) how absurd it is of her to take him so seriously, (*e*) what a brilliant film it is to get away with such nonsense, and (*f*) how nutty we must be to chuckle at it. Their mere appearance side by side isn't just one joke, but a whole battery of jokes, and they haven't even said anything yet.

Yet, however absurd a film's idiom, there can be no jokes without a dramatic undertow, for there can be no incongruities if there is no emotional tension. The dramatic elastic has to be wound up before it can quickly unwind in sudden laughter. In many films it is never allowed to unwind completely—or, if it is, it is promptly tautened again. The gags in *Slap Happy Lion* are full of suspense, a suspense which survives the spectator's total disbelief in the film's realism. Many Harold Lloyd films have a high terror-quotient. Will he fall to his death sixty storeys below? will the clock's minute-hand break off under his weight? will the cigarette-end burning away between his shirt and his back make him writhe so madly he falls off the window-ledge? In Elliott Nugent's *My Favourite Brunette* Bob Hope is pitted against Peter Lorre, Sidney Greenstreet and a gang of heavies playing relatively straight. The simple substitution of Alan Ladd for Bob Hope and a greater sobriety in style during the climaxes would have made of the film a perfectly adequate straight thriller. Indeed, the heavies are a scarier lot than their dramatic models, in John Huston's *The Maltese Falcon*. In the Bob Hope and Danny Kaye comedy-thrillers it's far from rare for minor characters to be killed quite convincingly and gruesomely—many a corpse with a nasty little flick-

---

[1] Under the influence of William Empson's *Seven Types of Ambiguity*, it's tempting to say that if a good joke stands repetition, it's because there's always another aspect to notice. But more probably, we laugh at the same aspects all over again.

knife in its back has fallen from many a closet into the anti-hero's arms to serve as a pretext for a little fantasia of comic panic. The seriousness of the scene is sabotaged by, and only by, the hero's absurd reactions. Everyone else plays absolutely straight, affecting not to notice the hero's improbabilities, or registering it in a stereotyped way, e.g. lifting one eyebrow as if to say, 'The fool,' as masterminds will, but carrying on deadpan. Thus the film thrills even as it amuses.

Conversely, a dramatic film like Howard Hawks's *The Big Sleep* can accommodate comic relief, not only very near, but in the very core of, its dramatic climaxes, without sabotaging them. It takes only one facial expression, one remark, to swing a tense audience into laughter, and another to swing it back from laughter to tension. Thus Humphrey Bogart, all tied up, tries to persuade Lauren Bacall to free him from his bonds, on the grounds that the villains will kill him. He explains, 'First they'll punch me in the stomach and then they'll kick my teeth in for mumbling.' Astonishingly, this line functions as hilarious comic relief, largely because of Bogart's wry poise (in fact it's a possible criticism of the film that for all its qualities it doesn't stray deep enough into real terror). But the line of dialogue quoted is admirable in extorting a laugh while accentuating the tension. Earlier in the film Bogart finds a corpse and dials the cops, 'I've got some cold meat lying about.' It's a laugh, and it's wish-fulfilment nonchalance, but the gag is also spiked with a chill about the cheapness of human life in the criminal jungle.

Since the line between comedy and drama is so fine, even where it exists, confusion is easily possible. A Swiss audience watched *The Lady Killers* in silence, with bated breath, for half an hour before it began to dawn on them, tentatively at first, then—yes, it was a comedy—oh ho! ho ho ho! Or a film may become a comedy involuntarily, being built round a greater intensity of dramatic tension than it makes an audience feel. Many silent movies amuse today's film society audiences because, owing to then current moods and idioms, the characters react in a more paroxysmatic ('weak') style than today's audience can feel in itself. Thus the film becomes a rather clumsy comedy. Conversely, one of the more recondite forms of meta-meta-humour is smiling at film critics who think they are scoffing at the clumsiness of certain horror films when in fact they are misinterpreting the moments of parody deliberately introduced by producers so that the audience's instinctive defence against horror-

suspense, laughter, can be satisfied, leaving them in the right inter-
ested frame of mind for the ghoulish climaxes.

A few years ago *Noah's Ark*, Michael Curtiz's 1927 silent epic, was
revived and given a limited release. Parts of it were still acceptable
spectacle, but elsewhere the sentiments were too rudimentary, the
acting too overdone, for modern audiences to take. The distributors
avoided the obvious approaches, of pleading for a respectful attitude
to this venerable old classic, or of making crude fun of it. Instead,
they dubbed a commentary which good-naturedly forewarned the
audience before too comically dated a bit of business, and introduced
friendly little asides like, 'This part is played by Myrna Loy who
before she became a leading lady played villainesses in B pictures or
small parts in productions like these.' The commentary thus dimi-
nished the incongruity between the seriousness of the film's mood and
the parodiac effect of its stylistic archaisms. The audience still
laughed, but more sympathetically than if the commentary had not
smoothed over the contrast. The film lost less than one might have
expected in straight story interest, and made up for it in aesthetic
interest. It's one of the few films to be released with talking footnotes.

8 · From Satire to Saturnalia

Comedy can cock its invigorating snook at the world only by appealing to our *other* feelings. Even when satire appeals to our moral feelings, it may so burlesque the disorder in society as to assert the deeper disorder lurking in our irresponsible nostalgias. Parody, satire and saturnalia, far from being distinct genres of comedy, have intimate affinities, and interweave from second to second in the same film.

From another angle: we affirm certain serious, consistent attitudes only because of the presence within our hearts of a secret opposition. So when comedy reverses our accepted ideas, and pretends to be a crazy comedy, it also tunes in to childish, zany, or immoral wishes or fears. It compensates for its obvious untruths by preciously reasserting these secret truths.

At first sight it might seem that nothing could be more unreal than the comic-strip universe of *L'il Abner*, the Norman Panama–Melvin Frank musical fantasy inspired by Al Capp's perennially popular comic strip. Its characters—dirty, feckless but generally contented hillbillies—and setting—the obscure rural town of Dogpatch—might seem just an extended skit on Erskine Caldwell's *Tobacco Road*. But the film follows Al Capp's practice of constantly multiplying the strip's references so as to include all aspects of American life. Perhaps I may here elaborate and develop in a different direction, some points made elsewhere about this fascinating (non-*auteur*) film.

The yokels are a disturbing collection. Instead of being, as American men should, clean, go-ahead, industrious, smart and prepossessing, Dogpatch males are almost to a man dirty, regressive, lazy, ugly and passive towards their females—of whose (albeit exasperated) affection they are, however, in complete command. So much so that the shapely maidens of Dogpatch, generally as glamorous and viva-

53

cious as their men are goofy and droopy (the Disney names impose themselves), compete every year in the Sadie Hawkins Day race, when the lovesick maidens pursue the 'fear-crazed bachelors' with lassoo, club, shotgun and any other means of friendly persuasion they can contrive. Any man they catch, they can have.

The film's hero, L'il Abner, is Herculean, kindly, dumb and placid, and can never quite get around to marrying the gorgeous heroine, Daisy Mae. He wants her to nab him each Sadie Hawkins Day, but, regularly, just as he feels her loving arms reaching out to grasp him, something deep inside him makes him 'put on mah usual burst of brilliant speed' and escape once more.

Thus, one way or another, Dogpatch males are a flagrant reversal of the American ideal. Certainly L'il Abner is hardly more dynamic but, clean, strong and handsome, has a kind of simple enthusiasm— he keeps asking himself what a 'real red-blooded American he-male would do', and he has a trusting boy-scout attitude to township and country. And that's why we laugh at him. He's forgotten to be sensibly cynical.

His Dogpatch companions are sexually potent (when they have a mind to be). But L'il Abner clearly has a mental block which is equally clearly sexual impotence. The key to these comic paradoxes is offered by Martha Wolfenstein and Nathan Leites in their *Movies; A Psychological Study*, where they establish the peculiar stress in American films of (*a*) sentimental conformism and Momism and (*b*) misogynistic heroes. They go on to attribute this to the extent to which American boys are trained, disciplined and set their goals, by their mother, their father remaining less authoritative than usual in the European family, more of an elder brother. So, in daydream films, the roles are often reversed. There, a diffident male refuses to seek the approval of a suppliant female, and he insists she prove herself. This keys the two faces of Dogpatch man. Those who reverse the all-American ideals are both indifferent to women and potent; L'il Abner, who exaggerates the American ideal of the trusting, benign Superman, is impotent—so, of course, burlesquing American puritanism and ironically turning the tables on the (apparently female) source of sexual tabu.

The Sadie Hawkins Day race is the matriarchal comeback. It takes the reversal of conventional sexuality to the point of (*a*) male masochism and (*b*) a derisive attitude to women, parodying the theme of 'marriage-by-rape' which, being associated with primitive virility and aggression, so interests Americans (as in *Seven Brides for Seven Brothers*), and (*c*) wish-fulfilment for the lonely, timid 'Bachelor Party' male.

The relationship between L'il Abner's parents, Pappy and Mammy Yokum, burlesques Momism more directly. Mammy Yokum, a mighty midget of a matriarch, puffs away at her pipe, like a female Popeye, and indeed she is second in strength only to her son (and far more belligerent than he is). Later in the film, she reveals herself as also a benevolent witch, weaving magic spells which allow her to see what is happening to her son miles away in Washington. (In reality, during World War II American army officers complained that they couldn't toughen up their recruits properly because of the vigilant tenderness of the monstrous regiment of Moms.) Pappy Yokum looks like Rip Van Winkle, and is first seen lying face downwards across Mammy's knees, while she stitches away at a hole in his pants (visually: spanking him? changing his nappies?). Throughout the film she bosses him and it isn't until disaster is imminent that paternal vigour contrives to reassert itself—and then, as we shall see, by a trick.

The trigger for the plot is a decision by the U.S. Government to find a new site for its atomic tests. Dogpatch is soon chosen, as 'the most unnecessary place on earth' (i.e. it is happy, disgusting, non-profit-making and non-utilitarian) and will have to be evacuated unless the villagers can justify its continued existence. What looks like a reason is the tonic on which Mammy Yokum has fed her Superman son. Made from the juice of the Yokumberry, which grows only in her garden, it succeeds in turning a weedy scientist into a muscleman in a few seconds flat. Scientists rush to test this valuable drug, this elixir of apparent masculinity, and Dogpatch is temporarily reprieved for the sake of the fruit on its tree, like a Garden of Eden in reverse.

The authorities reckon, however, without General Bullmoose, the smooth tycoon, whose flock of Yes-men sing, TV-jungle-style, 'What's good for General Bullmoose is good for the U.S.A.', when asked for their opinion by him. He plots with old-style Southern politician, Senator Jackass T. Phogbound, to steal Mammy's formula, patent the Tonic, and market it across the world as Yoko-Cola (without testing it). General Bullmoose (rhymes with 'Motors' and 'Electric') is of course the spirit of Big Business. Further, many of the film's characters are city slickers, out of the Damon Runyon bracket:

Available Jones, Stupefyin' Jones, Evil Eye Fleagle and Appassionata Von Climax. Available is a modest young man with a sprightly innocence of manner reminiscent of Harold Lloyd (we assume him to be as unspoiled). He lives in Dogpatch, and has built his own intercontinental ballistic missile, which he keeps in his backyard (in the American tradition of brilliant woodshed inventors who invent better mousetraps and have the world beat paths to their door). But he's a Harold Lloyd who's learned a thing or two; he's available, i.e. corruptible ('American small-town idealism isn't as idealistic as patriotic cliché has it'). He accepts bribes impersonally from both Daisy Mae and General Bullmoose.

Stupefyin', his cousin, is a (literally) dumb dame whom he keeps in his ICBM like a doll in its package. This puppet-cum-pin-up has a form so fair and a shimmy so shattering that any male who sees her perform is promptly paralysed where he stands. (It's odd, yet somehow 'right', that this paragon of feminine allure should emerge from something as technologically phallic as an ICBM; her femininity is masculine in attack, reminding one of the psychoanalytic assertion that the American taste for large and protrusive breasts is camouflage for a longing for the 'phallic woman'.)

Appassionata Von Climax is mistress to General Bullmoose (by whom she is 'bed and bored') and also (*sub rosa*) to his chauffeur. Essentially a gold-digger, she is also a muscles-crazy sexpot, and ravenously determined on enjoying the favours of L'il Abner. When, in his innocence, he fails to notice, let alone respond to, her advances, she falls in with Bullmoose's plan for cornering Yokumberry Tonic, which, conveniently, will require her to marry L'il Abner (until he gets bumped off). It's left vague whether she lusts most for loot or L'il Abner; one motive seems to apply as soon as the other lapses; in this respect she is very much in the Mae West tradition, reflecting a quite common American assumption that in women lust and avarice go together—both being admirable but naughty and dangerous. Of course, the wicked witch is a universal stereotype, at least in children's stories, but American puritanism seems to stress and continue it into adulthood in a characteristic way.

Evil Eye Fleagle is a stunted, slimy character clearly spawned in the slums and bred in the speakeasy. His eyes have a peculiar potency. He can so use them as to paralyse his victim by a glance, or, for a special fee, of course, turn on him a truth-drug glare. Truth being just as strange as comedy, there is in fact a character in New York Boxing

56

circles known as Evil Eye Finkel, self-styled 'No. 1 Hex Man of the Sporting World'. (As those who have seen William Klein's *Cassius Le Grand* will know, he put the evil eye, not only on Sonny Liston, but on the entire German army during the Battle of the Bulge.)

The film's first climax, which may read clumsily but works very rapidly and smoothly, occurs during the Sadie Hawkins Day race. Daisy Mae, balming L'il Abner's disinterest on what she supposes, incongruously, to be a lack of physical charm on her part, goes to Available and hires Stupefyin' to paralyse L'il Abner and save him from his burst of brilliant speed. General Bullmoose meanwhile hires Fleagle to keep an eye on L'il Abner, until such time as Appassionata, though hampered by her too-tight skirts and snooty *nouveau-riche* languidness, can toddle up and claim him. She will marry him, learn the formula and . . . be widowed.

Since Daisy Mae is not only attractive but half-undressed to prove it, clearly all she lacks is not Stupefyin's form, but her stripper's bumps and grinds. Her hiring a stripper to stun a man into matrimony on her behalf is supposed to show a becoming lack of vanity, rather than a cynical exploitation of sex-appeal (since L'il Abner wants to marry her *really*). It's as if good girls are tasteless, only very bad girls are sexy. Indeed, Wolfenstein and Leites make a special point of the way in which, from 1945 to 1950, American films showed the good girl appearing in situations which make her seem sexy, bad—and interesting (her goodness reappears in time for the happy end, but not early enough to become boring). This is the distinction between Daisy Mae and Stupefyin'. A deliberate, grinding-out provocation is the effective feminine riposte to male diffidence.

Further, an awful lot of *looking* is going on. If Stupefyin' don't git yer, Fleagle will. And Wolfenstein and Leites again come to our rescue, in their chapter entitled *Looking is Enough*. 'The enjoyment of the pin-up girl . . . illustrates another tendency. Looking at the picture of a beautiful girl under conditions where girls may be unavailable (in various Army situations, for instance) can presumably be pleasurable only if it does not evoke too strongly the impulses which require more than looking for their satisfaction. Americans cultivate to a high degree the capacity for the enjoyment of looking, without the evocation of longings which would end in frustration and resentment against the tantalizing stimulus. . . . Looking becomes on the surface at least free from tension and is accompanied by the feeling that one only wants to look.' This placid voyeurism is celebrated also in the song 'Standin' on the corner, Watchin' all the girls go by . . .', and the serenity goes with, one might add, a certain obsessiveness. In this comic context, looking becomes what, perhaps, the unconscious feels it to be—a sort of explosiveness. Stupefyin's is petrifyin', an amicable, assembly-line Medusa, a gorgeous Gorgon.

But what of Evil Eye, with his creepy, jiggering, snaky gait? Here, of course, is the situation, common, not only in American melodrama, but in American history, of Mr. Big hiring the hoodlums to do his dirty work. He's a little man in green, traditionally the colour of the supernatural, specifically, fairies—a double meaning which, however fortuitous—isn't irrelevant, and of jealousy. Though only little, he seems to writhe along like that well-known phallic symbol, the snake. His glance has a power which, by its symmetry to Stupefyin's, is sexual—but homosexual. Maybe it's not for nothing that, earlier on, L'il Abner, in his regretful diffidence to Daisy Mae, sings 'I'd rather have my brothers—than anything else I know'. The male turns from the demanding mother to relaxation with his buddies, his pals, his bachelor party. Fleagle is their nightmare form.

Evil Eye is in cahoots with Appassionata, like whom he is working for Bullmoose. The evil, writhing little gangster is in cahoots with the smooth, respectable father-figure. Bullmoose's father-figure role is underlined by the fact that he *really* possesses Appassionata, who is to be L'il Abner's bride. Where European literature tends to come up with wicked stepmothers, Bullmoose is, so to speak, a wicked step-father whose oedipal overtones intriguingly reverse the traditional pattern. Here father tricks his son into marrying their common woman. This squares with the partial abdication, under Momism, of 'pop' from the prohibition role, and with the denial of jealousy exemplified in the 'looking' situation.

Bullmoose's foul plan succeeds. But L'il Abner is saved on the eve of his wedding by the intervention of his unsuccessful rival for Daisy Mae, one Earthquake McGoon. McGoon is a sort of transition figure between L'il Abner (like whom he's Herculean) and his fellow-yokels (like whom he's dirty rather than clean-living). But he's as malicious as his fellow-yokels are amiable (indeed he proclaims himself 'the world's champeen low-down-dirty wrassler'). Earthquake promises to save L'il Abner from Appassionata if Daisy Mae will marry him. He gatecrashes the wedding reception in Washington, ricochets Fleagle's stare from a silver salver on to Bullmoose, who confesses and is led off by the cops. Nothing like a bit of honest brutality to save one's hero from the sneaky fairy (just as toughness is not only a development of American individualism, but also defence against fear of being cissy). The repugnant Earthquake, incidentally, is the only sexually normal male in the film.

By now, laboratory tests have proved that while Yokumberry Tonic has turned all the scruffy Dogpatch husbands into prime sides of beautiful beefcake, it has also deprived them of what Dr. Johnson was said to have described as 'amorous propensities'. Now Mammy Yokum realizes her tragic error. She has given her boy his wonderful physique at the expense of his love-life. Her poisonous tonic has made him sexually impotent (a wicked-witch type thing to have done, albeit unintentionally).

Demoralized, she listens, for once, to Pappy Yokum. He maintains that he knows the secret formula for another old folk tonic. This was invented by the Dogpatch civic hero, General Jubilation T. Cornpone, the Confederate Commander who single-handedly won the war for the Federals. Cornpone's 'potent rejuvenating and passionizing potion' will restore L'il Abner's git-up-and-go—although, Pappy chuckles to himself, 't'aint nothin' but a drop o' dirty old crick-water . . .'. In short, the secret that the fathers pass on to sons is that American-puritan substitute for virility—the old I-think-I-can-I-know-I-can Samuel Smiles sunnyside-up optimism. 'I want, therefore I can.'

But now that L'il Abner's wedding to Appassionata is off, Daisy Mae's with the loathsome Earthquake is on. Earthquake, surely, is a cousin of the Rod Steiger character in *Oklahoma*, the lonely, knife-drawing pariah whom the film condemns, with surprising savagery, to perish on a burning haystack. In a sense he is the 'manichean' opposite of L'il Abner. L'il Abner is a rustic virgin Hercules, a type not rare in American films (cf. *Bus Stop, Seven Brides for Seven Brothers, The Unforgiven*). Develop some of his characteristics in a less pleasant way, mix him with a dash of Earthquake's malice, and one arrives at the narcissistic, bicep-flexing homosexual hoodlums of *Murder by Contract* and *The Sound of Fury*.

At the last moment Daisy turns the tables on McGoon, by making it a condition of the marriage that all their even more loathsome relatives will come to live with them; this appals even Earthquake, resulting in the neat poetic justice of the biter bit. Then Washington officials arrive and find in Cornpone's statue a grateful testimony from Abraham Lincoln; this turns it into a national shrine and saves

Dogpatch. The merry wives of Dogpatch get their husbands back, lazy, dirty and amorous once more. Daisy Mae and L'il Abner are all set for their wedding which, true to the Fabian tactics of the comic strip, isn't actually shown, for the film finishes with seven or eight last-minute delayings of weddings—if Daisy Mae isn't fending Earthquake off, sudden interruptions delay her wedding to L'il Abner.

Earthquake has, after all, saved L'il Abner from Bullmoose, an act which may be selfish but deserves a little appreciation. Here there is a reference to the tension between city and hick America, in which the small towns of the South and Middle West maintain that they are a fount of folksy virtues, as opposed to the corrupt machinations of the city, big business and gangsters. The film to some extent accepts this myth: Bullmoose, Appassionata and Fleagle are big city characters. Still, Senator Phogbound is a rustic figure, Available is middle-class small-town and Earthquake is not only a (city) 'wrassler' but a feuding hillbilly. As the folksy strong man, brutally and healthily, exposing the sneaky, hypnotic machinations of sophisticated America, isn't Earthquake a bit of a Joe McCarthy (so that a recent panic about Communists is related to a fear of the homosexual enemy-seducer? Such a formulation might well throw some light on, for example, aspects of Moral Rearmament, with its common bracketing of commies and homosexuals).

But if the film accepts the country-city dichotomy, it is to subvert it. L'il Abner stands to attention and salutes whenever he even thinks of the U.S.A. This is a good example of parody-exaggeration *becoming* reversal, for super-patriotism leads to audience laughter. Again, small-town jingoism leads to Cornpone being revered for all the wrong reasons (which of course are also the right ones, since American patriotism demands that the South should have lost the war). Much as Addison and Steele in the eighteenth century ridiculed the Tory party by inventing such lovable old buffers as Sir Roger de Coverley, so Al Capp ridicules naïve know-nothing patriotism by inventing lovable L'il Abner.

The film's attitude towards the U.S. Government is ambivalent. On the one hand, Dogpatch, the disreputable paradise, the South Sea Island of the U.S.A., must be saved from the earnest, coldly efficient prigs of Washington—scientists, officials. National Shrines are ridiculed (L'il Abner innocently remarks that Washington is so full of National Shrines that you can hardly spit without hitting one). And there is a quiet sarcasm in the view of the Capitol from Bullmoose's window, during Appassionata's wedding reception, where the visual 'framing' suggests, Washington belongs to Bullmoose. But, for all its faults, naïvety, priggishness, ruthlessness, Washington is infinitely fairer than Bullmoose. It gives the Dogpatchians their chance. It sternly but valuably spots the flaws in Mamma Yokum's tonic. And finally it concedes defeat, Dogpatch is saved. Thus the film is even more anti-big-business than it is anti-government, for the government can be benevolent, if *resisted*. It is a 'city', Democrat film; but it is in its ambivalence that it's truest to American tensions, and it's not in the least surprising to see Al Capp satirizing the anti-Vietnam-war protestors as savagely as he can contrive.

The film is surprisingly complex in other ways. Earthquake, though loathsome, earns a little of our sympathy in his frenzied passion for Daisy Mae. L'il Abner is both adorable and ridiculous. Mammy Yokum is both a fairy godmother (with her crystal ball) and a wicked stepmother (with her toxic tonic). The characters are only strip-cartoon outlines, but their traits, and our feelings about them, are agreeably mixed, so that, in true folk-art style, their simple, striking personalities show plenty of intriguing contradictions.

Even the physical effects of Fleagle's gaze have a certain complexity. When one of his patent glances hits you, 'Your bone-marrow frizzles, your pancreas petrifies, and your red corpuscles stop dead in their tracks.' In short, it's radioactive fallout. His other glance is a truth-drug. The fairy wizard has space-age weapons.

Of course, no spectator stops to think, 'How extraordinarily complex, Evil Eye Fleagle = No. 1 hex man in the sporting world + atomic warfare + Big Brother + a gangster + homosexuality.' But if the lines get such admiring laughs, and his personality has such intriguing resonance, it's because they jerk the mind quickly through all sorts of incongruous emotions. Part of our pleasure in comedy is in the way the jokes dart about and confuse us. We are lost and giddy, creatures of contradictory impulse and fancy, at once as innocent and as shameless as children.

9 · The World turned Inside-out— and On

Apart from its satirical streak, *L'il Abner* offers us another kind of pleasure—the pleasure of living in a sort of spoof Utopia, a place where all kinds of crazy and incompatible things occur. According to Aristophanes, Cloud-Cuckoo-Land is where you can not only beat your father but then get praised for it. Like so many comedies, it acts as a Saturnalia, which Fowler explains as 'the Ancient Roman festival of Saturn in December, observed as a time of unrestrained merry-making with temporary release of slaves . . . scene or time of wild revelry or tumult . . .'. Not only slaves, but inhibitions, were released, as, every year, 'on December 17 to 24 a reign of topsy-turveydom obtained, restraints were abandoned, and masters and men diced and drank together. The mighty put down from the seat, the lower classes were given the utmost licence . . . at the Kalends, a New Year festival, the same sort of disorder prevailed, but now for three days . . . revellers carnivalled in animal-skins or dressed in women's clothes . . .'.

In medieval Europe the custom of periodical Saturnalia remained part of folklore. As A. P. Rossiter explains, 'As Rituals they remained part of the perpetually resisted, persistently recurrent pagan underlay of subsequent Christendom. . . .' In 1445 the Dean of the Faculty of Theology at Pisa protested against days 'when priests and clerks are seen wearing masks and monstrous visages at the hours of Office: dancing in the choir, dressed as women, panders or minstrels, singing lewd songs. They eat black pudding at the horn of the altar next the celebrant, play at dice there, censing with foul smoke from the soles of old shoes, and running and leaping about the whole church in unblushing shameless iniquity; and then, finally, they are seen driving about the town in carts and deplorable carriages to make an infamous

62

spectacle for the laughter of bystanders and participate with indecent gestures of the body and language most unchaste and scurrilous'.

Any such loss of restraint is more severely frowned on today, although vestiges of the old revelry remain, fadingly, in some old village ceremonies, in Guy Fawkes' Night, on New Year's Eve in Piccadilly Circus, and Rag Days at universities. The entertainment media have taken over their function. Screen comedy often uses satire as springboards to vicarious Saturnalia, where routine acts and emotions are hilariously upset. Fun breaks out with the Marx Brothers at the *Opera*, at the *Races*, in the *Big Store* or in Freedonia; it explodes in *Hellzapoppin* and in *Million-Dollar Legs*, in the dancing numbers of *Singing In The Rain* and *42nd St.*

Less 'farcical' or stylized, and therefore nearer, in a sense, to the serious reality of classical and medieval revelry, *Never on Sunday* is a fine example of a modern 'Saturnalia' comedy. Its huge international success is no freak. In London, it ran for twenty weeks at the London Pavilion, where the usual run is from two to three weeks, and recovered its cost from this one showing alone. Although it was partially subtitled, still on release, as Josh Billings reported, 'High, low and middlebrow are lapping up the Greek comedy. . . . *Never on Sunday* has taken an incredible amount of money, and much has come from those who don't normally go to the "flicks". In spreading the picture-going habit, *Never on Sunday* is alone worth a place in film history.'

The heroine is a Greek prostitute (Melina Mercouri) who only makes love to men she loves and doesn't worry too much about the money. She believes in combining business with pleasure. Her professional pose conceals the lover of love. All her lovers are friends together and seem to spend most of the day celebrating the fact, by foregathering in the local café and dancing and getting drunk, with occasional fisticuffs to vary the pleasure. A handsome young Italian who really loves her will surely be successful in the not-too-far-distant future. The heroine is kind (but not too sentimental), generous, independent, temperamental, childish, wise. She is played by Melina Mercouri with such caustic yet warm exuberance that no one could not believe in her; she delights the ladies as she enchants the men.

The film's hero, Homer Thrace (Jules Dassin), a cultured and very earnest American, represents our moral misgivings, in their most charitable form. He is fond of the heroine, he wants to improve and reform her, to endow her with his appreciation for finer things. But she converts him, and, at last, the missionary of sweetness-and-light throws sublimation to the winds and cries with the joy of the newly liberated, 'From the first moment I only wanted to sleep with you!' But his moral earnestness has been just a little too precious, a little too ridiculous, for us to share. His desire to improve her has led him to take, unintentionally, the side of a gangster who is trying to organize the local girls, against her spirit of freedom. His misgivings paraphrase ours, he is the fall-guy for our prejudices—but we recognize ourselves in him, and, when he leaves Greece, without her, we feel we are leaving, and losing her, with him. The film's wistful end is more satisfying than a happy one.

One little running gag shows Melina's lovers in their happiness constantly smashing glasses—either deliberately or accidentally; and promptly the glum café proprietor rings up its price on the cash register. These pleasantly trivial little acts of destruction, whose cost is rigorously calculated, has a kind of freedom-within-glumness which is both 'absurd' and 'solid'. So when the missionary of higher things at last admits that the prostitute has converted him it's not only Melina's other lovers who, on the screen, applaud his apostasy, but, 'e'en the ranks of Decency could scarce forbear to cheer'. A reviewer in *Annunciation*, the British Roman Catholic magazine, devoted to entertainment and its moral content, opined, 'The fact remains . . . that in spite of the basic amorality of the film there is nothing really unpleasant about it. This is mainly due to the light, humorous touch with which the whole affair is handled, the infectious high spirits of all concerned, and principally to the acting of Melina Mercouri as the prostitute . . . she conveys a warmth and generosity and love of life which seems to make absolutely credible the character she portrays. . . . The film is not altogether without moral value in that it is through the genuine love of one man and not through "culture" and the more obvious approach that she is, redeemed. Unobjectionable as the film is, one may also ask oneself whether any film ever painted vice in more attractive colours, or celebrated more gleefully the rejection of any number of the values on which society is founded, and so on. What an insidious effect this recruiting poster for prostitution must have on impressionable teenagers who, of course, don't know that prostitution isn't always like this! "When prostitution is a joke, the public's sense of humour has been depraved! And for that the film industry is largely responsible." In fact, of course, comic immorality antedates the cinema by a good few centuries, and will survive it by as many.

Part Two

THE GREAT AMERICAN SILENCE

10 · The Founding Fathers

Slapstick, like so many other things which we now think of as 'characteristically American', e.g. the Western, the gangster film, Pearl White serials and Cinemascope, was a gift to America from France. Years before Mack Sennett, French comedies swarmed with comic stuntmen called *cascadeurs*, who, in Nicole Védrès's words, 'really did perform the plunge from the third storey into a tub of washing; and at the exact moment that the floor of a room fell through, each man knew precisely where to leap—one on to the piano, another on to the aspidistra—silk hats still in their hands, lorgnettes dangling, beards a-quiver'. There was even a comic Emergo, 'one saw the *cascadeur* on the screen of the old Gaumont-Palace pursue his unfaithful wife from cab to cab, arrive at the door of the Gaumont-Palace itself, be refused entrance because of his disorderly dress, and resolve to get in over the roof. The screen darkened, the lights went up, and there, in the auditorium, shinning down on a rope from the ceiling, in person, was the very same *cascadeur* . . .'.

In 1907 Nonguet set a flotilla of nannies racing their prams across Paris rooftops (prefiguring the London–Brighton pram race in Michael Bentine's *It's A Square World!*). A charming little film starring Little Moritz had the very Mack Sennett idea of an entire house cascading into ruins under the energetic efforts of two irate men, one tugging away at the inside of a wall with his chest expanders while the other simultaneously hauls irately at a jammed bell-rope. The floors flap like so many trampolines, the walls stagger groggily and the chandeliers bob about like cutglass yoyos. From Italy came the equally inspired films of her Mad Mafia, André Deed (Foolshead in Britain), Tontalini, Polidor, Tweedledum and Bloomer.

Thus the Latin cinema broke through into the freedom of destructive absurdity, while American comedies were still 'cabin'd, cribb'd, confin'd' by the framework of the music-hall sketch. Mack Sennett studied the early French films, which were triumphantly cascading through American cinemas. Being a true genius, he not only acclimatized their style, he went on to intensify it. By 1912 he was beginning to establish the unholy trinity of American screen comedy: parody (of other films), ridicule (especially of noble virtues and lofty sentiments) and visual knockabout (which he lifted, by insistence and inventiveness, to the level of poetic fantasy).

Originally, the taste of crazy comedy was a speciality of uneducated, proletarian audiences. The French cinema abandoned it as its audiences became more respectable, and it continued its development in the U.S.A., with its vast city audiences of illiterate immigrants. As, in the 30's, American audiences in their turn became 'middle-class' (in aspiration and ideas, if not always in fact), crazy comedy, as we shall see, faded there too (or changed character), only to stage a comeback in the 60's, when affluence brought with it a more general feeling of being thoroughly at sea amongst all sorts of social, spiritual and sexual absurdities.

The mainspring of crazy comedy seems to be an awareness of quick, crazy tensions between man and man, man and society. Hence, perhaps, it has always been a shared taste between the proletariat and the intellectual. It seems to go with individualism, but with that individualism which feels lost in a crowd. So slapstick is soon identified with the land of immigrants, not only from all over the world, but those who poured from all the log cabins into the big cities.

Since 1914, French comedy has generally found its inspiration in the human touch, in interplay between people. The dominant mood of René Clair, long the nearest French artist to slapstick, is of a wistful loneliness. The slapstick element is a counterpart to this mood. But American slapstick traditionally drew its inspiration from the interplay of people with things and tasks. In France not only does Paris constitute a huge hothouse of emotional sophistication, but, via education, it profoundly influences a peasant and *bourgeois* nation. Instead of Paris, America had a rustic puritan past (with its simple-minded emphasis on industriousness and success), the rough and ready cultural melting-pots of the cities, and a middle-class ethos which was stiff with its conformist, rationalist, optimistic ideals. Thus American comedy continues to derive its poetry from coupling simple and violent human attitudes with a delirium of physical and mechanical knockabout.

Even within the actual sphere of physical action it's possible to point to a difference of emphasis between French and American physical humour. The French films were about chaos caused by people, Sennett's about people caught up in chaos. In the Little Moritz film, the house is pulled apart because people keep pulling. Though catastrophic rage isn't exactly unknown in Sennett still the name Sennett recalls speed gone mad, fandangos of disintegrating flivvers, spraying Keystone Kops to right and left as they swerve between converging streetcars, of jalopies stuck on level crossings as expresses charge nearer at supersonic velocity, of a crazy world, of a ballistic nightmare. An archetypal scene occurs in the Larry Semon comedy *Kid Speed*. A tired sheriff snores contentedly in bed (his badge pinned to his nightgown, naturally) until woken by the back-firing of Larry's 8-h.p. Snoozenburg being garaged next door. Larry promises to start her up quietly, but unfortunately starts her up in reverse. His car crashes through the wooden wall into the sheriff's bedroom, and hooks its back bumper over the sheriff's brass bedstead, which is soon being hauled along the public highway at 60 m.p.h. The rudely awoken sheriff leaps around on his bed waving his fists, only succeeding in getting tangled up and stumbling about in his sheets.

Much of Sennett's comedy is about the shock of speed, its insult to man. Again and again he turns the human body into a projectile, or into a package to be manhandled by physical laws—gravitational, ballistical, geometrical. Trees, cars, people alike are analysed down into objects whose fates become matters of weight, mass, trajectories, momentum, inertia, fulcrums and other impersonal qualities. Man's limbs become so many bars or levers, his body a cannonball. Even his skin becomes a flexible envelope, as when an over-zealous anaesthetist gives Ben Turpin so much gas that he swells up like the R101 and floats slowly around the room.

Sometimes slapstick makes domination of man by the machine even more marked. In an early Chaplin, *Dough and Dynamite* (1915) the human body is all but reduced to an apparatus for punching, kicking, ducking and dodging. It becomes a none-too-intelligent piece of protoplasm which has made a slap-happy adaptation to a civilization of crankshafts and flywheels. As Charlie's mate staggers under a sack of flour five times too large for him, and his legs begin to buckle, no one, not even the sufferer himself, thinks of so much as removing the sack from his shoulders, or helping him with his burden. They just push his legs back into the perpendicular, as if they were pit props. Often Charlie moves according to the most rigorous mechanical laws. If he wants to turn a corner at speed, he has to stick one leg out by way of counterbalance. If he wants to run away he has first to rev up by running on the spot. This, by contrasting with his desire for haste, gives us a curious impression that he's going backwards, like a car whose brakes are released. These things are based, of course, on physical experiences (the ballistic problems involved in running fast round corners), but the very stress on the physical problems of running has a materialistic tinge. We are not so far from the preoccupations of Muybridge and Marey. And the sharp, curt, pat, staccato movements of so many Sennett comics are vastly more machine-like than any form of comedy that had existed before.

Only a few years earlier the French philosopher Henri Bergson, in his famous essay on Laughter, had couched his view of comedy in the very terms which were to inspire Sennett. 'The attitudes, gestures and movements of the human body are laughable in exact proportions as that body reminds us of a machine . . . comedy arises from something mechanical encrusted on the living.' He was writing in 1900, before slapstick was so much as a gleam in Mack Sennett's eye, and said, 'On two occasions only have I been able to observe this style of the comic in its unadulterated state.' He found it in the most lowbrow medium of his day, the routine of two circus clowns. Clown wasn't then the respectable word it is now and Bergson describes their act with so sharp and friendly an eye that one can only hope he subsequently found his way to cinemas to enjoy his fellow-philosopher Mack Sennett's extraordinarily literal application of his theories.

Not that the mechanical is the only source of Sennett's humour. In the course of his thesis Bergson extended his notion of the 'mechanical' to include any maladjustment, any inept, inapt, or subadult response. Similarly the personages of *Dough and Dynamite*, amoeba-like, respond promptly to a prevailing stimulus—a beautiful waitress, a kick up the behind—but as abruptly recover from it after it has been removed, whereupon they await the next stimulus to prod them into action again. Affection and irritation spring up and die down, in split seconds, in a twinkling of the reflexes. There's certainly a reference to childhood impulsiveness, but the absurdity is so drastic as to go beyond that. It reduces man to the status of a mere package of conditioned reflexes. Pavlov's dogs are masterminds compared to those nippy little knockabout monsters, dashing about the screen with the rapidity of jumping fleas. As Bergson said, 'We laugh every time a person gives us the impression of being a thing.' Such a formulation, like Sennett's humour, is inconceivable before the materialism of the nineteenth century. Isn't the depersonalizing humour of *Dough and Dynamite* a reflection of the mental climate that produced Pavlov and Behaviourism? The harsh, callous indifference of the slapstick world is softened only by our laughter.

The shift in stress, by Sennett, from the music-hall's older comedy of character to the comedy of mechanized man, parallels the invention, not many years before, of time-and-motion study, by Frederick W. Taylor. Daniel Bell's fascinating account of the birth of 'Taylorism', since become the keystone of modern industrial culture, leaves us with the pleasant reflection that this apostle of American super-efficiency was himself a raging obsessional neurotic, who, even when he went out for a walk, compulsively counted his steps, so as to ascertain the most effortless stride (he was also a lifelong martyr to nightmares and insomnia—irrational nature taking its revenge?). His first triumphant demonstration of his method was in 1899, and Henry Ford established his assembly line in 1914. Thus Sennett's films register not only the shock of speed but the spreading concept of man as an impersonal physical object existing only to work rapidly, rhythmically, repetitively. But Sennett parodies the conception, to concoct a universe where authority, routine and the monotony of factory days are shattered, as cars burst into bedrooms and beds race down the highway. Comedy, by exaggeration, veers towards revolt, an orgy of disorder, a Saturnalia of chaos.

Bergson applied the concept of the mechanical also to the influence of habit—beautifully parodied when Chaplin, in *Shoulder Arms*, gets into his waterlogged bunk with short sharp movements as if he were still on the parade ground. In *The Idle Class*, Charlie plays a dual role, as a tramp, and a rich playboy constantly befuddled by alcohol. Much of the humour depends on his bringing the reflexes of the tramp into the role of the aristocrat. This humour of misplaced habit, as distinct from humour of character, is not absent from earlier humour, but has a special emphasis in twentieth-century comedy, as if we moderns are more conscious than previous generations of a gap between what we feel, what we do, and what we seem, between our hearts and our acts.

71

Vast sectors of Sennett slapstick are, of course, not centred on the mechanical at all. Indeed Bergson's use of the word begins to show severe signs of strain when he tries to extend it to include, not only childlike behaviour, but even dreamlike atmospheres. For what could be less mechanical, more organic, than childish impulses or dreams?

The extraordinary richness of Sennett slapstick comes, perhaps, from the juxtaposition of these various 'mechanism' jokes, with jokes depending on such un-mechanical things as childlike impulse, infra-dig feelings, dream fantasy and visual poetry. The bakery in *Dough and Dynamite*, whose denizens are all constantly being stuck, bogged down, or trussed up, in tubs or swathes of dough, becomes a nightmarish netherworld. The generally infernal atmosphere is reinforced by the red-hot oven wall on to which the characters keep backing. What could more closely reproduce the common dream situations, of peril or embarrassment, than the sheriff in his nightshirt behind the Snoozenburg; a ghost, by daylight, at 60 m.p.h.? or Ben Turpin and his bride in *Wedding Yells* aboard an automobile which, deprived of all four wheels, keeps getting parked on level crossings while express trains suddenly materialize out of hitherto empty horizons? or, in *A Laugh A Day*, a man running away from his neighbours while the barrel which surrounds his modesty, explosively disintegrates, back and front?

And, always, slapstick comedians are childlike, and in consequence act out the impulses which as adults we suppress. Hal Roach put it, 'Actually the great comedians are representing or portraying children or the things that children do . . . Chaplin's . . . hitting himself in the back of the head with his cane and looking around to see who hit him is the action of a child.' And accordingly they are as indecent as children. When Ben Turpin hangs out of a window with his breeches hooked over a turned-on tap, until his trousers swell up to a huge size and finally spurt little jets of water from twenty or thirty holes, the overtones of wind and wee aren't too hard to see. The latter are confirmed by a similar scene. Charlie Chase is about to empty his waterlogged plus-fours in the street, until, scowled at by a passing cop, he hurries quickly away, as if he had been about to commit, if not a crime, at least a nuisance.

Silent slapstick could reduce to utter absurdity any human activity whatsoever, from politics to the very processes of consciousness. Snub Pollard plays El Presidente of a bomb-happy South American republic, where bombs with smoking fuses materialize from under cops'

helmets, in socks and in street-urchins' footballs; one is even placed
in its target's outstretched hand as he signals a left turn. For American
audiences the real moral of this delicious burlesque of foreign politics
is that all foreigners are absurd; but, even if, as satire it's smug rather
than subversive, it becomes something rather more than satire, for its
atmosphere is quite demential. James Agee has beautifully described
the expressionism with which Sennett comedy presented its basically
rather cruel vision of man's thought processes. 'When a modern
comedian gets hit on the head, for example, the most he is apt to do
is to look sleepy. When a silent comedian got hit on the head, he
seldom let it go so flatly. So he gave us a . . . vision for loss of
consciousness. In other words he gave us a poem, a kind of poem,
moreover, that everybody understands. The least he might do was to
straighten up stiff as a plank and roll over backward with such skill
that his whole length seemed to slap the floor at the same instant. Or
he might make a cadenza of it—look vague, smile like an angel, roll
up his eyes, lace his fingers, thrust his hands palm downwards as far
as they would go, hunch his shoulders, rise on tiptoe, prance ecstatically in narrowing circles until, with tallow knees, he sank down the
vortex of dizziness on the floor, and there signified Nirvana by kicking
his heels twice, like a swimming frog.' The angelic smile, the beatific
trance, the frog's Nirvana, all due to a bonk on the cranium, exhibit
a sweetly ruthless irony about the human soul. Chaplin's *The Champion* has a similar joke about individuality and le style, c'est l'homme.
Each of the burly pugilist's sparring partners comes at him with an
elaborately different style of boxing—and each gets knocked out in
about two seconds flat by exactly the same, nonchalant, crude swing.

Although Sennett slapstick registers the shock of speed and mechanization it is by no means a protest against them. On the contrary, it
accepts them as children accept them, as conditions of life, and it
makes of them a source of festive disorder, a revenge which is a brief
mental liberation from its oppressive aspects. It hoists the 'enemy'—
the system—with its own petard. Yet the frequency of disaster in
Sennett is, by a paradox common in comedy, an expression of zest,
energy and ruthlessness of, in short, the American virtues which
Sennett himself possessed super-abundantly. In a sense, their message
is the opposite of that of the feeding-machine sequence in *Modern
Times*. Not, of course, that Chaplin's and Sennett's attitudes are
incompatible. Chaplin takes slapstick to the point of protest and
tragedy, so as to remind us that the consequence of mechanization

can be an outrage to the dignity of man. Sennett reminds us that, like his pin-men, we may be lucky, and survive this hectic world better than we sometimes fear. Even so, the fearsome bouncers, the punches, the kicks, the quick thefts and confidence tricks, the split-second utter lack of emotion, aren't as innocently childlike and stylized as the often only too sheltered critic may assume, and it's Chaplin who leaves us in no doubt that the usual inspiration behind slapstick is a stylization, not so much of childish innocence, as of the shifts needed to survive in a city jungle which, for immigrant and offspring, was an extremely chaotic and heartless one.

That mixture of confidence and callousness which enables Sennett to make his nightmares so outrageous and so funny, and which only an American could have taken so far, is beautifully summed up in the grand finale of MGM's *Hollywood Review of 1929*, where Buster Keaton, Marie Dressler, Bessie Love and the entire MGM roster of stars, all clad in yellow oilskins, cheerfully render 'Singin' in the Rain' while the rain pours down—before a backcloth, showing, on a mountainside, Noah's Ark. It's also neatly crystallized in the lyric Crosby and Sinatra sing at a party in *High Society*:

> '*Have you heard? It's in the stars,*
> *Next July we collide with Mars.*'
> '*Well, did you ever?*'
> '*What a swell party this is.*'

Only that spirit could dream up a scene where a series of cars roar into a one-track tunnel and a second later an express roars out.

Anyone can laugh at such a joke, but only an American like Sennett (or perhaps the odd Parisian) could have invented it, and hundreds of others like it. The art of slapstick lies in knowing (to hijack a phrase of Cocteau's) just how far to go too far. For however naïve slapstick seems, it isn't a naïve art-form (as innumerable British attempts at it only too lugubriously prove). Sennett repeatedly stressed the importance of some sort of possibility, of visual logic, in even the absurdest happenings. Lewis Jacobs records how Sennett had gags and scenarios explained to him verbally (never in writing), and, 'Often, during the telling of a story, Sennett, trailed by the writer, would go to the corner of the studio where his locales—lakes, rooms, fire escapes, etc.—were chalked out, and there work out the plan of the film. . . .' Clearly the mechanics of set-ups and things were more suggestive than those of character. Sennett himself said that he thought in terms of an idea rather than of individual personalities, 'Having found your hub idea, you build out the spokes; these are the natural developments which your imagination suggests. Then, introduce your complications that make up the funny wheel. . . .' He continued ruefully, 'We have tried famous humorists and I can say with feeling their stuff is about the worst we get.' One can't help feeling that this was not simply because of the screen's requirements, but also because of the newness and lowness of Sennett's humour, based as it was on a social stratum, on an experience of life, and a view of man, quite different from that of men-of-letters.

Not that his films are devoid of human interest. Even if his gags sprang from ideas and action rather than from character, Sennett knew the importance of gags not being out of character. His comedians passed gags on to one another, as more suitable for another's screen personality.

The best slapstick gags, however impossible, always have a kind of poetic rightness. Buster Keaton said, 'Nothing is worse than an ill-suited gag.' Larry Semon, thrown out of his car, which is leading the race, picks himself up and runs after it with such doggedness that he overtakes all the other cars and leaps into his driving-seat again. Larry defeats impossibility by running with all the 'I think I can, I think I can' earnestness of childhood. The impossible we do immediately: the inconceivable takes a little longer. Thus the 'gag' becomes a miracle deserved, indeed, compelled, by his sublimely dogged foolishness. Napoleon asked, before promoting an officer, 'Is he lucky?', and, similarly, Buster Keaton's aquiline gravity has the power to 'compel' luck, to turn it into fate. For poetry, even comic poetry, and superstition are profoundly connected, arising from the same springs of the imagination.

Speed isn't the only string to Sennett's bow. Much of the knock-about depends on a pigsty, barnyard, errand-boy, cabbage-patch, handyman frame of reference, vastly more meaningful when so many Americans had built their own homes, scratched a frugal living from dusty patches of soil.

With their variety of inspiration, Sennett's films have the richness to gain, rather than lose, from the sea-changes of time. To all their other charms, they now possess, not simply nostalgia, but a stranger kind of period charm. The tenderest absurdity now imbues Sennett's grotesque parodies of fashions and furnishings that no longer exist, parodies often far more delicious than the real thing. Particularly poignant, because of the slapstick context, is the grey, sober beauty of orthochrome and fixed-focus (in effect, almost deep-focus), which adds such an elegiac detail to the backgrounds of the action. There is that famous sequence of one tired old man pushing, not only his own stalled Model T, but a whole train of jalopies, forlornly up a gradient, not noticing they are dropping, one by one, over the edge of a precipice. The backgrounds of these comedies record a rustic America, of bleak shacks, of dusty hills, of flat horizons broken only by telegraph poles, of bare roads, of stores bulging with barrels and stoves. How poignant the contrast between this harsh, lonely world and the pranks and tricks performed by the human fleas—tricks sometimes less interesting than this vanished world, and setting it off with a soulless irony that's like a bitter elegy. . . .

The dreary slum frontages of *Easy Street* plunge us straight into the harrowing atmosphere of Arthur Morison's *A Child of the Jago*, and the very simplicity of the settings in *It's A Dog's Life* breathe a hopelessness no less terrible than the tragically bare workers' homes in the Tsarist Russia of Pudovkin's films.

Far from being a limitation, a sign of second-rate status, the (relative) absence of characterization in Sennett's films is of their essence. Depersonalization is part of their comic shock. In a sense, Sennett's humour is a preview of *Modern Times*. But it was his pupil, Chaplin, whose extraordinary eloquence restored a full humanity to slapstick and so made it simultaneously comic and tragic. You don't just laugh till you cry, you also laugh to keep from crying. And so, of course, your emotional defences collapse utterly. . . .

Chaplin wasn't, as is sometimes said, alone in bringing character into slapstick. But where lesser comedians had characters as simple and predictable as melodrama, Chaplin's reactions were a quickfire of nuances, shooting in a second from guttersnipery to romance, from fear to bravado, from brutality to pathos. His very walk gave the impression of being both mincing and bowlegged. His pantomimic skill must have owed something to the English music-hall (from the beginning his American colleagues admired his falling technique), as well as to the Frenchman, Max Linder, who, in turn, owed something to the Boulevard farces. The English music-hall comedians generally would seem ripe for revaluation; Bob Monkhouse, an authority on silent comedy, argues that there has been an unjustified neglect of Linder's foreign contemporaries. The French intelligentsia was quicker to appreciate such infra dig art forms as the music-hall, slapstick and Westerns than their English counterparts, who passed in silence over the equal or superior subtleties of, for example, Will and Fred Evans in *Harnessing A Horse*, 1912. Linder not only admitted to 'learning as much from Chaplin as he ever learned from me' but named Dan Leno and Bill Ritchie as 'the best masters of finesse to visit the Varieties'. Certainly the film sequences from the early 30's, of old troupers like Gus Elen singing 'It's A Great Big Shame' or of Lily Morris singing 'Don't Have Any More, Mrs. More' combine an immense verve with many subtly observed traits. It would be interesting also to explore the connections between the early screen comedies and the diverse music-hall styles in France, England and the U.S.A. After all, Bud Flanagan remarks in *My Crazy Life* that British music-hall artists had become heavily imitative of American as early as 1900, so one can't altogether rule out the possibility that much of what Sennett took from the Europeans was a development out of American ideas in the first place.

11 · Aimless Odysseus of the Alleyways

Chaplin may have derived a prop or two, and aspects of his character (the would-be dandy), from Linder, but psychologically his 'Little Man' is far richer and more complex (and, by 'realistic' standards, far more impossible). He is at once a tramp trying to be a dandy, and a child trying to be an adult. Despite his incessant failure, the delicacy and finickiness of his gestures are far more than a dandy's. They reveal a genuine, painful sensitivity, not at all unegoistic, that one can fairly call soul—a soul at the mercy of the cuffs, the cops, the bullies, all the gutter bestiary, and fate. It's an achievement to create such a character, but Chaplin not only created him, and in comedy, but contrived to gear in a tragic weight of nuance with the gross velocity of Sennettalia. Chaplin's short films are probably the only works of art ever created which can spin the spectator from laughter to tears and back in a *few seconds*. One wonders whether, if it weren't for the Mack Sennett forcing-house, Chaplin would ever have risen to the height he did—and have virtually re-created the art of mime.

While Sennett's slapstick is an art of objects, props, places and people-made-objects, Chaplin crosses it with that pantomimic virtuosity that delights in dispensing with objects altogether—as in his miming of David and Goliath in *The Pilgrim*. A fascinating example of cross-breeding props, mime and puppet-show is offered by the Dance of the Rolls in *The Gold Rush*. Two forks, stuck into rolls, parody legs executing ballet-steps. Sometimes they read as the left and right leg of one person, but sometimes they suggest two people. But if forks are legs and rolls are feet, then what huge feet the dancer has (recalling the huge boots Little Tich wore in the halls before the turn of the century). Moreover, the Little Man, seated at the table, also mimes the dancing with his face, head and shoulders—so that we

78

have a huge head, no body, tiny legs and huge feet, a grotesque caricature made out of both 'puppets' and puppeteer.

Here, as so often, a good joke includes all kinds of sub-jokes, that the conscious mind doesn't notice, but that the laughing mind does. . . .

Chaplin stands at a confluence of traditions. His pathos, and richness as a character, has its roots in nineteenth-century emotionalism whereas the cool callousness of Mack Sennett is more twentieth century. His sensitivity and his quixotism are as poignant as they are only because blended with scurrility, cynicism and all the comic vices.

Indeed, his films, the early ones in particular, abound in satire directed, bitterly, at pity and pathos. In *The Pawnshop* Charlie shamelessly exploits his boss's streak of tender-heartedness. He in turn is fooled by a ham actor whose sobs and groans make Charlie put an outrageously generous valuation on a ring—for which the customer then gives change from a vast bankroll.

Finally, when a lank, scrawny, mental defective brings in an alarm clock Charlie (once bitten, twice shy) examines it so thoroughly that he destroys it, and hands its debris back with a curt shake of the head, emphasizing the point by picking up a hammer and hitting his (completely inoffensive) victim smack between the eyes. If these early films had themes, that of *The Pawnshop* might be defined as *Beware of Pity* or, more scathingly, *Never Give A Sucker An Even Break*.

Raymond Borde points out that in certain scenes in *The Property Man* Charlie exhibits a cruelty rivalling anything in Bunuel. 'Charlie has to carry a very heavy trunk and doesn't fancy the task, so he approaches a colleague, a pitiful old man with an utterly humiliated expression. He loads the trunk on to the back of this human wreck. The man staggers forward, leaning on his cane. Charlie beats him like a mule, and the other collapses altogether, to lie, crushed under his burden, on the ground. To get him going again Charlie leaps up on the trunk, thus adding to the burden of the old man, who now resembles nothing so much as a pathetic beetle pinned to the ground by some sick wit. And *The Property Man* is no exception. In his short films, from 1914 to 1922, Charlie's sadism is incessant. . . .' And, one might add, no less serious, here, and in these terms, than thirty years later, in the verbal terms of *Monsieur Verdoux*.

Maybe this sadism is, by implication, excused by his pathos, but it's also true that Charlie's pathos enables him to be easily the cruellest of Sennett's comedians, with the potential exception of Fatty Arbuckle, whose face is rather more heartless than his actual acts.

So heavily has the stress been laid on Chaplin as a waif, as a sentimental clown, as Don Quixote, and so on, that criticism has all but lost sight of the complementary pole of his inspiration, a disconcerting matter-of-factness about basic, physical things. In *It's A Dog's Life* he hungrily tussles with a dog for a bone (if this isn't sick humour it's hard to see what is). In *The Vagabond* he not only washes the little waif's face, he searches in her hair for fleas, and he finds them. Chaplin remembers those vermin in *Limelight*, where Calvero has two performing fleas, called Phyllis and Henry.

Such humour may be charmingly 'picturesque' nowadays, but it must have had a much more realistic edge for the slum-and-immigrant audiences of the time—as we may have been reminded by the excellent Granada TV documentary, a montage of contemporary photographs evolving the extreme harshness of life for immigrants in the New York of the time, and their exceptionally high death rate, testifying to the traumatic shocks inflicted by the realities of New York's tenements and sweatshops.

Similarly, we tend to remember most of all the 'romantic' love-theme of *The Gold Rush*. But most of the film is concerned with more basic, physical problems of survival—food, warmth and feet. Whether by accident or design, feet acquire a Surrealist enormity. They blend with the theme of food when Charlie cooks and eats a shoe, and with that of warmth when, while he is entertaining Georgia, the rags wrapped round his foot go up in flames, giving him a hot foot and Georgia a (literal) hot seat (Charlie is never too busy for a scurrilous reference. Brushing himself down after being rolled in the dust in *Mable At the Wheel*, he pays particular attention to the seat of his pants, just as in *Limelight* he puns, 'What can the stars do but sit on their axes?').

Although Charlie appears as a gold-seeker, he, essentially, just wanders around the frozen North foraging as aimlessly as along the gutters and doorways of the slum alleys. The prevailing impression left by *The Gold Rush*, far from being, as, in view of Charlie's left-wing sympathies, one might expect, an indictment of gold-fever, greed and capitalism generally, is of tiny figures rushing about in empty spaces. The film's narrative may be about survival, but its visuals are about loneliness. This mood goes with innumerable trance-like situations: dreams (alone, Charlie dreams Georgia is applauding his Dance of the Rolls), hallucinations (starving Big Jim dreams Charlie is a giant chicken), amnesia (Big Jim has found a mountain of gold but can't

1. *Unidentified film, ca. 1930.*
   The involuntary humour of the thrill so excessive as to be reassuring. Or the laughter may hide the breaking of a basic tabu . . .
2. **The Gold Rush:** *Charlie Chaplin, Mack Swain.*

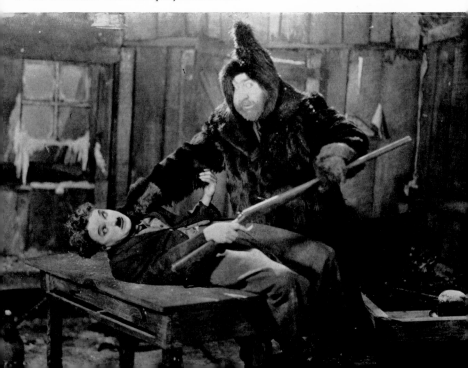

3. **Safety Last:** *Harold Lloyd*
   Man out on a limb, in a time-and-motion study world
4. **Romeo in Pyjamas:** *Buster Keaton*

remember where it is), and confusions of identity (millionaire Charlie dresses as a tramp for the news photographers and so not only meets Georgia again but can be sure her love isn't just a gold-digger's). Although the use of the 'double personality' isn't rare in Chaplin (in *City Lights* and *The Great Dictator*), *The Gold Rush* becomes a special meditation on loneliness, on who-am-I?, on am-I-real? The indefiniteness is enhanced by the featureless white wastes, by a scene where a hut is filled with slowly falling white feathers, and by another showing it being blown miles across country by a high wind, to end perched on the edge of a precipice, balanced on a knife-edge, like a seesaw, such that the slightest movement sets it swaying and tilting into the void.

There isn't a feeling that 'Nature' is the enemy. Nature, here, seems only part of a bad dream from which the characters are all trying to awake. More perhaps by a sure intuition of Chaplin's than by conscious design, *The Gold Rush*, with its loneliness, its confusions of personality, its universal indefiniteness, recalls the feelings of alienations in Kafka (albeit *vis-à-vis* an American chaos instead of a European bureaucracy).

It's interesting too that the *City Lights* idea of a rich man who's only amiable to a poor man when he's drunk was taken up later by the magpie Brecht for *Mister Puntilla and his Valet Matti*. Chaplin links the alienation theme to the greed theme very loosely, as loosely as Antonioni relates Monica Vitti's lonely-city-blues to his Marxist critique of the capitalist system and its gradual chilling of the soul.

It's interesting how often crazy comedy, in its general mood, precedes 'highbrow' message films, presumably because, offering irresponsible exaggerations, it has a fair chance of anticipating the eventual development of current trends.[1]

Modern Times is more 'topical' in its time. Again, one might expect it to be a message film, about the need for workers' solidarity, but it's nothing of the sort. Charlie gets arrested for waving a red flag at the head of a militant mob, but he was only trying to attract the attention of the lorry-driver who'd dropped it. The mob fell in behind him entirely of its own accord.

The film's spirit is thoroughly anarchistic. Its theme of unemployment is subordinate to that of deliberately contracting-out of society. Certainly there is the subsistence theme (food), but here it's not in short supply. On the contrary it's there in abundance for those who

---

[1] Those exaggerations which are non-prophetic come to detract from the comic's appeal, or have a nostalgic effect, or aren't noticed.

will accept the grotesque postures forced on them by the machines. Charlie is put in a feeding-machine. His mate gets trapped in another machine during lunch-break, and has to be fed by Charlie. Charlie later becomes a singing waiter who, caught up in a mass of dancing couples, can't get his food over to his impatient customer.

The theme of home is more agonized, expressing security and independence rather than survival. Charlie and Paulette camp in the luxury 'rooms' of a department store, then make do in a rickety old shack (which he dreams is a country cottage), and finally do without a home altogether. But this time there are two of them to walk off down those long, silent-film roads, towards hills, as bleakly grey as coke-tips, but lightened by a few shafts of sunlight. Even on the road, two people are—home.

In *Modern Times* the Little Man's berserk revolt is against being spoon-fed or mechanical shovel-fed. It is as anarchistic as Harpo Marx's and indeed, resembles it. Just as Harpo would have done, Charlie spreads disorder among his workmates, and he menaces a passing woman with a disquietingly sadistic eroticism (brandishing his spanner like Jack the Ripper's knife and threatening to twist the buttons off her clothes). Even when society sends, not cops to arrest him, but ambulance men to care for him, he, and we, revolt against them, just as the Marxes revolt against kindly Margaret Dumont, because, through our comic heroes, we sense the smothering quality of such 'niceness'.

Some critics of the time reproached Chaplin for seeming to blame the machines rather than the system that misused them. But by doing so, Chaplin attacked the enslavement of man to dogmas of productivity, whether under a profit system or a Stakhanovite one. *Modern Times* is now more modern than ever, for it anticipates that anarchistic faith in the couple, that semi-militant beatnickery, that is increasingly prominent, not only among the Anglo-Saxon young, but also among the youth of Communist countries. *Modern Times* is a layabout's manifesto. . . .

To over-idealize Chaplin into an inoffensive Little Man, all pathos and lovable mischief, a sort of Saint Chaplin, is not only to miss half of his humour and meaning, it is to make nonsense of all that really can be called Chaplin's comedy of the misplaced soul. To be misplaced, it has to be perched in someone who's incongruous and unworthy, who's infra dig, who has a guttersnipe's reflexes and lack of scruple. The mainspring of Chaplin's genius is, in a sense, the spiritual vividness which he gives to the basic, undignified physical things, fleas, feet, sausages. His one semi-failure, *A King in New York*, is also the one film that cut loose from these basics and lost itself in generalizations *about* society. Deep thinkers are two a penny nowadays; but guttersnipes like Charlie are worth their weight in gold.

Although Chaplin's psychological complexity is unrivalled among the 'Sennett school', many other comedians had a real, vivid presence. Marvellous indeed is that startling squint of Ben Turpin's and the dervish fanaticism with which it imbues its possessor. His eyes seem permanently rolled in paroxysmatic emotion, while their violent dislocation endows him a kind of utter helplessness. Hence Turpin was the ideal parodist of high-flown romantic characters, like Valentino and Von Stroheim. Every squint has its own soul, and Ben Turpin's was completely different from James Finlayson's. While Turpin's was both wild and endearing, Finlayson's was as mean and dour as a Scottish dominie's. Fatty Arbuckle was that rarity, a fat man who was neither pathetic nor a bully, but, among all the usual slapstick stupidities, alert, aware and cool.

12 · Self-Help with a Smile

Where Buster Keaton and Harold Lloyd were 'doers', Harry Langdon and Laurel and Hardy were the helpless ones (not that these are hard-and-fast categories, of course: comedy is based on contradiction as much as on consistency). The most cherubic and passive were Harry Langdon and Stan Laurel. Oliver Hardy was a 'tackler', or at least a bungler, so incompetent that he's an honorary member of the helpless club. But Keaton and Lloyd often came off best in their bouts with chaos, and much of Keaton's humour, particularly, is about the neatness of his gambits *vis-à-vis* the impersonal objects amongst which he gambolled. His humour depends on the combination of extreme bungling and extreme skill. His famous 'impassivity' is truer in the spirit rather than the letter. For his craggy, doleful face does change expression, his staring eyes are as eloquent as Eddie Cantor's, and his body is flexible and eloquent—indeed in moments of panic his limbs shoot out all over him like porcupine's quills. In his quiet style, he can be surprisingly versatile—*Sherlock Junior* has a beautiful shot of Keaton, as a suave detective, pressing an electric bell with a fastidious delicacy worthy of Dorian Gray fingering rose-petals.

Keaton said, 'I just concentrated on what I was doing.' This seriousness is a very different thing from the deadpan, and only apparently akin to a clown's mask. Rather Keaton's 'Old Stone Face' seems to blend the traits of America's original inhabitants—the silent solemnity of the Red Indian brave, the gloomy persistence of the Calvinist pioneer. Bleak and woebegone, his countenance holds at once a dour hopelessness and an undaunted never-say-die. He has a kind of childlike promptitude in performing his duty, and brings an almost ecclesiastical solemnity to the outwitting of machinery, to, as it were, redeeming it from its fits of Original Sin. His solemn face conceals the whirring gyroscope of inner-direction.[1] Buster brings a zany genius at lateral thinking to such obsessional tasks as chasing runaway locomotives, becoming a trapezist (in *Blue Blazes*) or trying to sign on for the Confederate Army. Of all the American comedians, he has the most one-track mind. Many of his mistakes spring from it, e.g. he keeps shovelling sand under the locomotive's skidding wheels even after it's moved off. He's as rural-American as the Model T, and has the calmly glum seriousness of the Abe Lincoln generation. He has a log-cabin loneliness and persistence. Yet in his general air of being *too busy* to feel emotion, he oddly anticipates the matter-of-fact dedication of Howard Hawks—which also seems to be modern, cool, derivative from American pioneer puritanism.

Keaton, in action, brings to knockabout both a balletic grace (he is the Fred Astaire of slapstick) and a Euclidean wit. He's a geometrician —in his own words, 'After all, to be able to scratch your ear with one of your toes requires a good dose of discipline, and all discipline boils down to mental discipline. . . .' All his epic battles between man and machine—whether a balloon (*The Balloonatic*), a deserted ship (*The Navigator*) or a locomotive or two (*The General*)—seem built around an *idée fixe*. It's not that they work their way through every comic corollary of a given proposition, for as Montaigne remarked, 'L'art de bien écrire est de sauter les idées intermediaires.' But only Harold Lloyd, matched with skyscrapers, could find as many 'gag-gambits' in a given object. *The Navigator* has been called a '*Robinson Crusoe* in reverse', and it's also the story of Jonah in a mechanical whale.

Keaton virtually directed most of his own films; all have an ascetic, yet dashing, beauty. Perhaps *The General* is the most beautiful, with its spare, grey photography, its eye for the racy, lungeing lines of the great locomotives, with their prow-like cowcatchers, and with its beautifully sustained movement (notably Keaton, astraddle his locomotive tender, chopping away frantically, obliviously, as his locomotive steams through the battlefield, past a contrapuntal pattern of drifting smoke, retreating Confederates, and advancing Federals). In spirit it's not unlike a John Huston film—the young civilian earning his 'red badge of courage'—and it's amusing to imagine what Keaton would have done with the situations of *The African Queen*.

---

[1] Inner-direction is the name which David Reisman in *The Lonely Crowd* gives to that old-fashioned conscientiousness which asks no reward but that of doing what conscience bids. He contrasts the contemporary trend to other-direction, a concern with popularity and conformity to the consensus.

Perhaps his strangest film is *Sherlock Junior*, where he plays a cinema projectionist who scrambles into the film, so getting caught up in (to borrow Jeff Keen's phrase) the movies' space-time warp. He tries to step into the film drawing-room and the door is slammed in his face. As he leans on a pot in the peach-spangled garden, cut, he falls into the middle of a desert. Just as he's picked himself up and is beginning to adapt to that, cut, he's marooned on a spray-soaked black rock. He dives bravely into the angry ocean, only to end stuck head-down in a snowdrift, out of which his black legs kick forlornly. Keaton's aquiline solemnity gives such *Hellzapoppin*-type gags a quite different atmosphere, more reminiscent, perhaps, of the *Ficciones* of Borges.

His face, as mysterious as the statues of Easter Island, hints at his inner realms of dream, and of the emotional reserve suggested by his name in France, Frigo. Bernard Stora comments that, 'His procedure consists in protecting, at all costs, that portion of reality which immediately surrounds him. . . . In this perspective, the sequence of *The Navigator* concerning his subaquatic expedition reveals its full meaning. The liner's propeller being damaged, the young girl who accompanies him on this weird voyage persuades him to don a diving-suit and examine the damage. Having arrived on the ocean-bed, he immediately tries to control this new element by strictly applying the laws which rule that which he has managed to control. He meticulously puts out a sign, "Danger—Men At Work" and carefully washes his hands in a pail of water—which he then empties—under the sea.' The hero has freed himself from his rich youth's maladjustment (no practical sense), only to adopt another maladjustment (a plumber's habits, underwater). Stora sees in Keaton's constant 'trying to reduce life to a structure of habits' a stiltedness of the heart, springing from the same root as his awkward reserve with women. For the virtuoso with machines is a gawk with girls (indeed with people generally). In *Sherlock Junior* he finally treats the screen love scene as an instructional, imitating it move by move, baffled only when it cuts from a passionate kiss directly to the arrival of twins. At the end of *The General* he has to turn his right arm into a saluting-machine so as to kiss his girl undisturbed. But it's also as if part of him is trying to sneak off and become as robotized as the machines which obsess him. Keaton's achievement is to move into this territory, as strange as science-fiction, yet never for a second lose his startling intensity of feeling. Against all these spaces and processes, he acquires all the desperate simplicity of an everyman; as poignant in affirmation, more genial in invention, he becomes as basic an archetype as Beckett's tramps. The New York avant-gardist Alan Scheider built his version of Beckett's *Film* round Keaton's silent eloquent back, and, as Robert Benayoun remarks, 'I don't know if Beckett thought of Keaton in writing this *Film*, but it's unthinkable that any other actor could have played this role, so adapted is it to his physique, his legend, his essential themes.' But perhaps Keaton's real swansong is *The Railrodder* where he traverses Canada on a diesel runabout, as pure, as worried, a totem at seventy as forty years before. This extraordinary sense of time passed, yet revived, of experience marked in this man's face, is, of course, laceratingly part of the film itself, for, by recording personality as it does, the movie medium possesses an aesthetic dimension with which theories relevant to literature, music and painting, are ill-equipped to deal. Cold as he may seem, Keaton's presence is strangely barbed with a quality of stoic elegy, and surely he's not so much the second genius of silent slapstick as the poker-faced compliment to the quicksilver Chaplin.

If Keaton, with his lean, knobbly, mule-face, always has something of the log-cabin loner about him, Harold Lloyd is slapstick's small-town Samuel Smiles. Lloyd played many different characters, from chefs to professors. He might be basically shy and he might be brash; but all his characters have the bounce and pluck of the self-help generation. 'Step right up and call me Speedy' he brags, to cover his shyness. He's a small-town Pollyanna shaping up to all the hectic opportunities of the roaring 20's, and is almost a comic variation of Douglas Fairbanks, who, at the same period, owed his popularity, not to the expensive swashbucklers with which he's now associated, but to his eupeptic playing of unstoppable guys next door. If Keaton is fired by duty rather than ambition, Lloyd is the eager-beaver with pasteurized hopes.

Lacking any hint of introverted depths, he offers less fertile ground for criticism, which has, perhaps, underestimated the resonance of his complete identification with the aspirations of his time. *A Lifetime of Comedy* offers snippets from a fascinating film in which Harold applies time-and-motion-study tricks to his morning journey to work. Darting back into the house for something he's forgotten, he leaves his car circling the lawn; running into a flock of sheep, he leaves the car creeping forward while he scrambles out over the bonnet to shoo them out of the way.

Occasionally a sense of strain becomes predominant, as in *Safety*

Last. Harold, whose trip to the big city has ended in failure, wants to impress his girl with his success. He sets out to win part of a 1,000-dollar prize for climbing a skyscraper. He plans to climb the first few storeys after which his more agile pal will take over, and they will split the reward. But a baleful cop and other bystanders force Harold to complete the climb alone. True, he's thus entitled to 1,000 dollars instead of only 500 dollars. But he only wants 500 dollars and with every floor his chances of death increase. It's a good symbol for the rat-race: you have to risk everything for big success, you can't settle for a modest reward and safety.[1]

Like Buster Keaton, Harold Lloyd made movies almost through to World War II, and he briefly emerged from a prosperous retirement when Preston Sturges concocted a characteristically disenchanted comedy about hearty hopeful Harold, twenty years on. *Mad Wednesday* is almost a slapstick equivalent of *Death of a Salesman.* Its first reel is the last reel of *The Freshman,* one of Harold's silent hits, and shows milksop Harold winning the match for his college. He is offered an executive position by an excited businessman who, by the next morning, has sobered down, and tells him, 'I'm going to give you a chance to succeed in the good old American way—right from the bottom. I was unfortunate, my father left me the business, ah well. . . .'

Twenty years on finds Harold, despite all the optimistic mottoes and slogans on his walls, still a lowly clerk, who has loved, and lost, each of seven beautiful daughters in turn. His boss, in yet another two-faced speech, 'retires' him. Realizing that all the homely small-town virtues have betrayed him, he goes 'mad', and does everything condemned by the small-town spirit (whence the film's American title, *The Sins of Harold Dibbledock*). He falls in with some city slickers, he blows his savings, he drinks hard liquor, he bets on horses, he buys loud check suits, he bullies bankers by storming into their offices with a lion on a chain, and at last becomes a success. The inner-directed ethos of diligent, self-help is ousted by a more cynical outgoing parade of irresponsibility, trickery and bluff. The release delays often associated with Howard Hughes productions, Sturges's not always successful blending of Runyonese and slapstick (e.g. too many quick-cut changes of angle spoil the flow of physical action), and a slackening of spiritual tension in the second half, took the edge off a nonetheless fascinating film.

---

[1] It's interesting that his cheating isn't felt by us to disqualify him for the reward.

13 · I was a Middle-Aged Water-Baby

Of the dreamers, Harry Langdon is the arch-apostle, with his wryly delicate mouth, his apple cheeks and moomin eyes. Bursting out of his suit like an overgrown baby, this sleeping prince is as virginal as Lillian Gish. By contrast Stan Laurel is a city slicker. And whereas Buster, especially in his moments of scarecrow limbed panic and jejune gawk, has something of the wizened timidity of a child that has experienced hurt, Langdon's childishness has a tremulousless, as if he'd always been too afraid to be hurt. Perhaps his complement is Fatty Arbuckle, the hard, energetic, cynical fat boy. To Buster's and Fatty's songs of experience, Harry pipes up his songs of innocence, 'I am not yet born, Oh hear me . . .'.

Whether in the guise of a small-town adolescent, a *City Lights*-type tramp or the only American sentry who doesn't know World War I ended a week ago, he seems, by some dogged self-abstraction, to have retained an embryo's immunity from the outside world. That strange blink of his eyes, the shy, quick dawn of a smile, imbues all he sees with the insubstantiality of a dream. And dream he constantly does. He takes too many pills in *Tramp Tramp Tramp* and thinks he's dreaming his way through a cyclone which devastates a town; he dreams he is still in his seat as everyone else leaves the theatre in *All Night Long*; in *Three's a Crowd* he tries so hard to watch over his sweetheart and her baby that he falls asleep, and while dreaming that he's putting his rascally rival to sleep with a monster punch, he sleeps through the gentle, prodigal father's return. But the swathes of dreaming sleep through which he has to perceive the world are only a special form of conscious bewilderments, which, progressively, become not only absurd, but tragic, and archetypal, man's inalienable alienation from reality. Our consciousness is a dream from which we don't know enough to awake.

The theme of innocence versus experience, of dream versus disillusion (and of its social metaphor, small-time niceness versus urban corruption) had long been a central motif of American literature, and Harry's mere presence intensifies it into paroxysm. It's paroxysmatic because it's complicated by his curious sense, pervasive, but unstated, of the perversities at the core of innocence. His invisible innocence wouldn't be even faintly tragic were he merely a cherub in man's clothing, a Little Lord Fauntleroy who'd flown off with Peter Pan to Never-never-Land. But there's no real absence of evil intent in Baby Face Langdon. The small-town Master Bovary in *Long Pants* is longing to slough off his innocence, to which end he locks himself in his parents' attic and reads Byron's *Don Juan*. Dazzled by the city vamp, it is with blissful serenity that he plans the murder of his sweet fiancée, and lures the unsuspecting girl out into the woods. There she closes her eyes and puckers her rosebud lips for a kiss, while he gets the pistol stuck in his pocket, loses it in the autumn leaves, can't aim because his hand's shaking, gets his hat jammed down over his eyes, falls into a barbed-wire fence, and catches his ankle in a man trap, from which he has to be rescued by his intended victim. Of course the comic, typically, acts out the impulses which only cross our minds, and of course accident, i.e. fate, plays, as in this scene, the role of our moral repressions. But of all American innocence, funny or serious, in any art form, only Langdon comes so near an adult's recreation of that *absolute state* of baby greed, baby gloating and baby blandness in selfishness. The Surrealists are quite right to claim him for their own, for there's never any real reason why he shouldn't, if it suited him, perpetrate the archetypal Surrealist act: taking a revolver and firing at random into the street. There's something so irresponsible it's almost evil when, dressed as a (monstrously tiny-headed) baby at the end of *Tramp Tramp Tramp*, he shakes himself until the giant cradle in which he's lying loops the loop. At those moments when he is a half child, if half adult, in an adult situation, his surprised, passive eyes set up complex reverberations of erotic hysteria. When, in *Long Pants*, the city vamp crawls maternally, treacherously, over him, not unlike Marilyn over Tony Curtis in *Some Like it Hot*, he is stunned into a wide-eyed immobility which simultaneously suggests (*a*) a total intellectual blankness as to any possible reason for such puzzling behaviour, (*b*) an arrested development whose other name is impotence, (c) a delicious paralysis, as at dawning awareness of ecstasy, and (d) the uneasy suspicion that a treat so sudden must have an ulterior motive, and be as dangerous as it's nice.

The world confronting Langdon's dreaming, milk-white countenance is often his accomplice in poetry. Seen from a bird's-eye view the small-town hero cycles slowly round the automobile in which the vamp sits. She looks straight ahead of her; he performs his small-boy cycling tricks. *Three's A Crowd*, perhaps less moving than *City Lights*, has no less magic. Its sense of a slum district is chokingly bleak and the long-flighted staircase leading up to Harry's drearily, sagging and lurching cabin is worthy of *The Salvation Hunters*. In *Tramp Tramp Tramp*, a short-cut takes him up to a fence marked 'Private. Keep Out'. Briskly scaling it, he turns around prior to descending the other side, without even noticing that when he drops to earth he'll plummet straight down a 500-foot precipice. The man who put such a notice on such a fence had a demoniacally pedantic sense of private property, and an extraordinary viciousness infiltrates what is in any case a virtuoso passage of gag logic.

In *The Chaser*, which Langdon directed, some elaborate tracking shots, of rare formal beauty, astonishingly anticipate Renoir's in *Boudu Sauvé des eaux*. Keaton's sense of railroad rhythms is paralleled by Langdon's flair for slow, wavering movements, with their hallucinatory poetry. His period of stardom was cut short by sound, though he continued a prosperous career concocting gags for Laurel and Hardy and many others. In a sense, his intelligence had a wider range than his screen *persona*; if his stories are less moving than Chaplin's, it is because his screen self couldn't always provide a holding, a linking, centre for his pathos and his gags. There seem, now, odd jumps, gaps, lacunae, rather than smooth transitions, between his other-worldly aspects and his this-worldly entanglements, between his pathos and his immunity, between his lunar, his adolescent and his adult responses. He lingered just a little too rigidly, perhaps, within his baby register. Stan Laurel occasionally capsizes into his crying act but most of the time he thinks like a man, or like a boy.

Yet Langdon, like Chaplin, like Keaton, like Stan and Ollie as a pair, bears the stamp of comic genius. His gestures, vague, yet clipped, brightly hopeful yet squidgily inept, sketch, vividly, a baby attitude untranslatable into any adult code, a strange condition of being pampered and lost, expectant and malicious. In pace, he anticipates

W. C. Fields (whose mind, more disgusted with reality, plunged right out of this world, to appoint its owner dictator of Klopstockia, or to hurl him headlong from an airliner washroom on to the ivory tower of Mrs. Haemoglobin). Harry Langdon gropes, from some virginal limbo, over the threshold of our mad, half real world, opening up weird spaces and emptiness all around himself, and within us. If Langdon was in some ways Stan Laurel's *alter ego* (he once replaced him as Ollie's mate) he also anticipates Jerry Lewis, even though his hysterias are silent and slow motion. In *Tramp Tramp Tramp*, he carries placards of the star (Joan Crawford) whom he adores, anticipating the Anita Ekberg-crazy Jerry in *Hollywood or Bust*, as surely as Harold Lloyd's Freshman ages into Harold Dibbledock.

Langdon's slow *tempi* remind us that slapstick and speed are not at all synonymous. If Sennett's *accelerandi* tend to fantasy, many silent comedies dwelt on bucket-and-ladder jobs whose homeliness was intensified by Sennett's great rival impresario Hal Roach. While Sennett piles one fandango situation on to situation, a Hal Roach two-reeler puts its characters in one simple plight and watches them, methodically, not get out of it. While Sennett's characters are well on the way to being pin-men, the slower Roach pace goes with a genial relish over reactions and character. Thus Sennett's semi-abstract Keystone Kops contrast with Roach's individualized Our Gang. If the 20's are Max Sennett's years, the talkie brings the Hal Roach idiom to full bloom. Though so many Laurel and Hardy films were made during the 30's, they had found their style by the coming of sound. Indeed, their talkies have a quality as of silence into which dialogue of sub-title simplicity is interjected.

14 · Beau Chumps and Church Bells

Mr. Laurel and Mr. Hardy are the simplest, the homeliest and the great, exponents of the Hal Roach style. Not that their career isn't diversified by such flights of fantasy as *Swiss Miss* and *Flying Elephants*. But even their absurdest moments are firmly anchored to our heroes' actions and reactions, which are essentially plodding and homely.

And never more so than in psychological paradox. How absurd yet how strangely persuasive are those 'tit for tat' sequences, where Stan, Ollie and an antagonist or two, often James Finlayson, each take it in turns, and irately allow the other, to rip off his clothes, tear his jalopy to pieces or ruin his shop or his home. Each lets the other do his worst before retaliating—perhaps in obedience to some strange relic from the Code of the West; perhaps deliberately stoking up his own indignation and therefore strength; perhaps out of bravado; perhaps out of obedience to some streak of masochism which, if Laurel and Hardy films are any guide, must be more compulsive in human nature than unaided common sense would have us believe. The ungentle art of self-destructive escalation was worked out by Stan and Ollie long before Herman Kahn applied its logic to nuclear war.

Laurel and Hardy must number among screendom's greatest gluttons for punishment (even including the soap-opera queens). Stan suffers because he's timid and inoffensive, Ollie suffers because he's pompous and rude. Stan is the 'child', Ollie is the 'parent'. But Stan's meek awkwardness is regularly more destructive than Ollie's irate bungling. It's possible that, if children predominantly identify with Stan and think Ollie rather fierce, parents identify predominantly with Ollie, surprisingly patient victim of Stan's childlike 'helping'. Not of course that Mr. Laurel is without any means of defence. He can, on occasion, when pressed too far, or when the wind is blowing from the right direction, be both adamant and violent. When, in *You're Darn Tootin'*, Mr. Hardy keeps punching Mr. Laurel in the stomach, Mr. Laurel retaliates by kicking Mr. Hardy on the ankle rather hard, so that our two friends come to perform between them a species of stooping-and-hopping ritual, further diversified as tensions mounted, by trouser-ripping. This spreads compulsively, from one passer-by to another, like an Artaudian plague, until the whole street is thronged with ducking, hopping and ragged-trousered misanthropists. Their natural level is proletarian, and even their mayors have the minds of bottle-washers.

A kind of quiet fruitiness, bringing music-hall 'presence' back into screen comedy, makes Laurel and Hardy perhaps the supreme screen practitioners of the *temps-mort*.[1] One of the funniest moments in *County Hospital* (a gem of sick humour) has Stan, simply, swallowing a hard-boiled egg. The duo loved to combine such inanities of detail with dramatic ironies. Thus, in *Brats*, we know that Stan and Ollie (filmed child-size) have left the tap on after being given their bedtime bath by Stan and Ollie (filmed parent-size). Ollie, overflowing with sentimental fondness (irony 1) sings the dear children a lullaby, 'Go to sleep, my ba-ha-by'. Ba-ha-by asks, 'Can I have a drink of water?' (irony 2). Stan, helpful as ever, says, 'I'll go,' (irony 3), to which Ollie replies sternly, 'No, I'll go, you'd only spill it' (irony 3). None of these ironies on 'flood' would be half so funny if Mr. Hardy didn't speak weightily, and complacently, and pause. Not that their slowness is a mere device for milking three audience laughs out of the gag. It is psychologically right, it establishes the obliviousness of their innocence, pompous in one case, meek in the other, and dim in both. It inflates every moment of time to the strange distensions of childhood's subjective clock. Typically, the most catastrophic events (like Stan reducing Ollie's house to a smoking ruin in *Helpmates*) ascend from the little slips and forgetfulnesses to which children are especially prone.

The inexorability of disaster has a poetic quality of its own. *The Music Box* takes a simple labouring job (two men carry a piano up a long flight of stairs), and makes it a perfect little epic of monotonous futility, ornamented with odd little lyrical moments (as when the manhandled music box seems to mutter to itself, melodiously, sul-

---

[1] *Temps-mort* is a *nouvelle vague* term for moments when nothing at all is happening, story-wise, and nothing much emotion-wise.

lenly, or when, having fallen from a balcony, it sways gently in the shallow waters of a little pond). It's the myth of Sisyphus in comic terms, a little hymn to the uselessness of work, a study in absurdity that one has not the slighest hesitation in ranging alongside the few best examples of the theatre of the absurd.

So strong is this aspect that certain images, from Laurel and Hardy films, qualify as visionary crystallizations of the human condition. Thus the plight of art is summed up by the scene where Laurel and Hardy, as street musicians, patiently render 'In the Good Old Summertime', while the snow falls, and falls, and falls. On human respectability: as a jealous husband fires a shot at our (innocent) duo, a jump cut shows every window in the street fly open while a horde of nightshirted lovers leap into the street below (*We Fall Down*). All the inadequacies of human friendship are summed up by the muffled anguish of Ollie's cry in *County Hospital* at the delicacies thoughtfully brought for him by Mr. Laurel. 'Hard-boiled eggs and nuts! Mmm-mmm!'

The gap between the ultra-high-brow 'theatre of the absurd' and these ultra-low-brow comedies is narrower than it may seem. When Kafka read his stories to his friends, he and they used to roar with laughter at the ridiculous conduct of his heroes. Samuel Beckett obviously derives a great deal from music-hall techniques. Perhaps it takes the atmosphere created by the high-brow pieces to make us so fully, so uncomfortably, aware of the strangeness or sinister aspects occluded by our hilarity at these 2-reel comedies. But the obscurity, and complacency-in-despair, of many *avant-garde* plays needs, in turn, completing by the crazy comedies, whose blend of disquiet and reassurance, of absurdity and homeliness, confers a tone which, while other, is no less satisfying than, that of the *avant-garde*. And it may be that the low-brow form is, in the end, less petulant, more mature, truer of the general run of humanity. For Laurel and Hardy, whether they're street musicians or mayors, life isn't, after all, devoid of all meaning or feeling, as it is for Beckett's tramps. However obscure their goals, however brief their satisfaction, however petty their (in)dignity, life goes on, and it's a sign, not of their escapism, but of their truth, that Laurel and Hardy were never simply laughed at by their fans, but loved by them. In his biography, John McCabe quotes Stan's account of the pair's arrival at Cork in 1953, 'There were hundreds of boats blowing whistles, and mobs and mobs of people screaming on the docks. We just couldn't understand what it was all about. And then something happened that I can never forget. All the church bells in Cork started to ring out our theme song, and Babe looked at me, and we cried. . . .'

15 · Krazy Kat Daze

Primitive cartoons bob up a little earlier than slapstick, in America as in France. They thrive on the same tension as slapstick, being drawn between, on one hand, the fuller freedom of their purely graphic, arbitrary, world, and tied, on the other, by the need to relate to its spectators' experience. (Even cartoon animals are mainly domestic pets or familiar Aesopian icons—lion, beaver, etc.) But if slapstick rapidly became the major genre, it was partly for purely technical reasons. The movie cartoon is vastly more laborious and expensive than the photographic film, and hardly moved from the one to the two-reel format; indeed, the feature-length cartoon had to wait on Disney's *Snow White and the Seven Dwarfs* in 1938.

Slapstick action approached the modern cartoon not only in its high velocity action but in its visual impossibilities, and Sennett went as far into cartoonland as photographic techniques allowed. A boiler, to which Ben Turpin is firmly trussed, swells up like a balloon before exploding, and Disney's use of cartoon animals is prefigured in Larry Semon's *Golf*, with its parody of a golf-match between two (ouch, the pun) gophers. But the cartoon could bring crazy humour through into a whole new realm of impossibilities and visual puns (like the 'elephant gun' in *Field And Scream*. After firing a cannonball, its barrel droops with fatigue, but braces itself, curls up and back, and picks up another round, like a trunk grabbing buns. Hence it's an 'elephant gun').

Criticism owes to Raymond Borde the rediscovery of Charley Bowers who flourished between 1926 and 1928. 'Physically he resembles Keaton—lanky, lean-faced, with black and abundant hair like Keaton, he's often in overalls, and his trousers—a circus inheritance?—are too wide. On the screen, he incarnates an imperturbable inventor who actualizes his delirious conceptions. . . . He is the heir of Snub Pollard, who often used little inventions—systems of pulleys and strings for boiling eggs or scratching his back. He is also the heir of Keaton, that virtuoso in the art of putting objects to impossible uses . . . but with Bowers things go further. They take on a disorderly life of their own, obeying nothing but the logic of dream. Unequal, sometimes tedious, his films are suddenly transfigured by strokes of the imagination. . . . Whereupon, thanks to all the devices of animation and single-frame exposure, the impossible come true. . . .' Bowers's movies are one of the silent cinema's innumerable research problems, since even Borde himself can't give the English titles of the films whose French versions he possesses. *Pour Epater Les Poules* revolves around a device for making eggshells pliable. Because he's put the eggshells under his automobile bonnet they give birth to tiny black creatures which turn into mini-cars, and hide under the coachwork, whereupon the whole car protectively softens, like a mother-hen. *Non Tu Exagères* (*Now You Tell One?*) centres on a club of tall tale-tellers. One swam the channel on the shoulders of a cyclist, another describes an instant tree sprouting so fast that it spears up its sower's trouserleg, sprouts branches through his sleeve, and crucifies him in midair.

Maybe because the infant muse of the silent cartoon was so soon outshone by her younger slapstick sister, maybe because the shadow of Disney's technical inventiveness lies so long and heavily across the cartoon's history, the earliest cartoons are very rare birds even in film-archive programmes. It's regrettable, because several series were closely related to some of the most interesting specimens of that collateral line in graphic narrative, the newspaper strip-cartoon. Winsor McCay, whose *Little Nemo* series is an astonishing blend of Lewis Carroll and M. C. Escher, made his first cartoon *Gertie the Dinosaur* in 1908, followed by a *Little Nemo* cartoon in 1911. 1912–13 saw a *Baby Snookums* series drawn by the newspaper cartoonist George Mc-Manus, working in collaboration with the French cartoon pioneer Emil Cohl. The human figure was not the stranger in these early cartoons that he later became, when Disney's success with animals banished almost all but the redoubtable Popeye from the graphic world. At the other extreme, a few cartoons made regular play with the Pirandellism that comes so easily to the cartoon. In a 'mixed media' film, *The House That Jack Built*, a quaver hovers in the air, its tail wriggling like an animal's, to catch a sleeping man's attention. A cow in a picture hanging on a wall gallops away. A running man's hat bobs up and down in a neat and sustained counterpart to his steps.

Perhaps the best remembered silent cartoon series is Pat Sullivan's *Felix the Cat*, from 1917. In *Felix Wins and Loses*, Felix, hotly pursued by a police-stationful of cops, resourcefully employs the question marks which emanate from his cheeky inkblob face, and the gags generally have a free-and-easy quality which Disney deliberately obliterated. Both use impossible gags, but Disney's respect a systematic continuity, e.g. time and space are continuous and systematic, whereas the earlier series switched like dreams. Felix's head, all cheeky points and apexes, and his curly limbs and grin are one degree nearer the doodle-line, with all its chirpy freedom, than the oval and circular forms which were to sweep the cartoon in emulation of Disney's developing smoothness. The earlier cartoons, being weightless lines in a flat space, enjoyed a delicious graphic freedom, which may have come to seem crude and monotonous when Disney's fuller background and perspective effects were new, but are much nearer the possibilities of our post-UPA-Steinberg era. Indeed the 20's is the best period for America's 'cartoon of the absurd'—a genre which is endowed with an intermittent existence, most successfully in the hands of Tex Avery, until it enters its golden age with the advent of the intellectual cartoonists of Europe in the 60's—Lenica, Borowyzck, and others.

The series of *Krazy Kat* cartoons, around 1916, and in the 20's and in the 30's, were at least an echo of the astonishing strip cartoons by George Herriman. Their principal characters are Krazy Kat, Ignatz Mouse and Offissa Pupp. The trio inhabit a mesa which is also a cartoon 'everywhere-land'. Krazy Kat believes that Ignatz Mouse loves him and won't be shaken out of his blissful ignorance by the bricks which Ignatz heaves at him, unerringly and with maniac obsessiveness. Offissa Pupp is fond of Ignatz and constantly foils Krazy's schemes. Gilbert Seldes likens Krazy Kat to Parsifal and Don Quixote, Ignatz to Sancho Panza and Lucifer. From a less philosophical, more sociological, aspect, one might see this epic and unending battle as a ying and yang between two forces which are like the demiurges of the American cinema: the optimistic sentimentality which is a mainspring of human nature, but particularly connected with middle-class, do-gooder America, and the rough guttersnipe cynicism of the asphalt (or garment, or city, jungle, or the wide-open towns of the wild west). Not even a veritable torrent of brutally accurate bricks will persuade the Panglossian Kat that Ignatz doesn't love him, that cats and mice aren't friends rather than enemies, that this universe isn't, ruled for all the odd misunderstand, by harmony and love. Our sympathy goes to the violent if diminutive Ignatz, not just because he's merely a mouse, but because as the voice, and arm, of stark simple truth, he has both the Kat and the Pupp to contend with. Ignatz's language has that grotesque, that immigrant's, grammar, which is a keystone of the earlier strips:

'Golla, I always had an idea they was grend, and magnifishint, and wondafil, and mejestic . . . but my goodniss! it ain't so,' while Krazy Kat tends to the schoolmarm's flowery:

'I will unveil my heart—a heart too long, still—too long silent—too long hidden in the shadows of secrecy.'

The arena for the action, the Protean mesa, transcends all specifically Western reference, becomes a few shacks and a horizon under a sky as weird as another planet's. This lunar loneliness hints, by a kind of dream opposition, at the spiritual loneliness of the immigrant, in a strange land, where communication has all the abruptness of a brick arriving out of nowhere. *Gertie the Dinosaur* (improbable heroine!) embodies the same spirit of clumsy, docile, grotesque, alienness. But the screen history of the Krazy Kat series typifies the fate that befalls too many of the popular arts' most haunting and poetic examples when transferred to the screen.[1]

Disney's role in the cartoon is an ambivalent one, and perhaps he is less to blame for his too-crushing influence than his emulators. But, as Benayoun reminds us, the earliest Mickey Mouse, now forgotten, by Disney, by critics, by audiences, was a cheekily, rascally, scruffy-lined fellow, more Felix than Mickey. His occupations are proletarian in reference (*Building a Building*, *Steamboat Willie*), but through the 30's he becomes more cheery, innocent, confident, his situations more middle-class, his shape rounder, blander, smoother. And since the 30's are Disney's imaginative heyday, it is under that period that it is most convenient to glance at this Disney spirit.

---

[1] A newspaper reader can skip a cartoon if it exasperates or bores him. A cinema spectator can't. Trying to amuse all, Hollywood compromises, dilutes, bowdlerises.

The less stylized a comedy, the more its evasions of reality are apt to jar. For to say realistic is to say dramatic, and the cultural tabus on drama began to sap and edulcorate the comic vigour.

The movement of realistic comedy is very much like that of 'straight' drama, indeed, it's impossible to draw any objective dividing line. Hence the tendency to feel that comedy necessarily evades dramatic material (whereas, at its best, it proposes a different attitude to it), or to perpetuate the classical distinction whereby what isn't tragedy is comedy. This older definition describes as comedy what we would now call drama with a happy end, and farce covers both farcical and comic.

The change in the meaning of 'comedy', from meaning serious but happy, to meaning happy but frivolous, seems to be a reaction to the current predominance of the happy end after suspense over the tragedy of inevitability. Suspense, by its nature, queries the whole distinction between comedy and tragedy, not only as the ending is concerned, but, by back-formation, throughout the play's tone. Shakespeare's tragedies and comedies may be considered as intermediate between the classical definition (which lingered on in criticism) and more modern attitudes, no doubt reflecting the Elizabethan era's transitional status as between a medieval, hierarchical, 'religious', resignation and modern, bourgeois secular optimism.

The shift in meaning is strengthened by the increased stress on the gag. The gag certainly isn't absent in Shakespeare, but, in the music-halls of the late nineteenth century, it seems to acquire a new energy, and, in the twentieth century, and particularly in Hollywood, effects a new more intimate junction with the comic mood. As Albert F. McLean, Jnr. remarks in his insightful study of *American Vauderville as Ritual*,[1] the late nineteenth-century influx into America of non-WASP immigrants, called the New Folk, and the consequent social implosion of the cities, is associated with what was called the 'New Humour'. In contrast to the leisurely, folksy, humorous style of the old humour (with which we would now group Mark Twain and Stephen Leacock), the new humour was sharp, rapid, cynical, often cruel, reflecting a faster, quicker-witted world. Rapidly, the gag made its way up the social scale, not simply because vaudeville increasingly drew the middle classes to its ever more palatial halls, but also because the business explosions and the automobile drew ever more prosperous Americans into the roaring pace which gave the 20's their sobriquet. The gag, like obsessively syncopated music, and tearaway movie rhythms, expresses a kind of brisk, alert, perhaps slightly dehumanized, attitude to life. As McLean indicated, the pre-1900 joke takes its time in setting up the human aspects of the story, whereas in the post-1900 gag, these exist only to 'set up' the 'punch line'—a significant description. The gag represents, in a sense, a de-personalization of emotional release, it depends on the very rapid recognition of emotional stereotypes. In splitting humour from character, it brings comedy towards the condition of farce. But, unlike farce, it can gear in very exactly with the mental aggravations of realistic social life. The new genre expresses both the brutalization of comedy and the new shrewdness in farce. Life is becoming a matter of rapid manipulation of feelings rather than a full experience of them.

Nowadays, we need some sort of distinction between dramatic comedy, comic comedy, farce and slapstick. But it's a distinction of prevailing tone, and many a work in one genre includes interludes in others.

Used of the comedies of the pre-war era, 'realistic' is apt to be something of a misnomer, for it is at once a little more realistic (in the indignities which the spectator shares) and a little less (the balance of portraiture and caricature) than the dramas of the time. Like theirs, its principle source was not the comic strip, but the playlets of the vaudeville houses. Socially, though, the material was less elevated, just as the humble nickelodeon was rather lower than the opulent vaudeville palaces. The morally normative setting was the honest working man's home, the sentiment critical of the rich, and of The Idle Class.

---

[1] A book far more valuable to the student of the American cinema than its title may imply, because of the close links between the two audiences, and the two sets of performers.

Race frictions, already a major feature of city life, underlie such early vaudeville and cinematic successes as *The Cohens and the Kellys* and *Abie's Irish Rose*, both dealing with tensions between two major early waves of immigrants, the Irish Catholics and the East European Jews. The ethnic mixtures of big city life are comically reflected in the composition of Hal Roach's *Our Gang*. Griffith's *True Heart Suzie* pokes gentle fun at the foibles of rural America, but is no less a celebration of its rustic puritan values: humble contentment, thrift and innocence. Basically rural, too, are those early comedies which established Mary Pickford, as 'America's Sweetheart'. These canny but not insincere mixtures of sentimentality, comedy, drama and sermonizing, laud the virtues and spirited contentment of the poor.

Subsequently, in the later 20's, Marie Dressler, Wallace Beery, Polly Moran, and others, brought to the regional comedy the warm, ripe sentimentality of their expansive, Dickensian personalities; and the generosity of their playing survives many a contrived story. For obvious reasons, regional comedy has not had the same appeal for sophisticated audiences as the sophisticated comedies of Lubitsch, or the more serious regional dramas—themselves too rarely shown— like *Tol'able David* or *The Wind*; and a review of the genre may well reveal buried treasure; though whether we will find an equivalent of Pagnol's Marius trilogy, or of Dreyer's *The Parson's Widow*, is another matter.

'Her charm, her sweetness, and her golden curls glorified her rags and dirt,' writes Lewis Jacobs, and Arthur Mayer and Richard Griffith add, 'What was it that set Miss Pickford apart from all her contemporaries, imitators and competitors? . . . Her sweetness and light were tempered by a certain realism. . . . She played . . . Pollyanna . . . not so much saccharinely as vigorously. In spite of her creed, the Glad Girl knew that it was no cinch to make everything come out right. Nothing could have been more in tune with combined limitless optimism and a belief, that what was called "Git up and git" was necessary to make optimism come true.'

The mood became a staple of 20's comedy. Before the costume epics for which he is best remembered, Doug Fairbanks played innumerable variations on a boy-next-door, bursting with pep and good cheer, charmingly able to parody himself or goof while hardly faltering in his determination. If Fairbanks paraphrases ruthlessness by zest, and makes the rat-race seem as clean and hearty as an Olympics event, his hopeful swashing isn't too inaccurate for the booming and expanding America of the 20's. In this optimistic context, Fairbanks sunnily contrives to square puritan ideals of self-improvement and self-advancement with an exuberant sociability and a Don Juanism which doesn't so much defy puritanism as roar cheerfully past it at 100 m.p.h. For Fairbanks all that impeded access to every kind of happiness, success and self-improvement was a few gloomy old notions which could soon be thrown overboard. Isadora Duncan's idea that a world-wide chain of dancing schools would retread a tired olde worlde is a more intellectual version of Fairbanks's cruder spriteliness. His is a bourgeois Futurism.

The extension of this spirit to the emancipation of women and of sex is carried through in the flapper, and flaming youth found its girl-goddess-next-door in the fetching figure of Clara Bow. The meaning of her comedies lies mainly in her personality, for their often third-rate scripts used implications of immoral intent rather than affirmations of immoral conduct. They simply outflanked the scruples of the older generation, and of the staider young. They abounded in ambiguities which l'homme moyen sensuel could take as emphatically as he wished, and no more emphatically than he wished. But Clara's notoriety leaves no doubt that a thoroughly libertarian interpretation was placed on her films by a large section of the film-going public. *Little Miss Thrill* (*My Lady of Whims*) is almost an instructional on flapper behaviour and values. She looks at a man from top-to-toe, she coolly pushes her hand forward for a man to shake, she Charlestons, she smiles at one man as she kisses another, she teases a would-be sugar daddy with a finger-kiss from her butterfly lips, even as she gently takes pity on him. Her style is 'Git up and git' applied to sex. Maybe she succumbs to the puritanical detective sent to trail her: but maybe her assent to his moralizing is as much due to delight in submitting to a male as to a change of heart; or maybe submission *per se* leads to loving. Parallel equivocations underlie Victor Fleming's *Mantrap* where city shop girl Clara follows dumb ox Ernest Torrence (physically, the 1920's William Bendix) out into the wilds, where she subjects him to all her feminine wiles. Because she merely fancies him? or to tempt him into marriage? These theoretical alternatives fade under the impact of the star whose nickname 'It Girl' was bestowed upon her by that literary lioness, Madam Elinor Glyn. Budd Schulberg described her as an 'emotional machine' because of a screen test in which she switched from laughter to a torrent of tears and back at, quite literally, a snap of his fingers. The hysteric com-

plexity implied by this virtuoso celebrity endows her performances
with far more depth than most of her screen writers needed to ack-
nowledge, and imparts to her mostly superficial roles a fascinating
admixture of sensitivity, insincerity, dolefulness and single-mindedness which is at once tongue-in-cheek and desperate.

A devil-may-care vo-de-o-do was far from being the only comedy
mood of the 20's. Scarcely less numerous were such quieter pieces,
solidly rooted in mainstream middle-class morality, as *Ella Cinders*,
with Colleen Moore as a modern Cinderella, *Young April*, with
Bessie Love a gentler, homelier, variation on smart comedies, or *A
King On Main St.* with Adolph Menjou as a visiting Ruritanian
potentate discovering the simple joys of purchasing one's own ice-
cream cornet and sauntering along incognito, in an American small
town. Sam Taylor's *Exit Smiling* is an agreeably madcap piece with
Beatrice Lillie as maid-of-all-work in a wandering rep troupe.

Still charming, these comedies are probably less congenial to
modern taste than those which, like Howard Hawks's *A Girl in Every
Port*, express the dourer, more ruthless and competitive aspect of the
American ethos. Victor McLaglen and Richard Armstrong play the
competitive, scrapping pals so dear to American popular mythology,
putting each other down with mighty punches, before combining to
fight anybody and everybody—policemen, foremen, rival crews. . . .
This time their rivalry stimulates their transoceanic philandering; in
fact their girls are reduced to hurdles in the race between the two male
rivals. Eventually, the more successful falls for a gold-digging trapezist (Louise Brooks), from whom the other has to rescue him.
Hawks's and Louise Brooks's style, cool, limpid, cynical, matches
60's modernity, while the male camaraderie, no doubt intended to be
subtly off-key, has dated so outrageously as to have acquired a
bizarre charm (like the men swearing to be oppos for life, or Victor
McLaglen's way of pulling his rival's outstretched finger). Yet these
traits are surely based on accurate observation of waterfront mores at
a time when middle-class puritanism had not yet exchanged certain
concessions to heterosexual impulses for a hypochondria which has
made almost every strong emotion between men seem meat for the
couch, thereby freezing it deep below conscious zero.[1]

---

[1] The contrast appears even in a Sam Goldwyn musical comedy, *Kid Millions*
(1934), where a pair of confidence tricksters pose as Eddie Cantor's mother and
uncle. His smooth, glamorous, fast-talking 'mother' (Ethel Merman) kisses him,
and then tells her awkward plugugly accomplice to kiss Eddie. The burly bruiser

17 · Spoof and Satire

The American cinema is often supposed to have had an innocent era, before moral controversy reared its sophisticated head. But Lewis Jacobs describes an item featured in the Edison catalogue for 1901, and entitled, *Why Mr. Nation Wants A Divorce*. Mr. Nation, henpecked spouse of Carrie Nation, the fearsome Prohibitionist agitator, baby-sits for his campaigning spouse, and seeks consolation for his lowly lot by tippling from a bottle of spirits. 'Just then,' runs the synopsis, 'Mrs. Nation enters and is horrified at seeing her husband drinking from a bottle. She smashes the bottle to the floor, and turning her husband over one knee, spanks him soundly.' As an attack on respectable morality, the film is the exact equivalent of the satirical sketches which caused such controversy in the mid-60's.

Probably we underestimate the virulence of early satire, in its period and context. Its broader and more obvious traits now look more like farce, or have taken on the charming quaintness of old Valentine and greeting cards. But much slapstick doubles as satire. Sennett's characteristic procedure was to take a serious hit of the time and burlesque it, and the procedure has remained a comic staple. Thus, Bob Hope's *My Favourite Brunette* parodies Huston's *The Maltese Falcon*, just as Will Hay's *Ask a Policeman* parodies Hitchcock's *Jamaica Inn*, and *Carry on Cleo*, *Cleopatra*. Not that parody is necessarily satire; often,

---

promptly grabs Eddie by the nape and gives him a smacker full on the lips. It's a queer gag all right, but it has another meaning. Such salutations, between male members of a family, at intense moments, are the practice in some peasant cultures. Thus the principal catchment area of this joke is the embarrassments, in a slick, tough, prim America, of peasant emotionality. It's useful to remember, whenever thinking about Hollywood movies, that the comic relief (and the villains) are usually more realistic than the (idealised) behaviour of the heroes.

the reference works the other way, and the formulae can yield comedy-thrillers rather than parodies. But slapstick parody can work up a fine satiric charge, as in Ben Turpin's mockery of Valentino and von Stroheim. In fact, Turpin's fussy gestures and wild squint are relevant to absolutely every human emotion, activity or state of soul.

The most celebrated silent satires are probably the Fairbanks movies scripted by Anita Loos and by their director, John Emerson. Thus, *American Aristocracy*, satirized 'bean can nobility' (the *nouveau riche*) and *Reaching for the Moon*, the enthusiasts of 'New Thought', a philosophical equivalent, on the pseudo-intellectual level, of the Dale Carnegie philosophy.

The dichotomy of rural naïvety and urban sophistication is nicely touched on by Raymond Griffith, of whose work, now almost unavailable, *Hands Up!* is an appetizing example. As a suave master-spy bent on winning the Civil War for the South, he parades his evening dress and opera cloak through the deserts and sage brush of the wild west. The film burlesques martial law ('Captain—we've caught a spy!'—'Call out the firing squad!'), heroism ('If I don't get through—send the medals to my mama!'), the spirit that won the West (pioneers civilize the Indians by teaching them to gamble and tap-dance), the Civil War (just as our hero saves the South, Lee surrenders), the gallant Old West (driven off his stagecoach seat by two old ladies, our hero 'strap-hangs' and reads the paper, like a rush-hour commuter). While his girl's father is being made to dance on red-hot coals, and a brave tries to scalp him with his teeth, our hero, gambling with the Indian Chief, shows a perfect composure and a dapper aplomb which comes very near complete indifference to the old man's miseries. He resolves his hesitations in love by meeting Brigham Young and becoming a Mormon, while this must be the only American film to caricature Abraham Lincoln and his entire Cabinet. Satire apart, the comic invention is often first-rate—thus a man and two girls terrify one another with ghost stories inside a stage-coach while those on top fight off Indians, and mistake the whizzing of arrows which they never quite see for an annoyingly unswattable bee. The film also builds, quite logically, to such incongruous images as a man being pushed by a darkie on a trolley, with a burning candle clipped to his top hat. By and large, it lasts much better than Ford's *The Iron Horse* and the other Westerns which it so smoothly mocks.

A rather more sharply realistic tone appears in the films of James Cruze, now best remembered as the director of a typical epic Western,

The Covered Wagon. The satirical comedies which he produced throughout the 20's are almost unknown now, and even the encyclopaedic Andrew Sarris lists him under 'Research Problems'. But from their description by Lewis Jacobs, they seem well worth rediscovery. His *Hollywood* (1922) was the first of the long series of movies in which Hollywood, with the cheerful masochism of sublime self-confidence, offers itself as a comic scapegoat for all America's virtues and vices. Cruze commented tersely, but bitterly, on the treatment accorded Fatty Arbuckle by studios and public alike, and, through a burlesque dream sequence, on the 20's foible for romantic and megalomanic daydreams. In 1923 he introduced Edward Everett Horton in the first version of *Ruggles of Red Gap* and experimented with expressionistic satire in *Beggars on Horseback* (another satire on the *nouveau riche*). Cruze was a close friend of von Stroheim, and such titles as *We're All Gamblers*, *On To Reno* and *City Gone Wild* (all 1927), suggest that he may be an important link between von Stroheim and the Wellman–Sturges–Wilder tradition, streamlining Stroheim's heavy, Victorian, exotic-romantic impulse down to something faster, more modern, sardonic and indigenous.

18 · The Lubitsch Touch

Sophisticated comedy implies, not only a certain sophistication on the part of audiences, but also a positive relish of all the finer points of human behaviour—at least as long as they also imply a certain frivolity, a certain irony, a certain cynicism, an unusual degree of social assurance, a reasonable love of worldly parade, of material comfort and of pleasure. For the opposite of 'sophistication' in this sense is not so much naïvety as earnestness. If sophisticated comedy is so often set in upper-class, or royal, circles it is because these gratify the daydream materialism to which Hollywood has, from the end of World War I, been consistently, not to say monotonously, responsive. It is also because only those well above the middle middle-class can remain openly likely and nonchalantly impervious to puritanical earnestness, yet retain that elegance and *savoir-vivre* which disarm and charm even those bourgeois matrons who most sternly uphold middle-class morality.

Before World War I sophisticated comedies were hardly possible. After World War I the mood had changed. The middle-class had begun to come to the cinemas, America had begun to question and overthrow her rustic puritan heritage. America became fascinated with the European aristocracy, as urban(e), snobbish, frivolous and thrillingly decadent.

The cinema's first sophisticated comedy is, as usual, European: *Erotikon* (Sweden, 1920), directed by Mauritz Stiller, who was shortly to discover, and mould, the young Greta Garbo. His comedy of manners created a scandal by its justification of adultery as a stepping stone to divorce. Too audacious for American film-makers, though not for actual American manners, such unbiblical notions are lengthily indulged, but of course condemned, by the more serious

109

studies of moral decadence, from von Stroheim to de Mille. Otherwise, the characteristic Hollywood treatment of high life is romantic.
And it is yet another European who acts as trend-setter for another
form of sophistication. Not that Lubitsch's reputation should lead
one to overlook the existence of, for example, Sam Wood's 1923
version of *Bluebeard's Eighth Wife*, remade by Lubitsch in 1939. The
60's developing rediscovery of silent Hollywood will doubtless reveal
many celebrated auteurs to be less isolated than they now seem—
peaks in a range, perhaps. At any rate, Lubitsch's Hollywood contemporaries readily accorded him the leadership in bringing high life
down from the realms of moral problem and romantic fantasy, and
various combinations of the two, and gave it a tone at once light,
comic yet classical. Ernst Lubitsch's first American movie *Rosita* in
1923 starred Mary Pickford, already evolving from her pre-war
Pollyanna image. His silent movies range from 'royalist' satires (*Forbidden Paradise*) and operettas (*The Student Prince*) to matrimonial
satires like *Kiss Me Again* (with Clara Bow), or *So This is Paris*. A
sophisticated Berliner, pleasing American audiences with stories
taken from French farces or from German or Hungarian romantic
comedies, Lubitsch's cosmopolitanism underlines the effortless stylization of his world. In his—silent—adaptation of *Lady Windermere's
Fan*, 'the director establishes the sentiments of his personalities . . . by
leaving us to guess them, almost entirely through the effort which
they make to conceal them' (Jacobs). Indeed, the famous 'Lubitsch
touch' is misleadingly named, for it is not so much a something added
to a story as a method of telling a story through ellipse and emphasis.
Omitting the obvious presentation, Lubitsch substitutes allusive detail, and then emphasizes that detail, not simply to be sure that even a
hick audience gets the point, but in such a way that the sweet nothing
becomes an ornamental equivalent of the dramatic sense. As one of
the censors bitterly complained, after the Hays Code had clamped
down in 1933, 'you know what he's saying but you just can't prove
that he's saying it!' In *Trouble in Paradise*, the lovers in a hotel
bedroom rise from their supper to kiss, and the light throws their
shadows neatly on to the pillows of the double bed. The charm is just
that little more than charming; its effect of turning aside from the
kiss gives that kiss a delicacy perfectly conjugated with the wistfulness
of that clean, fresh, luxurious linen. The shadows are their inner
desires. Or perhaps they did. . . .

That his style was a matter of conception rather than inflection is demonstrated by the fact that Cukor directed most of *One Hour With You* from Lubitsch's plan, and Borfage directed *Desire*, which Lubitsch produced; both are virtually indistinguishable from the productions Lubitsch directed himself, which suggests, not that none of those concerned is an auteur, but that an auteur may work as producer as well as a director.

If Lubitsch's work, until his last film in 1948, was respected by intellectuals and adored by shop girls, it was because, apparently so simple, it concealed an exact, a delicate, a classical balance between contrarieties. He conjugates the sumptuousness of de Mille with the space and lightness of Clair. The palatial halls, the hotel bedrooms as large as aerodromes, are relieved of all weight by whiteness, by the neat spacing of columns, of bouquets, of ice-buckets, by the soft light playing upon the people and props of 30's romance, a light now glittering, now veiled to lightly indicate the shadows banished from his realm. The planes and props disposed in space so pleasantly, but not too carefully, draw attention, not to themselves, nor to the composition, but to a free, light languor in the atmosphere. So, in the talkies, the words, quite simple and direct, seem heavily annotated by little silences around them, by an easy suaveness, by all sorts of possible alternatives from which they have been nonchalantly selected. The protagonists are puppets, but puppets in the best sense—the delicately nuanced puppets of a genre whose limitations are not simply its charm but its *raison d'être*. Like René Clair he loves to pull his camera back until his characters are pin-men, gliding, in large, high rooms, by large, high windows. His heroes and heroines recall the winning silhouettes of his compatriot, Lotte Reiniger, but in white on white.

These flat characters are interesting because, as painters know, tensions can exist on two dimensions. In *Desire* a rascally old lady (Alison Skipworth) cadges drinks from Marlene Dietrich, 'I could be your grandmother. And if your grandmother called on you, what would you do? You'd offer her a drink, of course. You know I never drank until I went to jail. You know when people are afraid of dying —a brandy will see you through. . . . You know I need another brandy. Thank you. Now I'm sober again.' The cat and mouse game between comedy and tragedy, between the sadness and the glamour of senescent criminality, is so smooth that, like all the best film dialogue, it seems, on the page apparently meaningless. Of Maurice Chevalier, star of his *Love Parade* and *One Hour With You*, Lubitsch said 'he

111

can make even the most scabrous situation acceptable', and this tribute to Chevalier's style is a tribute to his being, 'le style, c'est l'homme'. In *Trouble in Paradise* it is with an air of infinite regret that Monescou (Herbert Marshall) goes about his business of being a crook; but it is an air of regret, neither of shame nor guilt.

The light banter is possible only because of an easy mastery. The mastery is a condition of yielding to pleasure, but delicate enough to be a part of that pleasure. Herbert Marshall, a gentleman thief, woos Kay Francis, a thief masquerading as a lady over supper. He is gracefully taken aback when she reveals that she knows he has robbed the gentlemen in rooms 203, 205, 207 and 209. He ripostes by expressing his awareness of the fact that during their conversation she has stolen his watch. He then reveals that he has stolen her garter which, with a kiss, he keeps.

In his sense of personal relations, Lubitsch heroes and heroines subscribe to a hedonistic code whose blend of amorality and generosity is well known to us all but is curiously absent from philosophical tradition. His films are too sentimental to recall Restoration comedy (another tacit defiance of ambient puritanism), are too concerned with the sensual and the material to recall the comedies of Sheridan or Goldsmith (but have their watch-maker's precision), are too bold and rectangular for rococo (although the camera, gliding as on a silver salver, contributes its aesthetic elegance to the proceedings), are unconcerned with moral and social mores for neo-classicism (but also keyed to the clear, the reasonable, the decorous), and too shallow for any comparison with Mozart, the honour of which belongs, rather, to René Clair, his sadder, austerer French counterpart. The Lubitsch world is as formal as the flowers in their vases, the servants who, during a peace conference, deprecate, with profound shock, the table manners of the Bolsheviks. A light correctness, masking sadness but not fun, is part of the film's pleasure, all the more since such correctness facilitates a superb insolence. Lubitsch does not so much avoid the coarsened forms of hedonism, as balance them against one another, supply. The glorification of youth and beauty is mitigated by a mellow eye for the older characters, and by that eloquent deployment of etiquette which is a privilege of experience. Any mechanization of charm is avoided by a certain gentleness, even in deceit, and an alert respect for one's quarry, in seduction as in all other Macchiavellian games. The bland amorality is deliberate, i.e. it is never the result of a lack of consideration for others; just as concern and remorse are

5. **When Comedy Was King:** *Chester Conklin*
   Lords of misrule
6. **Days of Thrills and Laughter:** *Ben Turpin*

7. **Bonnie Scotland:** *Stan Laurel, Oliver Hardy*

   While Hollywood dramas daydream, slapstick peeps in at the everyday—cramped quarters and rustic plumbing

8. **The General:** *Buster Keaton*

acknowledged only with the smooth frankness which isn't without
its Nietzschean aspects.

Wealth and happiness are never confused. If Lubitsch life is lived
at so lavish a level it is only for high spirits and suave courtesies to
dance together with a freedom no less significant for being, in reality,
so rare. Lubitsch's films, no less escapist than they seem, are also
amiable, winning manifestoes to the effect that the *summum bonum* of
human life lies, after all, in possessing the advantages which figure so
largely in the hedonism of l'homme moyen sensual: high spirits,
personal attractiveness, wealth, poise and humour, a kindly insolence,
the generosity of heart needed to appreciate most people, flirt with
many, and love not a few. His enemies are the spiteful, the mean, the
dried up, and the slaves of systems as well as the uplifters, the
puritans, and the Commissars of left, right or centre. Not that
Lubitsch is aristocratic for one moment—on the contrary, he is bourgeois, Jewish, *nouveau riche* to his finger-tips, to the tip of his fat
cigar. His pleasure in good living may be an anathema to the puritanism implicit in so much criticism, but looms large in this sad
world. It is, after all, to a Lubitschian nonchalance that Chaplin's
Little Man aspires.

It is no doubt Lubitsch's limitation that he never throws even a
satirical light into the shadows of his world, though it is perhaps not
without significance that a successor who does, Billy Wilder, describes his own style as a curious cross between Lubitsch's and Stroheim's. Reality peeps in through the windows of the Lubitsch world,
like, not a skeleton, exactly, but a shadowy form, at a feast. In *Angel*,
the camera pauses for a second on the old flower-seller with her
wrinkled countenance, and her lined hand on the lovely money—and
then, having struck its mingled chime of commiseration, cynicism
and anti-sentimentality, moves smoothly on its sparkling way.
Trouble in Paradise opens on a venetian gondolier operatically
warbling his arias as he propels his gondola, which is piled to the
gunwhales with garbage, to the local rubbish dump. High society is
corrupt, businessmen are crooks, officials are bribable—of course. . . .

Lubitsch's career has taken us ahead of our chronological order,
for his work has the coherence of an auteur—a *petit-maître*, perhaps,
like Hitchcock, but a *petit-maître* all the same. The comedies which
constitute the bulk of his work follow the mood of their times. They
are robustly saucy or extravagantly romantic in the 20's, and more
concerned with upper middle-class life in the 30's. Though he stood

H 113

aloof from the political and class comedies which were sparked off by the Depression, the late 30's brought a new, and an advanced, asperity into his style. *Bluebeard's Eighth Wife* (1938) gives the sex-war comedies of the epoch a more outrageous tone as when Claudette Colbert not only has her multi-marriage Casanova (Gary Cooper) beaten up by pluguglies ('but don't hurt him') but finishes by kissing him into marital submission while he struggles vainly inside a strait-jacket. *Ninotchka* (1939) with a bitter-sweet double-edgedness, sketches the moral downfall of a too-serious Bolshevik (Greta Garbo), but the representative of capitalist hedonism (Melvyn Douglas) is the playboy gigolo of a none-too-lovable Countess.

Part Three

WHO'S AFRAID OF THE BIG BAD WOLF?

19 · Lightly and Politely

By the time sound (introduced in 1926) had percolated down to all grades of Hollywood production, the roaring 20's had roared their way into the Great Crash. Thirties comedy, from 1929 until America began rearming in 1940, exists under the shadow of the Depression—a catastrophe represented, in so many political cartoons, inspired by Disney, as the big bad wolf huffing, puffing and blowing down the houses of the three little pigs. The Depression backcloth bears remembering, if only because the screen's comic tone switches less drastically than one might expect. Throughout the 20's, grinding tenement poverty had endured. Rural America had known extensive local depressions. Rat-race morality had justified hardboiled and bitter movies, and bums, tramps, hoboes, starving men had trooped across the screen. *Easy Street* (1917) is as gruelling, under its hilarity, as *Modern Times* (1936).

If anything, the comic tone took an upbeat turn. The earlier movies took poverty matter-of-factly. But when it became a national problem too, and the subject of optimistic pronouncements, from complacent Republicans as from dynamic New Dealers, a more optimistic frame of reference was introduced. The cinema had, from its very beginnings, been steadily rising in the social scale, and the middle classes are far more decorous and squeamish about the seamy side of life than the lower classes; the Hays Code (1933) marks middle-class dominance. Further, the grimness of life made everyone all the more responsive to sentimental escapism.

Moreover, the vast majority of Hollywood producers favoured the Republican cause. They positively wanted to allay any bitterness arising from the new tensions between rich and poor, between big business and the unemployed.

At the same time, the more realistic view of high life, held by the middle class, the quickening undercurrent of resentment at high finance, and the increasing concentration on the domestic horizon, blended to shift interest nearer home. The Ruritanical operettas, the whimsies about nobility remained popular, but gave ground to American, middle-class, themes (even within the genres, the old fascination with exotic customs was replaced by a stress on American-type ideas beneath a sumptuous surface). The operettas survived as musicals, with their additional stylization.

Otherwise, the mere presence of dialogue quickened a tendency towards realism, clipping the wings of silent pantomime. The royal and aristocratic comedies, à la Lubitsch, continued to flourish, but increasingly the centre of the stage was taken by those intimate upper middle-class settings and styles, which still shine so brightly in everyone's memories, or notions, of the 30's.

Simultaneously, slapstick begins slipping, from the A feature to the B feature and, by the 40's, from the B feature to the two reeler. Increasingly the comedians' place is taken by an influx of character comedians from vaudeville and radio. The semi-fantasy genres give ground to realism, but this, in its turn, becomes more respectful than hitherto of the moral daydreaming of the middle class. This daydreaming, which is conveniently summed up by the Hays Code, but is by no means restricted to sexual subjects, and extends to the whole range of tones and topics. But if comedy is less free than before, or, fortunately, since, there are certain compensations, of style and grace, perhaps enhanced by the spiritual limits.

Ironically, the first effect of King Mike is to deprive the sophisticated comedy of the sophisticated style with which it had imbued its silence. Not only was primitive acoustic apparatus extremely cumbersome, but Hollywood found many talking problems raised by King Mike new to its mute stars, writers and directors. It turned to the 'legitimate' theatre, whose talents were often, alas, unused, or uncongenial, to the cinema medium, as to the cinema audience, then far remoter now from the interests of the Broadway theatregoer. The 'teacup comedies' didn't amuse contemporary moviegoers. Even Noel Coward's stiff-upper lip way with emotion seemed far too cold fish for the land of Clara Bow, and a latecomer in the genre, the 1934 version of *Private Lives*, fell flat, despite the presence in the cast of Norma Shearer and Robert Montgomery whose smooth, informal style might have seemed admirably equipped to translate Cowardese into American.

The Lubitsch comedy survives the Depression without difficulty. His heroes skate on the thin ice of their assumptions, but they need, one feels, only a musical cue to move into a tap-dance as suave and lively as Fred Astaire's. The condition of such lightness is all the assumptions of privilege, money, or their equivalent, impudence. But Lubitsch uses the paraphernalia of high society in an almost abstract way (again, like Fred Astaire), so that his films, while pointedly diffident towards social egalitarianism, relate to no particular class code, nor even to fun morality (for which his characters are too relaxed, graceful and considerate), but to a hedonistic magnaminity whose cynicism is not unkindly and which is the reverse of snobbish. The smart hotels in which his characters evolve are the meeting grounds of Dukes, and of Duchesses-for-a-day, of businessmen, of jewel thieves.

Of the Lubitschian films of the 30's, Rouben Mamoulian's *Love Me Tonight* is perhaps the most charming exercise, variegated by its borrowings from European comedies of the period. The song 'Isn't it romantic' is tossed from tailor (Maurice Chevalier) to customer, from customer to taxi-driver, from taxi-driver to composer, from composer to marching soldiers, from soldiers to gypsies, and from gypsies to the heroine, sitting at the window of her country chateau. The use of such a lietmotif to link diverse classes is clearly inspired by Clair's *Sous Les Toits de Paris*, while the song's picaresque trajectory is no doubt suggested by Erik Charell's *Congress Dances*.

It suggests the intriguing possibilities of highly mobile plots, appropriate for the chaotic mobility of the Depression years, with its hoboes, its jobless men trekking from town to town, living in transit camps, or driving, like the Joad family in *The Grapes of Wrath*, long distances in search of a job. Even within Mamoulian's framework, acute points could have been made. However, the film settles within the chateau, and the tailor's pose as a nobleman and the predictably egalitarian marriage. Mamoulian decorates it with some charming filmic effects—a whole fox hunt, shamed out of its blood lust by the spirited heroine, galloping away in soundless slow-motion, to express its new found consideration for animals; a sudden high angle gives a God's eyeview of footmen fanning out over a chess-board floor; and the direction's pastiche of Lubitsch would confound even an auteur-conscious eye. A boring operetta becomes a gentle ripple of cinematic grace.

Distinguishable from the Lubitschian line are those comedies

which celebrate not dissimilar personal qualities in their more specifically American form. In film after film, with almost any director,
such players as Katherine Hepburn, Claudette Colbert, Jean Arthur,
Carole Lombard, Cary Grant, Robert Montgomery, William Powell
and James Stewart, turn and glide in their moods as lightly and
exhilaratingly as swallows on the wing. The dialogue of these movies
is celebrated for its wit, but in itself, on the page, it's more often
direct to the point of flatness. Its play of contradictions is likely to
seem crudely arbitrary. The air of wit comes rather from the playing,
from the very smoothness with which contradictions are reconciled.
It is by an impudence of style that Katherine Hepburn, as the wilful
society girl in *Bringing Up Baby*, pursues absent-minded paleontologist Cary Grant. 'But I'm engaged,' he objects, and then, more petu-
lantly, 'Engaged to be married.' 'Then she won't mind waiting,' La
Hepburn purrs, and quickly scatters his protesting stammers with, 'If
I was engaged to be married to you, I wouldn't mind waiting, I'd wait
forever.' Only a lordly lady could have made up her mind so quickly,
and have dared announce it, could have stated it so nonchalantly and
endured, without a flicker of impatience or resentment, the inevitable
protest, not to say snub. The mixture of bland docility and irresponsibility, of passivity and brashness, in her 'I'd wait forever' exemplifies
dramatic wit (working against the situation) as distinct from literary
wit (expounding the situation). On the personal level all these qualities are based on an almost dream-like (rather than merely wish-
fulfilment) triumph over inhibition and embarrassment. They were
used as instructional manuals in behaviour by a whole generation of
adolescents, and very much more *àpropos* they were than much
official teaching in meaningful human relationships.

Katherine Hepburn moved through comedy after comedy, like a
radiance of contradictions: blandly rich, but matter-of-factly democratic; incredibly clumsy, but smoothly clever; as briskly authoritative as a schoolmarm, but also capable of instantly re-vamping all her
assumptions without pausing for breath; edgily masculine, but
bathed in a bright feminine glow. Similarly, Cary Grant contrives to
undergo every form of exasperation, humiliation, or tension, while
maintaining a clipped irascibility which, while blander than more old-
fashioned styles, is more masculine than the merely cool. Reluctant to
reveal her identity to her travelling companion, Katherine Hepburn
won't accept a parking ticket from a cop. She baffles the law by
pretending ownership of the adjacent car. But, because he's

watching, she has to steal it. Eventually she reveals she will return it, by chauffeur, from her destination after dark. If her quickwittedness celebrates, without apology, the aristocracy of money, it also elevates *savoir-vivre* to the highest level of a considerate anarchism. Any American audience, though relatively underprivileged, can participate in this exhilaration, not only by identification, but by overcoming its own stabs of envy. For more classbound European audiences, all this happens in 'America', in a land, that is to say, where the poor are rich, where every adult is happily infantile, and which refers only to its own screen conventions or to personal questions in everyday living.

Bringing Up Baby is almost a pure exercise in this personal style. A series of comic episodes is festooned around a farcically empty centre. Baby is an escaped tame leopard; the dog has hidden the paleontologist's precious bone; a fierce leopard is perilously mistaken for Baby. This abstraction isn't gratuitous as, Arthur Mayer and Richard Griffith put it in *The Movies*: '. . . if what went on in these private worlds was mostly nonsense, what sense could be found in the great world outside, where economic crises and the threat of approaching war barred all the conventional roads to achievement and happiness? It is hard to describe today what these films meant to a Depression-bred generation, and it is not surprising that the "screwball comedies", as they came to be called, usually ended in slapstick or violence. They mirrored a world of frustration.'

A mellower air, a gentler domesticity, imbued *The Thin Man* series, with William Powell as Dashiell Hammett's eccentric private eye and Myrna Loy as his long-suffering spouse. Directed by W. S. Van Dyke —another 'research problem'—the films used the overlapping dialogue often thought to be the exclusive property of such, perhaps, excessively 'cult'-ivated directors as Orson Welles and Howard Hawks. Like many apparently simple entertainment movies, *The Thin Man* series had more than one facet. Deems Taylor attributes its 'instantaneous success' largely to the fact that 'To a movie audience that had been brought up to see marriage, in the films, as an ordeal, the sight of two ultra-smart, sophisticated people, very much in love was reassuring and oddly moving.' From this angle, *The Thin Man* series is an ingenious and needed hybrid between sophisticated comedy (with its immoral overtones) and the sentimentality which also led to the Victorian revival. Mayer and Griffith also observe that 'Two seemingly routine films of 1934 revolutionized film comedy in the

30's. The first was a purported murder mystery, the second, one of a short-lived cycle of pictures about bus travel' (the hobo theme). 'But both *The Thin Man* and *It Happened one Night* featured something new to the movies—the private fun a man and a woman could have in a private world of their own making. A new image of courtship and marriage began to appear, with man and wife no longer expecting ecstatic bliss, but treating the daily experience of living as a crazy adventure sufficient to itself.' The craziness, being voluntary, paraphrases, and matches with contented aplomb, that social chaos, which, in real everyday life, disrupted, or threatened, private fun.

20 · Old Wheelers, New Dealers

A number of these sophisticated comedies might as well be described as political, since, however important the purely personal style of the protagonist, however unreal or special these specific stories, they are quite openly about the unemployed, about the rich, about social responsibility and individuality.

The most celebrated of such films is undoubtedly Capra's *Mr. Deeds Goes To Town.* Confident in his flair, Frank Capra ventured to break the Hollywood tabu on political themes. And he proved that the safe formulae are only one way of arriving at a critical and commercial hit, and a relatively expensive and hackneyed one. Wherever a tabu exists, it reveals the existence of strong feelings, which, like all feelings, crave expression; so that the producer who is willing to take the risk of a massive flop has the chance of an overwhelming success. The lowest and the highest scores are side by side on the board. The creative producer must pluck the flower pleasure from the nettle resentment.

Mr. Deeds (Gary Cooper) is an amiable smalltown bachelor who earns a living by writing verses for Christmas cards and plays the tuba in the town band. On inheriting a few million dollars from a deceased uncle, he travels to New York where creditors of every kind assemble about him. Two rival, but equally crooked, firms of lawyers offer to administer his estate; an opera company wants him to subsidize its massive annual deficit; three highbrow poets conspire to ridicule him; the butler whom he has inherited from his uncle fawns on him; a girl reporter (Jean Arthur) lets him fall in love with her so as to spy in his life, and find a basis of sorts for her newspaper's lies.

Deeds, disillusioned, decides to retreat to his smalltown privacy, but as he packs his bags, a distraught stranger bursts into his mansion brandishing a gun. This climatic form of persecution leads, in effective dramatic style, to a prompt reversal of move. Overpowered, the intruder breaks down, weeps, apologizes, explains he is a small farmer, hard hit by the Depression, that watching his family starve has driven him nearly out of his mind. Deeds realizes that his retirement was selfish. Instead, he embarks on a gigantic plan for capitalizing small farmers, on private enterprise lines, by giving each individual his own two acres and a cow. The disgruntled lawyers issue a writ accusing him of insanity. In court, Deeds is at first too despairing and disgusted to defend himself from the snaky testimony of a foreign psychiatrist, but he finally yields to the entreaties, not only of the now repentant, and amorous, reporter but also of the farmers, and successfully vindicates his private enterprise 'New Deal'.

The film illustrates several wish-fulfilment paradoxes. It deals with the Depression, yet our hero begins by becoming a multi-millionaire. In the confrontation between Deeds and the farmer, our hero enjoys every wish-fulfilment privilege, and it is the minor character who represents the general experience of the Depression. Because too accurate a description of the Depression would run the film head on into all sorts of depressing controversial reflections, Deeds's enemies are all unconnected with the industrial and financial world (his financier uncle dies as the film begins). Consequently, the film paraphrases industrial and financial malfunction by blaming journalists, lawyers, socialite opera-lovers, psychiatrists and poets. Thus it shifts its attack from big business to the big city, and from the rich to rich highbrows, and it does so, not in sentimental ignorance, but with very sure calculation of the extent to which dramatic thinking is associative rather than analytical. Richard Griffith, in his other, and less interesting, collaborative role as alter ego to Paul Rotha, relates the film to the 'fantasy of goodwill', the idea that if Americans could only feel trust and goodwill the Depression could be licked with none of those quasi-Bolshevik proposals for state control which were being peddled by F.D.R. and his New Deal. The Great Crash was in fact triggered by a crisis of confidence, and the Republican thesis was that 'we have nothing to fear but fear itself'. Capra's solution is a compromise. Too many of the rich are snobbish, self-regarding, frivolous, but if only the responsible-minded became fully aware, then private enterprise could do the job. On the other hand, of course, Deeds is saved from himself, by a gang of small farmers, who, as victims of the Depression, might be a very Democratic group. It is sufficiently ambiguous for a New Dealer hardly to notice, or care, that, on balance, it is propaganda for a moderate, concerned, Republican point of view.

The film's terse suggestiveness is often dismissed as Hollywood craftsmanship, but is in reality a style, in the profounder sense, in which neo-classicism or the baroque is a style. For example Deeds makes a modest but comfortable living by writing verses for greeting cards. Thus the film defends middle-class sentimentality by linking it with Coop's cowboy physique and solemnity. If his inspiration comes slowly, he coaxes it along by playing the tuba, which he also plays in the town band. Thus his individualism goes with a responsible, and voluntary, neighbourliness and community spirit. The townsfolk gather to see Deeds off at the station; loyally and logically, he puts the oompah into the tune played in his honour. As the train steams out of the station, he keeps playing gallantly, the sound becoming lonelier and lonelier, as he will become.

Deeds's musical modesty contrasts with the pomposity of the opera company. And his refusal to subsidize them, on the grounds that culture must make cash, is obviously intended to provoke a rousing cheer from the audience, as if the simple Deeds were at last, and rightly, rounding on his cunning tormentors. Deeds's encounter with the highbrow poets cleverly reiterates the same theme. They invite him over to their table in a chic restaurant, and lavish praise upon his verses, imagining he's too simple to appreciate their irony. They are mean-faced, plump, small and old. Deeds leaps up athletically, punches a pair of them in the face and stalks off disgustedly. Again, the audience is expected to cheer, and even intellectual audiences do, for, if three men gratuitously gang up to humiliate a stranger in a sneaky way, they can't grumble if he retaliates in his own, and man-lier, terms. Still, Capra has foreseen the audience's uneasiness. So the third poet, as yet unscathed, toddles beaming up to Deeds and re-quests to be socked, for kicks. This ratifies Deeds's action, and proves that intellectuals generally are bafflingly and reprehensibly weird, i.e. deserve socking. But it also raises some intellectuals, at least, in our estimation, since, given the opportunity, they can show an un-expected sporting spirit, a manly delight in brawls and excitement, all the more admirable in persisting though having been starved for so long. And this third poet goes on to prove himself 'one of the boys', showing Deeds round the town's hot spots.

As the film progresses, Deeds's too-forthright way is clearly meant to make us even uneasier. At various intervals during the film, he has been asking the too-servile butler not to kneel to help him put his trousers on. Eventually, Deeds wakes up, depressed, hungover, bleary, fuddled and raps, 'Don't kneel,' with an irritability which has suddenly become a tycoon's petulance. While planning, with an understandable egoism, his return to his small town, he harshly ticks off his domestics, and abruptly notices that the vast, empty rooms of his mansion produce a quaint echo. He stops short and amuses himself listening to the echo—then he makes all his trembling servants say 'Ooh-hoo' too. The whimsical detail restores a comic tone to a sour scene. But the empty, solitary 'ooh-hoo' is in disturbing contrast to the communal 'oom-pah'. Deeds's home is beginning to echo like Xanadu. He has, briefly, become the bullying, irresponsible, lonely millionaire, of anti-capitalist sentiment. Deeds sins again in his understandable, but excessive, in fact his suicidal, passivity during the trial. This time, it is the farmers who, massing to rally him out of his silence, save him from himself. 'For the decent idealist, irresponsibility is moral death.'

The film comes up against a basic snag in the 'fantasy of goodwill' argument, and, indeed, in American idealism generally. If mere goodwill could put the system right, then the real enemy is illwill. A hunt for scapegoats begins. The scapegoats in *Mr. Deeds Goes To Town* are mainly intellectuals, and if we extend the category to include such brainworkers as lawyers and journalists, entirely intellectuals. Capra has already found his way to the classical scapegoats of McCarthyism. Capra seems to have sensed this, and takes care to skate round it by placing people of goodwill even among Deeds's persecutors: the girl reporter repents, a lawyer's aide turns out to be decent, one of three poets will be 'one of the boys', and so on. A similar plot informs his *Mr. Smith Goes to Washington*. This time James Stewart proves it's all the fault of those lazy, isolated, cynical or defeatist politicians, rather than of the sum total of social pressures, i.e. the system. Capra's fantasies of goodwill reach an O altitudo! of absurdity in the solemn *Lost Horizon*, where a group of Americans learn wisdom from a mysterious Tibetan monk who preaches a few Christian truisms amidst cardboard décor.

The Depression is approached from another angle in Gregory La Cava's *My Man Godfrey*. When high society playboys and playgirls, scattering for a party scavenger hunt, pick up a 'forgotten man' (an unemployed war hero) the flightiest of them all (Carole Lombard) stumbles across William Powell, living in rags down at the rubbish dumps. She takes a liking to him, and, despite the pretexts of her *nouveau riche* family, hires him as their butler. He proves to be a perfect one, and shows up the rich for the vulgarians they are, although the daughter of the house is sufficiently frivolous to be no snob in love. Thus, the body of the film might well answer the description given by an American critic, writing under the pen name of Cancer, in that perceptive *avant-garde* magazine *Kulchur*: 'This time the rich get it, or at least the mean rich do, and the manners of the bum and the butler are revealed as preferable to those learned at finishing school.' But the film goes on from there. If William Powell is the perfect butler, it's because he's a millionaire playboy himself, who only got down in the dumps because he was crossed in love. 'It's amazing how fast you can go down hill when you're feeling sorry for yourself.... There are two kinds of people; those who fight the idea of being pushed into the river, and the other kind.' However, this bracing philosophy leads not as one might expect, to a Darwinian *laissez faire*, but to a compassion for those of the poor who are deserving. The ex-butler will give them the chance they deserve, and organize, no, not a government New Deal, but a syndicate of those businessmen who are prepared to put the provision of decent jobs, and homes, for the deserving poor before immediate dividends.

Cancer not only sees it as a vindication of bums and butlers, but remarks, 'It's interesting that a very serious social idealism could underlie the crazily funny comedies produced during the New Deal without either spoiling the fun or degenerating into caricature. Perhaps having a political ideal was so cheering that one could permit oneself comedies—at any rate, there have been no good comedies of this type since in American films.' And although the screenplay, closely followed, yields a definite Republican moral, it is easy to see how it can be interpreted in another sense. For most of the time, the butler seems to be an ex-bum, the man who has been given the chance. Powell's triple character Bum-Butler-Playboy doesn't only show that 'A man's a man for a' that', it could be felt, in an irrational, but potent, way, as the complete vindication of bums.

Ambiguity appears again in the contrast between the comparative fewness of the amiable rich (hero and heroine) and the ridiculous and/or snobbish nature of most of their family and friends. One might estimate the film's sympathies by its 'statistics', and see it as an anti-rich film. On the other hand, hero and heroine express what ought to happen; they are our principle identifications; they loom very large in the foreground; and, in fact, the hero, after stealing a necklace, selling it and making a killing on the stock market, takes charge of the film in the final reel. The general feeling is not even so radical as that a spell in the rubbish dumps never does the over-privileged any harm; it is, rather, that nothing sets any man up like an honest day's work. The rich should be educated to face reality, instead of living like dolls in luxury. The moral appears in another form too. The rich husband is a pompous, henpecked, money-grabber; his wife a near-lush, the daughter frivolous; her friend, Cornelia, a monster of cold pride. Their trouble is not their lack of basic character, but the moral unreality of their existence. (In this connection the film works a neat motif. The scavenger hunt is for a forgotten man; and mother and daughter keep stressing that they keep forgetting everything.) But reality is defined in terms of justifying oneself in doing a good job. Once our rich hero does that everything puts itself right. He goes out of his way to stress how conscientious many bankers are and the film's sharpest animus is reserved for his rival for the girl, a Russian aristocrat who awes the family on which he spunges by his formidable displays of temperament—artistic, of course, which, like so many things artistic, is phoney. For example he eats an orange, while singing a soulful dirge to his own pianoforte accompaniment. He moans, 'Money, money, the Frankenstein Monster that destroys souls,' in imitation of German expressionist drama, then still popular in left-wing intellectual circles (and whose idealism is burlesqued also in *Sullivan's Travels* and in *Room Service*). As with *Mr. Deeds Goes To Town*, Depression problems are evoked overtly but obliquely; by concentrating on the problems of a playboy turned butler!

In fact the film's main challenge to the system comes in something of an aside, which normally one would pass over as a mere detail, or comic licence, or an acceptable sentimentality. The butler induces the better sort of businessman to join his syndicate, which will consider the provision of steam-heated apartments for the poor as more im-portant than dividends. At this point, the film goes beyond the general Republican notion that economic individualism leads to the general good, and may even seem to be advocating welfare-state housing. That La Cava meant this very seriously, but not exactly in a New Deal sense, is suggested by his *Gabriel Over the White House*, made in 1934, at a very dark moment in America's fortunes. It was clearly intended as a serious, if desperate, remedy. An inspired Presi-

9. **Modern Times:** *Charlie Chaplin, Paulette Goddard*
   Chaplin and Lubitsch: men of the world . . .
10. **Angel:** *Marlene Dietrich, Melvyn Douglas*

11. **Forbidden Paradise:** *Pola Negri, Rod La Rocque*

Woman disposes—Tsarist style (above), Greenwich Village style (below)

12. **My Lady of Whims:** *Clara Bow*

dent appoints himself dictator and solves all America's problems. The great appeal of a good dictator is, of course, that, as a strong man, he can overrule all the problems caused by economic individualism. (Before dismissing La Cava's film as absurd and hysteric, which it is, perhaps understandably, one should remember that his arguments, and even his terms, aren't basically very different from Plato's.) By the time of *My Man Godfrey* the American solution showed more signs of hope, and possibly La Cava would by now have repudiated the earlier film solution as too Draconian. But the insistence on luxurious apartments for the unemployed underlines the thoroughness with which individuals must renounce orthodox ideas. Hence *Gabriel Over the White House* might seem to some a New Deal film; those who accused Roosevelt of being a Socialist, a Bolshevik, a Stalin were also saying that he was interfering, unwarrantably with big businessmen's freedom to be irresponsible.

But the basic reason why Capra's and La Cava's films could seem to be New Deal, rather than more or less right-wing Republican, was one of popular mood. The Republicans could offer no solution to the Depression, only the hope that sound business management (which had already failed) would restore prosperity. The mere fact that a film could accept the possibility of a radical shake up, could look on such a shake up optimistically, was enough for many to associate it with a progressive, New Deal attitude. Hence, the uncompromisingly Republican attitude was that adopted in *Soak the Rich*, neatly summarized by Griffith and Mayer: 'Most message pictures were frankly New Dealistic, but a few, such as this by Ben Hecht and Charles MacArthur, derided or deplored the rising tide of liberalism and radicalism. In an ad. for this film which pained the more sober-sided radicals, Hecht and MacArthur were depicted singing "We're the guys who wrote the yarn/And here's what it's about/Class ideas don't mean a thing/When love kicks them out".' All 'fantasy of goodwill' pictures posit love as part of the solution, but, with the Capra and La Cava films, it's only part of the solution: class ideas still mean a thing. In essence, both right- and left-wing comedy in America attack class barriers. But the former stresses the importance of self-help, the latter the importance of group action. The right justifies the example of riches as a spur, the left the role of class distinctions as a barrier. The Republicans stress individuality, the Democrats stress solidarity. In so far as spectators in either camp usually felt the pull of the contrary ideology, both views make concessions to the other. Thus, right-wing films cheerfully condemn the irresponsibility of rich people, a left-wing film will tend to deny the existence of so mean an emotion as envy. Conversely, even those who felt that the rich were largely to blame accepted the films' conspicuous lack of animosity towards them, as part of the new, self-confident, generous spirit. But the films' elaborate avoidance of non-Republican solutions suggests that the New Deal mood was a common sense, pragmatic, rather than an ideological response to a crisis, and didn't represent as much of a shift to the left as it may have seemed.

21 · The Politics of Personality

Political thought is, after all, only one particular aspect of an ideology which appears, less obviously, but no less firmly, in very many of one's personal attitudes.[1] La Cava's *Stage Door* sets a similar issue in the purely personal terms of a running duel between two chorus girls in a theatrical boarding house. Ginger Rogers plays the tough, hard-boiled, embittered (albeit golden-hearted), proletarian blonde; she expresses, vivaciously, all the audience's despair about the individual's ability to help himself. Katherine Hepburn incarnates the contrast to her defeatism and absence of private enterprise, and an unusually astute storyline endows her with every trait which contemporary audiences must have found most exasperating. To recap an earlier formulation, she is 'a top dog—stinking rich with unearned wealth . . . coolly and positively scornful of their envy . . . bossy . . . a self-righteous suffragette . . . an ambitious and none too talented career girl . . . an intellectual . . . arty. She gets another girl's part, indirectly causing her suicide and feels just enough genuine response (but no more) to make herself into a successful actress . . . the moral is: "if you're over-privileged, don't apologize—you probably deserve to be: for unto those that hath guts shall be given, and from those that hath not it shall be taken away".'

Cultural, rather than political, differences also inspire Leo Mc-Carey's *Ruggles of Red Gap*, another butler story, which, like all

---

[1] This isn't to say that one's every opinion is logically consistent with all one's opinions. On the contrary, the contradictions will tend to be reproduced in each sphere and there may also be contradictions between spheres. The point is that an ideology, by definition, tends to appear on several spheres. Nor is this to say that the basis of ideology must be a political one; obviously, many different factors go to make it up.

131

butler stories of the 30's, tends to express delighted surprise at the possibility of reconciling an intimate devotion to others' comfort with self-respect (the blend of physical closeness and class barriers imposes fascinating strains and stresses which have led several notable 60's movies to return to the situation of domestic service, archaic though it is: one thinks of Bunuel's *Journal d'une Femme de Chambre*, of Losey's *The Servant*). Charles Laughton plays Ruggles, the very English butler whom a *nouveau riche* goldminer wins in a poker game with an English Lord. With consummate tact, Ruggles defers to his new master's democratic instincts, and with a rare blend of integrity and diplomacy compromises between being his conscience and his accomplice. So lordly is his manner that the homely moneyed folk of Red Gap take him for an English aristocrat, and he calmly, respectfully, checks the lashback of inverted snobbery with a magnificently Laughtonesque rendition of Lincoln's Gettysburg address. Thus the story is a double conversion. Ruggles, smoothly, adapts to American egalitarianism and the rich hicks make a smaller adjustment less smoothly, learning that 'a man's a man for all that', even if he apparently offends every tenet of American individualism, by his identification with an aristocratic, traditional, deferential style. The vindication of smoothness runs through very many American 30's, and obviously has a double aspect: on one hand it implies a renunciation of the aggressive style appropriate to the jungle ethos, on the other hand it implies an acceptance of middle-class WASP norms.

In so far as manners are the badge of class, most comedies of manners are class comedies, and political overtones creep into even George Cukor's delightful *The Philadelphia Story*. Once again, Katherine Hepburn plays the spoiled rich girl, a Quaker heiress, whose idea of her own perfection has to undergo a comic comeuppance, while James Stewart is the left-wing journalist who has to cease being an inverted snob. As a comedy of Momism, a few lines, surprisingly sharp for the Hays Officer era, look forward to the 50's: 'You didn't want a bridegroom, what you wanted was a High Priest to a Virgin Goddess . . . they're commoner in America than people realize. . . .'

Cukor is responsible for perhaps the classic 30's comedy of the matriarchy, *The Women*, which amassed the redoubtable array of Norma Shearer, Joan Crawford, Rosalind Russell, Paulette Goddard, Joan Fontaine, Mary Boland, Marjorie Main and Hedda Hopper. The monstrous regiment of women was busy behind the screen as

132

well; the play being by Clare Boothe Luce, and adapted by Anita Loos and Jane Murfin. The film is an éxposé of gynocratic self-deception, rivalry and tyranny. As Jacques Siclier put it: 'Nuttiness is the rule in the pink comedies signed Capra, Leo McCary or Mitchell Leisen, but is it quite without premeditation that mothers are so often changed into amiable nuts? The fat rich woman who, in *Merrily We Live*, goes into ecstasies over her pet goldfish as it gives birth. . . . As for the terrifying Mrs. Sycamore in *You Can't take it with You*, she seemed nearer the mental cradle than the matron's throne. While her grown-up daughters think about marriage, she spends her time writing novels, so as to make use of a typewriter which has been delivered in error. She interrupts the motions of her fingers on the keys only to raise the little sleeping cat which served as her paperweight and quietly slides under its paws the new page of her ever unfinished opus. Or else, seized with a sudden desire for destruction, she organizes a monster carnival in her home. She takes no notice of any domestic matter.' *My Man Godfrey* illustrates the pattern. Hubby, his mind geared to business, is all but a negative force in the home, and hen-pecked, while his wife, both childlike and tyrannical, lives an unreal existence at once frantic and sentimental. The limitations of Cukor's picture are lucidly stated by Cukor himself; to an interviewer's question as to whether 'These portrayals reflect to some extent your feelings about a certain type of American woman', he replied:

'Well, some of them, yes. You get it out of the air, you get it out of the text, and there is a way of doing it without making it seem gritty or vulgar, or disagreeable. *The Women* is tough in its way, but it's not a masterpiece; it's rather a romp laid on with a great trowel. A lot of women set a city on its ear; the Merry Wives of whatever it is.'

The sex war in its turn takes on a social tone. As Geoffrey Gorer has remarked, the American male ethos, stressing the ability to survive in a tough, ruthless world, finds its contradiction, and complement, in the only too idealistic, socially very responsible, not to say inquisitorial, ethos maintained by the sociable circuit of middle-class wives, daughters and widows—the old girl network. The attack on Momism, sometimes a defence of masculine realism against feminine sentimentality, is, at other times, a defence of masculine amorality against feminine responsibility. The divisions and tensions help form that favourite 40's figure, the good-bad girl, the girl who's both a tough guy and a good moral influence, while also sexually more giving than the too-cynical hero (cf. Lauren Bacall vs. Humphrey Bogart).[1]

It's an ironic anticipation of post-war obsessions that the last and perhaps the best of 30's political comedy is Lubitsch's *Ninotchka*, with Garbo playing the Russian commissar who softens to affluence and love and to Melvin Douglas as the gigolo who typifies the irresponsible hedonism of the capitalist West. When rearmament began to clear up the last traces of the Depression, the class war could be approached more overtly, as in Sam Wood's *The Devil and Miss Jones*. The 'devil' (Charles Coburn) is the anti-union boss of a big store, and Miss Jones (Jean Arthur) leads her fellow employees in a strike. What's at issue is really his testiness and the film is universally inoffensive.

[1] It's ironic that the culture of co-education should be that which most stresses the sex war. But in so far as education instils notions of self-assertion, then the two things go together, particularly if reinforced by members (sons being educated by Momism and schoolmarms, and later taking refuge in stag and bull sessions—bachelor parties).

22 · The Cosiness Backlash

To the crazy comedies of the 30's, we may oppose their cosy comedies. The popularity of this artistically unrewarding genre seems to have been inspired by two major factors. The New Deal spirit, and the continuing Depression, created a taste for films which were optimistic but escapist, which offered the audiences the wish-fulfilment of that cosy, innocent, solid, family life which the Depression continued to destroy or endanger.

At the same time, the Hays Office, from 1933, made it impossible for films to deal with sexual topics except in ways congenial to puritanism, and showmen naturally resorted to the possibilities of astounding audiences by a mood of startlingly bold innocence. Child stars, and Victorian themes, flourished. Freddie Bartholomew played Little Lord Fauntleroy—another permutation on the cissy and poor-little-rich-boy themes—while Shirley Temple achieved the apotheosis of the genre with her tophatted rendition of *On The Good Ship Lollipop* (not forgetting her saucy three-year-old's burlesque of Mae West). Deanna Durbin ended the Depression for her father and his fellow musicians by persuading Stokowski to conduct an unemployed orchestra in *One Hundred Men And A Girl*. It may have been meant as a pro-cultural retort to the opera company in *Mr. Deeds Goes To Town*, but the suggestion that the Depression would be ended for thousands of American musicians if, in every town, a Stokowski concert set an orchestra on its feet, makes it oddly fitting that Deanna Durbin's speaking voice should be astonishingly like that of Mickey Mouse. Mickey Rooney and Judy Garland caught a mood of small-town innocence which made an adventure out of drinking milkshakes in the drug store; the *Andy Hardy* family series hit on a popular blend of traditional security and modern freedom. In their

135

best moments, the precociously womanly intensity of Judy Garland, with its quality of desperation, and the *Our Gang* vulgarity of Mickey Rooney, give the duo a relief which the rosy formula takes great care to leave covert. Among the adults, Katherine Hepburn turns up in *Little Women* and J. M. Barrie's *Quality Street*. If the suburban comedy prospers, the rustic comedy lingers on, through Wallace Beery, Marie Dressler, and various character actors. By 1940, though, the genre has virtually disappeared; even when setting and theme derive from rural traditions, they have that soft haze derived from that suburban, school-marmalized view of the countryside as idyllic, pure, genteel, lacking, even, in roughness, other than torn jeans, grubby face, or salty wisdom. The change reflects both the increasing numerical preponderance of suburban life *vis-à-vis* the (often depressed and depopulated) countryside, and the suburbanization, by radio as much as by cinema, of rural taste.[1]

Another change of tone may be exemplified by the career of Zasu Pitts, a tragic victim of von Stroheim's, and a heroine of the 20's. By the 30's, her air of helplessness, as appropriate to the softer, more nervous 'young old maids' of American rural life, as to the newly arrived immigrant families, could be accommodated only by her transformation into a scatty comedienne; while by the 40's Martha Raye transposes the same bewilderment into a more active, noisy, belligerent style.[2]

In general, the cosy comedy is something of an extreme genre, and hardly survived the war. In fact Louis B. Mayer's insistence on perpetuating it into the late 40's rapidly lost M.G.M. its leadership of Hollywood. The post-war Andy Hardy films, like the revivals of the

---

[1] Indeed, *Oklahoma*, which, on stage in 1943, seemed a return to regional roots, is, in retrospect, almost as kitschy as *South Pacific* and *The King and I*. Rodger's and Hammerstein's influence on the musical parallels that of Disney on the cartoon.

[2] A parallel repudiation of vulnerability appears in the hero-villain contrast in dramas. By the late 40's, almost the only normally vulnerable male in American movies was Zachary Scott, whose typical roles were as the scheming gigolos of Joan Crawford in her 'matriarch burden's' weepies. Following the usual rule-of-thumb about the relative accuracy of villains compared to heroes, he's a crucial figure of the period—in fact the relationship between Bogart and Bacall can't be understood without bearing in mind the Zachary-Joan one. (The secret affinities and contrasts between Hollywood stars are often interesting to follow up. In the same way, one can imagine a film in which Judy Garland and Martha Raye played two sisters frightened of being 'old maids'.) Throughout the early 50's, comedy increasingly indulges emotional vulnerability, heralding its return to drama; Jerry Lewis precedes, and heralds, James Dean.

Thin Man series, and of a collateral genre, the Ruritanian operetta, of which the last was a pachydermous production of *The Merry Widow* (1952), have a somewhat anachronistic air.

23 · That Touch of Tarnish

Such satires as William Wellman's *Nothing Sacred* and *Roxie Hart*, honoured in their time as social criticism, have since been all too rarely seen. Other—perhaps unjustly—forgotten genres include what we may call populist comedy (like the *Min and Bill* series with Wallace Beery and Marie Dressler), and those comedies which were as hard-boiled and cynical as the Code allowed (like Jean Harlow's and Clark Gable's).

Ironically, it is these critically eclipsed genres which are the closest ancestors of the Sturges-Wilder-Kubrick tradition and of the sex comedies of the 60's. No doubt, their very closeness to reality may have imposed evasions so conspicuous as to make the films less satisfying than the aloofer genres. As so often, it is in the sphere of the less stylized film that research problems exist. In the early 30's few film archives were established; their very limited prestige and resources allowed the acquisition of only those films which most pleased 30's critical taste and theory (since substantially transformed). And a temperamental exclusiveness is far from rare among archivists even today.

One would expect the worst sufferers of the middle-class tastes which form most film critics to be the hardboiled films of the immediately pre-Code era, as exemplified by Alfred E. Green's *Angel Face*. One of the attractions of the compilation film *The Love Goddesses* is the examples it affords of a genre almost unrepresented in the archives and unrecorded in serious cinema histories. Barbara Stanwyck plays a young gold digger who, in full Depression, begs a job as a lowly office girl, and then proceeds to titillate and sleep her way up to the executive penthouse with a crude speed that even nowadays would bring a blush to the cheeks of our censor (Baby Face's protectors solved the *Apartment* problem by using everything from the Inner Office to the Ladies loos). Something of the same spirit prompts Bette Davis in Michael Curtiz's *Cabin in the Cotton* to shock and mock shy Richard Barthelmess by singing *Willie the Weeper* while performing an off-screen striptease.

A similar tone informs *Forty-Second Street*, which, though correctly classified as a musical, keeps all its numbers for the climax, until which point it constitutes a classic example of hard-boiled light comedy. This original show-must-go-on, understudy's-big-chance story takes in several sharper references to the social demoralization of its time. The show's producer (Warner Baxter) has had to come out of retirement, which was forced on him by a bad heart, because his shares were wiped out in the Great Crash. The furtiveness and humiliations of the man whose wife (Bebe Daniels) has become a big star paraphrases the despair of the unemployed—as in another big Busby Berkeley production number, where the women sing, *Remember My Forgotten Man*.[1] The comedy is peppered with references to sexual ignominies: the seedy assistant director trying to date the knowing chorus girl, who just drawls, 'Quiet, please'; the guerilla warfare between a puritanical Irish landlady and her lodgers with their girlfriends; and scurrilous asides like, 'They call her Anytime Annie because the only time she ever said 'No' was when she hadn't heard the question,' or this exchange, between a chorus-boy and the girl sitting on his lap while rehearsing a number: 'Are you comfortable?'—'About as comfortable as sitting on a flagpole!'

But in so far as, at least in America, unabashedly cynical films tend to be made by people who are cynical about art too, the genre is going to be rapidly cut down by the Hays Code into a cheaply prurient version of itself. Such calculation certainly seems to underlie Garson Kanin's *Professional Sweetheart*. Ginger Rogers, as a lady of lax

---

[1] It's from this time that feminine dominance becomes a recurrent theme, and often an assumption of comedy. And it might be arguable that Depression unemployment facilitated a—probably inevitable—shift in sexual relations. It threw men out of work, just as women were increasingly employed; indeed, women found it easier to get work, since their wages were lower. Hence the theme of woman as holding the purse-strings and man as gigolo. But it would seem also that the gigolo theme which runs, covertly, through a surprising number of American films, in parallel to the comic contrast between feminine aplomb and masculine clumsiness, has its origin in the 'Momism' situation, whose social causes are rather different; and that Depression emphases are only an aspect of the emancipation of women.

morals (though less lax than you'd think), falls in love with a bluenose boy who spanks her into contented submission to the puritan creed on their wedding night. This denouement reiterated in *Angel* has an obvious ambiguity. In the Jean Harlow and the Clark Gable comedies the scenario tends to be unworthy of the robust cynicism established by the personal style of the two stars—a cynicism of which the Bogart–Bacall banter of Hawks's *To Have and Have Not* is the heir.

Frank Capra's *It Happened One Night* invests this cynicism with his sentimental core. The hardboiled newspaper reporter (Clark Gable) and the runaway heiress (Claudette Colbert) meet on a bus journey, giving the classic Depression backcloth of sleeping rough or in make-shift camps, hitch-hiking, dodging the cops, and travelling on. Gable instructs Claudette in the subtleties of making with the thumb. A short and jerky movement means you don't care, you've got money in your pocket; a very broad gesture means you've got a brand-new story about the farmer's daughter; a very long movement can have a pitiful effect, 'but you gotta have a long face to go with it'. In the event, Claudette makes the breadwinner take a back seat, getting their lift by showing her leg. With hunger at stake, these examples of hobo knowhow play more cynical than they may read. And when a driver concludes that they're a honeymoon couple on a healthy hiking holiday and chuckles 'young people in love are seldom hungry', his sentimentality justifies their stealing his car.

The satires treat a similar cynicism with moralists' rather than sentimentalists' tongs. Roxie Hart (Ginger Rogers), on trial for murder, postpones her trial by pretending to be pregnant, and her lawyer is shrewd enough to see that Momism can be brought into it. 'We'll demand the trial starts on Mother's Day!' Expertly the film sets the brutal mechanism of American justice against the sentimentality of American idealism; each exposes the other as a parody of sober common sense. A shrewd woman journalist, who writes under the pseudonym of 'Mary Sunshine', is altruistically in cahoots with Roxie's tricks. Her plea of temporary insanity gets some rough handling; she must have been 'sane all the time before and sane all the time after with just a little patch of insanity in between'. The cameo of a witness running through his evidence is curiously chilling and splendidly pithy lines abound, like, 'Laugh and the world laughs with you; weep and you look like a chump.' The film's brace of musical themes nicely sums it up; it alternates *When the Bough*

Breaks with *Chicago*.[1] Otherwise, the *Roxie Hart* view of life is represented by such actresses as Anne Sothern and Eve Arden, in sharp
asides imparting a welcome touch of acidity to a variety of generally
more sentimental comedies, including the 'true confession' soap-
operas of which *Roxie Hart* is a parody. And, in so far as they
deployed their emotional resources to pardon and palliate their
heroines' immoralities, *Roxie Hart* is both a cynical film and a
puritan's film.

Since every Hollywood satire aroused protests from the group
satirized, Hollywood often found it convenient to catch the public's
satirical mood by focusing its satire on itself. The process was less
masochistic than it seemed, since everyone thought Hollywood was a
nest of enviably outrageous eccentrics anyway, and the satires allowed
the film makers to posit, even in Hollywood, a small town, neigh-
bourly norm. Wellman's scathing *Nothing Sacred* is paralleled by
Tay Garnett's lesser known, but not inconsiderable *Stand-In* (produced by a company with the agreeable title of 'Masterpiece Productions'). Leslie Howard plays a banker's whizzkid, a desiccated
calculating machine, despatched by a banking firm to put a Hollywood studio on a profitable basis or sell out.[2] Humphrey Bogart
plays the gifted but self-destructive director who tries to save the
studio from the crooked front office executives, and Joan Blondell
plays a one-time child star, who has now sunk to stand-in status but,
cheerful and hardboiled, wises the banker up about the studio's situation, as well as his own emotional inhibitions. Transformed and converted, he saves the studio by persuading the employees to work for
two weeks without pay (needless to say, the reluctant labour leader is a
thoroughly bad hat). Not really more substantial than, say, *The
Philadelphia Story*, the film catches a tone of slick cunning, of acrid
camaraderie, of bleary idealism, of brusque worship of activity brushing aside all feelings which it cannot subsume, which seems more
typically American, and more intriguing. There is, for example, a
splendidly double-edged scene where the prim ex-banker drives the
alcoholic director round in a taxi, feeding him bottles of beer from
the crate in which he has prudently invested, while talking him into
redeeming himself.

[1] American movies have some surprising theme tunes. That of *Public Enemy*
is *I'm Forever Blowing Bubbles* (a choice repeated parodiacally, in *The Big Shot*),
that of of *Duel in the Sun* is *Beautiful Dreamer*.
[2] The type is a drier version of Harold Lloyd: Leslie Howard, here, briefly
evokes McNamara.

24 · Suckers and Soaks

\ Mae West and W. C. Fields came to the cinema from the regions
where theatre interbreeds with vaudeville, and top the bill among the
early 30's influx of vaudeville and radio comedians. Ken Tynan described Wheeler and Wolsey as the only American cross-talk comedians whose films will never have a season at the National Film
Theatre, but it would be interesting to see more of the comedies of
Joe E. Brown and Jimmy Durante (almost the last of the race comedians, indifferently Jewish, Italian, or East European), which may
well possess consistently what they possess in extract: the kind of
zany fidelity to grass roots reality which one finds in the correspond-
ing English tradition, of Will Hay, George Formby, Lucan and Mc-
Shane, Norman Wisdom and the *Carry On* series. Victor Moore,
Jack Oakie and others bring to 30's movies something of the brash,
down-to-earth, briskly accurate character vignettes which are as vivid
as they are limited, and catch much of the snap-crackle-pop of the
American style.

Mae West smilingly acknowledges the applause for her fairground
shimmy in *I'm No Angel*, and happily gurgles under her breath:
'Suckers!' The film is directed by Wesley Ruggles, but its credits
engagingly proclaim its *politique des auteurs*: 'story, screenplay and
all dialogue by Mae West; suggestions by Lowell Bernardo'. The
film's plot (pre-Code) is, on paper, ambiguous, but there is so little
mistaking its meaning that her films, more than any others, goaded
the do-gooders into their successful clean-up campaign.

Yet the film's morality is more complex than opposing the Legions
of Decency and the opulent Mae's prime side of high camp. In a climatic courtroom scene, Mae, at bay for her easy virtue, argues that if some
men gave her diamonds because of what they thought she was pro-

mising, they ought to lose them. The implication that the would-be clients of a supposed prostitute deserved to be bilked is clipjoint morality, and if Mae's male spectators can forgive her for it, it's for a variety of reasons. Certainly her victims are the sort of mean-faced characters who turn up as crooked bankers and sheriffs in B Westerns, and are clearly incapable of matching, even to their nearest and dearest, Mae's conspicuously loyal and generous way with her friends and lovers. Also, however, the film homes in on that challenging old saw which titles a W. C. Fields movie: Never Give a Sucker an Even Break. But as a result of Mae's forensic genius, it is respectability which finds itself in the moral dock. The prostitute's client is not only as immoral as the lady of easy virtue herself, but ten times as ignominious. And when she rounds on her beloved's ex-fiancée and forces her to admit that she wouldn't dream of returning his engagement gifts, she convicts the respectable matriarchy of clipjoint morality in its turn. The comedy's happy end is possible because Cary Grant is generous enough to accept, and to forget, what is, perhaps, most difficult for the proud male: the fact of Mae's close relationship with a man who is clearly a pimp type. Mae clinches her triumph by offering to let any of the jurors 'come up and see her'. But her lover she will ring—any time. . . .

The film manipulates the moral masochism of the mere male as deftly as the more usual blend of puritanism and is, in a sense, a libertarian riposte to it. Mae West is the Statue of Liberties, whose hourglass figure sent Old Father Time into a flat spin, and brought the naughty 90's back to the roaring 20's. Like Westerns, the films are partly exercises in nostalgia, with Edwardian razzamatazz, ragtime pianos trickling notes into the saloon office, music halls with big-voiced tenors and figure-of-8 chorus-girls with high boots and feathered hats. In the streamlined 30's, her sofa contours, her slow-drag way with wisecracks, evoke the epoch of Madams rather than Moms. Indulgent, undulant, monolith, she glides, her hips moving as sweetly as the paddlewheels of a Mississippi pleasure-steamer. Lucky all who sail in her. . . . Her mystery lies in this sumptuosity immingling with a slick, cool, mercenary ruthlessness, a Momist outline with feminine independence, a Nietzschean will to power which has too much humour not to be agreeably self-critical, and a generosity whose tone deliciously blends maternal indulgence and complicity. It's the perpetual possibility of any of these responses which gives tension and wit to lines which, on paper, could hardly seem more mechanical.

143

Her lover asks her what she's thinking of: 'The same as you, honey.'
Was ever the need to court a woman more smoothly put aside? 'I'm
crazy about you,' he adds. 'Yes . . . I did my best to make you that
way.' The wit in that line lies not so much in any revelation of female
scheming as in its almost maternal tolerance of manipulable little
boys. Baudelaire likened the superior lucidity of one lover *vis-à-vis*
the other to the relationship between surgeon and patient or torturer
and victim. Mae's view has a worldlier amiability. Mae's celebrated
'Beulah—peel me a grape!' occurs after a row with Cary Grant and
suggests that she is soothing herself after a slight heartbreak by a
self-indulgence in luxury and power—slightly provocative, perhaps,
in the era of *My Man Godfrey*.

Some lines are almost unanalysable, as when she tells Cary Grant
that she's come to a decision about their affair. That was very quick,
he remarks, to which she replies, 'Oh, I'm very quick, in a slow way,'
a line which might mean almost anything, particularly as accompanied by a broadly sensual resettling of her hips. But, whatever it
means, it refers to some blend of impulse and scepticism, of impulsive
passion and nonchalant reserve, of stalling and pouncing. The sexual
innuendo is a magnificent promise.

I'm No Angel concludes with Mae adorning herself with a white
bridal gown, a defiance of society as outrageous as Groucho's teasing
of Margaret Dumont, that anti-Mae West of yearning, lonely, innocent, respectability. One or two lines work on double-entendres of
sexual unorthodoxies much to the taste of the kinky sixties. Thus when
Cary Grant over-romantically asserts, 'I would be your slave,' she
amiably replies, 'That can be arranged. . . .'

The films themselves have aged and creak in every joint, almost
giving a curious double nostalgia. One good turn deserves another,
and Old Father Time has gallantly rejuvenated the outrageous Mae,
for her whole style has a bland, unruffleable cool only enhanced by
her archaic opulence.

Disreputable, disillusioned, dissolute and disgruntled, W. C. Fields
was Mae West's comrade-in-arms in bawdy comedy's rearguard
action against the galloping pasteurization of the 30's. Like Mae
West, he wrote most of his own screenplays, under such pseudonyms
as Otis T. Criblecoblis and Mahatma Kane Jeeves (and co-stars with
her in *My Little Chickadee*). But his bursts of slow-motion slapstick
and ethereal fantasy relate him to Harry Langdon, Laurel and Hardy
and the Hal Roach tempo. In the vaudeville tradition of pompous

3. **Never Give A Sucker An Even Break:** *W. C. Fields, Margaret Dumont*
   Lofty sentiments in ivory towers, and low cunning below the Plimsoll line
4. **Monkey Business:** *Harpo, Zeppo, Chico, Groucho Marx*

**15
Long Pants:**
Harry Langdon

Hick virgin, city slicker

**16
Earthworm Tractors:**
Joe E. Brown

fruity rascality, he may recall Will Hay and Wallace Beery, but his cultivation of a lordly Southern drawl irresistibly recalls the seedier sprigs of decaying gentry, and/or suburban pretensions to such gentility. His sourness at this Hays Code world recalls the Marx Brothers' way with La Dumont, but the butts of his satire are more solidly characterized than theirs. It's no accident that before Sturges, he used Franklin Pangborn and other preferred denizens of the Sturges world. *It's A Gift*, his study of small-town family life, is less hectic, but even more pessimistic, precisely because every humiliation has time to be winced from beforehand, and mused upon afterwards. His world has less warmth, more emptiness; in several films, his nearest approach to human contact is the dour complicity of fellow-topers. In contrast to Mae's all infolding narcissism, he can manage only a mumbling, but obdurate, paranoia.

This grognosed sourpuss is a sort of battered, half-defeated Uncle to the Marx triplets. Where Groucho's frankness is aggressive, Fields mutters to himself in an interminable monologue, compromising between anger and hopelessness. What may have started out with some hope of eventually counterfeiting an elegant Southern drawl has long since decayed, *à la* Tennessee Williams, to an alcohol-grated larynx rasping like a rusty lavatory chain. His extreme suspicion of the world is revealed in his bitter, lopsided lips, narrowed eyes, and the tentative, cagey gestures that give his rolypoly frame the crabbedness of an arthritic teddy-bear. He is a Sir Toby Belch cruelly misplaced in the Prohibition era. Malvolio now is no mere steward, taking orders, but that dread figure, the bank manager, and Olivia's household has become as petty and niggardly as the Bassonets of *It's A Gift* or the Sousés of *The Bank Dick*. Stout, and still as sour as Cassius, he wages a last-bottle-stand against almost everybody, but especially kids, Moms and bluenoses, that is, everything that the American way of life considers sweet and uplifting.

With Mae West, he shared an ultra-slow humour in which part of the joke was what wasn't quite said, but was, as it were, sidled around. He drawls complacently: 'There's been a catastrophe. He's fallen off the parapet. Yes. . . .' Or an enormous blonde waitress tells him: 'There's a something so big about you.' He waits, with misgivings, and in the silence it's as if a shell were whistling over from the enemy lines, where will it land? She says: 'Your nose.' He nurses his ego, and bides his time, while she bends over a table, and then he murmurs, 'There's something so big about you too. . . .' His retort's crudity, its quality of anticlimax, are all part of the defeated mood of the joke. Thus Fields has an odd quality of non-wit, as if wit required a kind of zest that he no longer possesses, because he despairs of mankind. His gags have an eccentric timing, or mistiming, all their own, sometimes loitering on indecisively, sometimes appearing out of nowhere and disappearing almost before one can laugh. Fields himself said that what's really funny is what one doesn't do, and he can almost claim to have developed the shaggy-dog joke to its highest pitch of inanity. (A clerk spends a whole scene wearing a straw hat without a crown, explaining in almost the last line, that he wears it that way because he suffers from hay fever.) His burring-and-slurring of gags combines a hopeless expectation of audience disapproval, with an ever-frustrated aggression which is nevertheless heroically maintained—as when he stands over an exasperating baby with a chopper in his hand, murmuring by way of excuse, 'Even a worm can turn. . . .'

It's A Gift, an unrelenting exposé of small-town life, includes a deliriously cruel episode where Mr. Bassonet (Fields) as the proprietor of a store, has to deal, not only with a baby who releases floods of sticky molasses from a barrel, but, simultaneously, with a customer who knocks over piles of glassware wherever he turns, because he is not only virtually blind but also virtually deaf. (Only Fields could get himself persecuted by creatures so helpless.) All the petty paranoia of the average man is crystallized in a dawn scene where Bassonet, driven out of his bed by his wife's indefatigable nagging, tries to snatch a little sleep on his balcony, only to be disturbed by, successively, the milkman, a coconut bouncing slowly down every tread into the ash-can, a baby in the balcony above bombing him with grapes and screwdrivers, an insurance salesman, his wife, a 'vegetable gentle-man', two females being maliciously polite to each other, and his own couch's collapse. In one film he spent eighteen minutes trying to hit a golfball. In a nightmare drive to a maternity hospital he gets his car stuck in a fire-engine ladder, and lifted off the road, but not high enough to spare passing traffic from suicidal swerves. This, a classic episode in the Sennett style, is matched by the automobile's racing up and down and around the corridors, staircases and elevators of the *International House*.

His slapstick homeliness brings him quite near Laurel and Hardy, whose taste he shared for absurd parody-realms. But just as in his 'homely' scenes, he exhibits a far more abrasive hostility to the way of the world (where Stan and Ollie just blunder along), so, these 'absurd' realms have, in Fields's films, a function of derisive liberation that anticipates goonery and its indefinable, but pervasive, affinities with satire. In both *Million Dollar Legs*, written by Joseph L. Mankiewicz, and in *Never Give a Sucker an Even Break* (originally released in Britain as *What a Man*), we are introduced to a crazy realm which matches Al Capp's Dogpatch as a parody-opposite of ours.

In the latter film, he falls out of an aeroplane washroom into a strange realm presided over by a Mrs. Haemoglobin (Margaret Dumont), a sort of respectable female Dracula whose ivory tower is equipped with hanging swimming-pools. *Million Dollar Legs* has Fields presiding, like the genially tyrannical Oz, over a Land of Cockayne where all the women are called Angela and all the men are called George (suggesting a happy extreme of democratic equality, and the idyllic community cohesiveness of a South Sea tribe). There's also a vamp called Mata Machri (deliciously played by Lydia Roberti). The million-dollar legs are not, as one might expect, hers, but, of all people's, Andy Clyde's, as an international athlete who, in the old Mack Sennett spirit, keeps in trim by outrunning express trains, and takes his super-superman speed absolutely for granted.[1] There is also a charmingly erotic scene where Jack Oakie and his girlfriend brush each other down with feathers. Such titillation is rare in Fields films, for, in the presence of women, Fields, though hardly lacking in deep dark desires, seemed in his amorous relationships paralysed by a suspicion that all women, however beautiful, were merely harridans in their butterfly stage. *Million Dollar Legs* isn't simply a Dogpatch: or rather it's a European Dogpatch, it's a last zany image of Ruritania, of the lands from which America's immigrants came. It bristles with secret police, yet everyone is content. According to Aristophanes, Cloud Cuckoo Land was the topsy turvy region where you beat your father and got praised for it. Klopstockia is the land where foreign, fuddy-duddy fathers turn out to be champion weight lifters and supersonic sprinters. Andy Clyde's philosophy is the absolute reverse of American earnestness, he's a deferential, almost feudally modest, messenger boy, and he can hardly be bothered to stir his stumps merely for the sake of winning. 'Have you ever studied astronomy?' he ponders, philosophically. 'Have you ever realized how short a hundred yards is?' Backwoodsmanship is in

[1] Are these quick motion effects, one wonders, a parody of King Vidor's was of slowing camera speeds to make his heroes run or work faster (in *Hallelujah*, in *Our Daily Bread*) at inspired moments?

147

there too, and Fields's slow, full-blown style, often nearer the anecdote than the gag, sometimes takes on an almost Mark Twain quality,
as in *If I Had a Million*. Fields and wife, having at last hit the jackpot,
drive round town, followed by a fleet of spare automobiles; after each
smash, they climb out and hail the next in line.

The homely and the exotic weirdly coexist. Fields hears a police-car
radio describing a wanted man as having 'apple cheeks, cauliflower
ears and mutton-chop whiskers' (shades of Arcimboldo); or he buys
shares in a beefsteak mine; or, as a bank dick, he dons a disguise
which consists mainly of a length of string running from the bridge of
his nose to behind his ear. These improbabilities are presented so as
to be quietly mulled over, rather than developed, and have a strange
halfheartedness which is itself a joke, and rather a sad one. Fields's
humour, instead of falling between two stools, of fantasy and satire,
wobbles uneasily, and intriguingly, on the edge of both. He seems to
be taking a subdued revenge on the real world by substituting for it a
fantasy one. Yet he's also too weary to develop the fantasy. It's as if
he introduces, into the familiar atmosphere, little 'air-bubbles' of
fantasy, which swell, and slowly subside, and at last burst, leaving a
sour nostalgia behind.

The passage of time has perhaps enhanced this effect, since his
films abound in parodic reference to genres with which later audiences
are less familiar. In *Never Give a Sucker an Even Break*, Fields leads
an existence weirdly split between a Hollywood director's and a small-
town spouse's; he has simply taken, to a *reductio ad absurdum*, Hollywood's picture of homely Hollywood. In *International House*, the
Chinese inventor obsessively trying to get a six-day bicycle race on his
'radioscope' (television) is an idiotically Westernized, passified and
cretinized Fu Manchu. Fields's flight in an autogyro, out of which he
keeps dropping empty beer-bottles, refers at once to the 30's fascination with long-distance solo flights and an outrageous defiance of still
vivid Prohibition. (It's easy to forget just how much any reference to
any alcoholic beverage, even the presence of a bottle and glass, meant
for Prohibition era audiences.) In one of its musical interludes, *International House* also has Cab Calloway singing about 'that funny
reefer man', a line whose subversiveness probably strikes more people
now than it did then. But the fact that it got there is one of those
happy accidents with which a kindly fate blesses those artists who
deserve it. It's ironical that *International House* would today have to
lose this scene, or be banned.

148

The one new innocent of the 30's is Eddie Cantor.[1] His *Roman Scandals* (for Goldwyn) started out in Depression America, from which town bum Eddie dreams his way back into the court of Poppeia, finally returning to save the poor from being evicted by the hard-faced businessman. The mixture of comic topicality and wish-fulfilment opulence is evident enough. Less characterful, less rooted in reality than Keaton, Lloyd and Langdon, Cantor had something of their touching intensity, and, in his personality 'aura' seems to have something of each, as if typifying the way in which the various sections, strata and racial groups of America were coalescing into— not the American ideal, for Eddie, like most comedians, was an anti-hero—but the 'little American'. There's a kind of scuttling nervousness about him which is very much of the period, too, with its hectic pace and its Depression. The stress lies on gags, and bluff-and-cowardice gags, in a way anticipating Bob Hope, a comedian with a slicker, more realistic style. But if *Kid Millions* now seems an awkward anticipation of the Bob Hope style movie, it is saved, like *Roman Scandals*, by the musical numbers of Busby Berkeley, which, in these and other 30's movies, are really little deliriums of the imagination, psychological counterparts of crazy comedy, but, with their lines of milky, healthy, smiling beauties, cosy as well as crazy. As the middle-class tide rises throughout the 30's, Berkeley's Freedonian regiments of lovelies yield, in their turn, the limelight to more intimate and 'cosy' numbers, based on the 'individualistic' couple-of-lovers (Fred Astaire, Ginger Rogers).

[1] He had made *Kid Boots* with Clara Bow in 1926 but the early 30's are his heyday.

25 · Four Against Alienation

Rather less melancholy and vastly more aggressive, the Marx Brothers found highbrow admirers from the moment of screen blast off. It's no accident if Antonin Artaud, prophet of the Theatre of Cruelty, subsequently so fashionable, called *Animal Crackers* that 'extraordinary thing . . . an . . . essential liberation . . . a kind of exercise of intellectual freedom in which the unconscious of each of the characters, repressed by conventions, and habits, avenges itself and us at the same time . . . a kind of boiling anarchy, a kind of disintegration of the essence of the real by poetry . . .'. A few years later, Dali presented Harpo with a harp whose strings were made of baked wire.

On their first appearance in London, at the Coliseum in 1922, the brothers, still billed as 'Herbert, Leonard and Julius', were so unpopular that the audience booed and threw pennies on the stage. Art houses apart, their cinema popularity here was, reputedly, centred on London and Leeds (a distribution presumably related to their often very Jewish humour). In America, of course (mainly through Chico) the Marx Brothers (though themselves German Alsatians) had a special resonance also with the many Italian immigrants struggling along in a strange land, feeling themselves to be 'crazy', by American standards, while contemplating, irreverently, its strange customs and institutions. Prominent among these latter, of course, is Margaret Dumont, the high society hostess with the well-meaning schoolmarm soul. She can never believe that life around her is as chaotic and cynical as it is, with the result that Groucho can insult her with impunity (in *Coconuts*, more by luck than by design, he saves her daughter from marriage to crooks). Through the Marx Brothers, immigrants could take a liberating revenge on that American xenophobia that made them feel third-class citizens until they had brainwashed and transmogrified themselves into conformity. Their successive films rake every aspect of American life; WASP snobbery and high society (in *Animal Crackers*), the campus (*Horse Feathers*), politics (*Duck Soup*), and so on, through the opera, the circus, the Old West, big department stores, and, in *Love Happy*, the conventions of the Raymond Chandler world.

But from the particularly American issue of immigrants versus conformism, their films spread out into a wider application of Bergson's 'mechanism' theory of humour. They also mock the maladjustments brought about by habit, assumption, social convention and hypocrisy. The Marx Brothers are flippantly, scathingly alive, whereas all their victims are half-mummified by a particular position in the social order—whether waiters or foreign ambassadors. The characteristic Marxist posture is opportunism and a bashless nerve. It is scathingly cynical rather than nihilist, for, although it finds nothing sacred (not even the underdog), its view of human nature is as tolerant as it is low. 'Sir, are you offering me a bribe?' thunders Groucho, adding, 'How much?' Well might he parody, in *Animal Crackers*, Eugene O'Neill's *Strange Interlude*, and interrupt a love scene to tell the camera his *real* opinion of the two women he's courting. For his Marxism is, precisely, a long 'monologue', an aggressive saying, and acting, out loud of everything the ordinary, responsible, hypocritical adult finds it easier not to say, and then, in the end, not to think, so becoming alienated from his own heart. Marxism is making instant, not proposals, but propositions, to each pretty woman in turn (or several at a time); it is exploiting and insulting the Margaret Dumonts of this world, as they try to soothe cynicism and reality out of existence; it is flying an airliner no hands, and, only incidentally, dishing the crooks. It may seem odd to describe this 'Marxism' as honesty, since Groucho is a con man, and Harpo is a born liar even though he can't speak. But they never fool themselves. Their hypocrisies aren't even skin deep. The transparency (to us) of their roguery helps blow the gaff and show that, from the point of view of mental freedom, respectability is dishonesty. It wouldn't take much, one feels, for the Brothers to rush into the auditorium of a cinema showing one of their films and insult all their fans for laughing at their jokes without applying the lessons of that laughter to everyday reality. For not to take Marxism seriously is precisely the sin of Margaret Dumont. Because she treats Groucho's truths as jest, she remains the eternal sucker.

The Brothers' least typical film, *Room Service*, throws a fascinating sidelight on their resonance. Here the Brothers are, for once, caught up in the cogs and gears of something resembling a plot (a Broadway comedy which is also the original of *Step Lively*). Impresario Groucho, hardpressed by creditors, shamelessly exploits all the pitiable characters—a pathetic waiter, a decent and hard-pressed hotel manager, the idealistic author of his play, and even the sentimental streak in a hatchet-faced accountant. The final fake funerals are in the hilarious worst of all possible taste. Into the conventionally intricate plot, the Marx Brothers contrive to slip a fair charge of fantasy while Groucho, in particular, sustains a *comic*, as well as *farcical*, characterization. The Marxes aren't so far from the Sturges world of *Mad Wednesday*. (As a footnote, it's strange too how their films found room for three actresses who went on to live hectic, libertarian or tragic lives: Thelma Todd, Lillian Roth and Marilyn Monroe.)

On the strength of their verbal and logical craziness, the Marx Brothers have, justly, and most detailedly by J. P. Coursodon, been called the true heirs of Lewis Carroll. Our surprise at the comparison stresses a difference. Lewis Carroll's common-sensical little Alice justified a childlike simplicity against the arbitrariness of adults, and her simplicity was a decorous, moral innocence. But Margaret Dumont is the matronly Alice of the Marx Brothers' Wonderland. She is the innocent voice of 'square' common sense. She feebly protests to Groucho, 'But I saw you go out of the room with your own eyes.' To which he retorts, scathingly, 'Well, who are you going to believe, me or your own eyes?' All Bishop Berkeley's philosophy doesn't confuse the issue more thoroughly or more instantaneously.

Thus the Brothers correspond to the Mad Hatters, the Humpty Dumpties, the tetchy Duchesses, and all the rude and unreasonable characters who plague Alice in Lewis Carroll. But their unreasonableness goes with their drastic honesty. Hence, they never attain the swollen malevolence of Jarry's *Ubu Roi*. They still have some of his characteristics—Groucho's fake front of respectability, Chico's sullen plots and plans, Harpo's shameless lasciviousness. Instead, they're more benevolent, particularly towards the young lovers, than all the 'straight' citizens, who, weighed down by responsibility, or soured by taking life seriously, have no time or wish to play truant.

In their vulgarity, they are nearest Chaplin (but without his pathos), in their sourness, nearest W. C. Fields (but without his defeatism). Harpo *constantly* does all the things that The Little Man does on running amok in *Modern Times* (only with Harpo it's not twisting off women's buttons, it's cocking his thigh up on to their hands). Chaplin's rollerskating in *The Big Store* is dreamy-idyllic (with hints of tragic danger), whereas the Marxist version in *The Big Store* is chaos come again. (There's also a counterpart of Chaplin's feeding-machine, when an Italian momma and all her brood keep getting trapped in automated beds, which, to add to the confusion, look like safes, automobiles and other absurd status-symbols.)

Between them the Brothers are everything that's disreputable in the city jungle. Groucho is the city slicker with the commercial or professional front. His moustache is painted, while his eyes are as shifty as ballbearings in an earthquake. His scathing cynicism about everything is an inversion of Yiddisher sentimentality. There's a touch, about his cagey leer and rasp, of the Humphrey Bogarts (another hard-bitten, disillusioned city-dweller), while his sneaky, bent-double walk-cum-slide isn't monkeylike, so much as physical metaphor for moral snakeyness. He's the Brothers' front man, and, as the most ambitious, constantly being victimized by Chico and Harpo. They usually descend on him, as a team, in the first reel, to offer their 'help', and, in the end, get him to help the young lovers—generally much against his will, for, of the three, he's the most contaminated by worldliness. He's almost Jack Lemmon before his time. As house manager of the Coconuts hotel, he's eventually ready, in sour, weary irony, to join the two agents of chaos in tearing up his guests' registered mail. He becomes more or less benevolent only after their crazy persistence has worn him down; but they are, in a sense, his fate, i.e. his real nature. He's the most Jewish of the three but he is also all the minority groups rolled into one; thus, in *Coconuts*, he leads the singing of *My Old Kentucky Home* and then adds, 'This programme comes to you from the House of David. . . .'

Chico, the most Italian of the three, has all the humble occupations —peanut-vendor, tootsy-frootsy ice-cream seller, dirty postcard-pusher, even 'the fish-pedlar from Czechoslovakia'. He has most of the practical ideas, and he concocts most of the 'artisan-type' schemes (burglary, theft, etc.). He is the link man between the deliriously articulate Groucho and the deliriously inarticulate Harpo, and he is also the 'ordinary' man, the workman of the trio, dour and solid. With implacable loyalty, he won't be separated from, and he always defends, Harpo, his idiot brother (cousin, pal). In family loyalty he could give points to another Italian immigrant, Rocco. A major scene in Visconti's film has Rocco not retaliating when beaten up by his brother. Similarly, when Chico and Harpo fight, Harpo always fouls, by squaring up with his fists and then kicking, whereupon Groucho says, 'Hey, whassa matter, thas-a-not-fair, you no fight downstairs.' But he never retaliates, just like a responsible but forgiving brother. Harpo's 'angry' looks (puffed out cheeks, gritted teeth, protruding tongue) is based on the mocking glare of a local cobbler at the boys who stared at him as he worked away in his shop window. Just under the surface of the Brothers' fantasy, a documentary is screaming to be let out.

Harpo is the dregs of society, the dumb tramp-cum-ragpicker, a character quite as handicapped as one of Samuel Beckett's, but happy with it, because not impotent. He's the St. Francis of the Rabelaisian hagiography, a moon-calf on roller-skates, the most aggressive of dreamers. Since he's a pickpocket and a sex-maniac, one can't altogether describe him as innocent, but he's the most *spontaneous* of the Marx Brothers. His impulses are the least affected by the world's hostility. He's a satyr in ragpicker's clothes. Pan had his pipes, and Harpo has his motor-horn. His red hair is a traditional symbol for lasciviousness; and he is a special master of such coyly suggestive gesture, such as parking his thigh in a lady's hands, or gently leaning forward to press the bulb of his motor-horn against the stomach of his interlocuter. If he's maniacal in his pursuit of blondes, he's indiscriminate in a kind of innocent-hypocritical sexuality, often smiling at villains and cops like a gurgling baby, while double-crossing, or parking his thigh on, them, too. He steals things like a baby grasps an adult's nose to play with. Like a baby, he tries to eat inedibles, especially telephones, and being a magic baby, invariably succeeds. If anyone frustrates him, his face becomes hideous with wrath, rather like a gargoyle's (by Christian standards, he is, indeed, a little demon). In *Animal Crackers* he does his level best to break a girl's arm, and also shoot several other young ladies, because, when there's more than one blonde in a room at a time, he can never decide which to chase. He also has a kind of nutty tenderness that never quite becomes pathos.

Thus the Brothers constitute a three-pronged attack on society—Groucho's 'front man' outrage of polite conventions, Chico's dour, proletarian scheming, Harpo's clown-and-satire glee. Their verbal humour includes execrable puns, which suggest an immigrant's difficulty with the English language. Harpo naturally combines it with an

154

even more primitive form of communication, gestures, which become a sort of punning sound language. He buzzes like a saw and then makes squirming motions, which means, 'bee' plus 'twist', i.e. 'Beatrice'. Not content with contorted verbal barbarisms the Brothers dwell with cretinizing glee on *faux-naif* bad jokes: 'How much do you charge to fall through an open manhole?'—'Only a cover charge'—'Drop in sometime'—'Sewer'. While reducing words to mere lumps of sound, they also create logical solipsisms: 'I know where the suspects are—they're in the house next door.'—'But there isn't any house next door.'—'Then we build a house next door!' and plan to put the roof in the cellar so as to keep it dry when it rains.

Thus they tear language, and all the conventions and assumptions which language incorporates, apart, in just the same way as logicians caution students against bad logic—by inventing plausible logical and verbal patterns which half-procure one's habit-blinded assent, but which lead straight into utter absurdity. Thus, as detectives in *Animal Crackers*, they reason their way from 'This portrait was painted by a left-handed painter' to 'This picture was eaten by a left-handed moth'.

Not that they're pure logicians—their abuse of polite tags, false modesty, idioms, the very sound of syllables, constitute a verbal barrage whose real aim is to devastate social custom. Every time La Dumont replies with false modesty to Groucho's amorous flatteries, he takes her seriously, and serve her right. 'Welcome to my humble abode,' she coos. He punishes her for this coy nonsense by agreeing: 'Now you mention it, it is pretty frowsy. Come to think of it you're not looking too good yourself,' and tries to sell her life insurance in view of her probably imminent death. He courts her with all the romantic flourishes, and when, playing hard to get, she simpers, 'You'll find some pretty young girl to go off with and leave me,' he retorts, 'I'll send you a postcard. . . .'

Unexpectedly for verbal comedians, Marxist dialogue doesn't read half as funny as it sees. In cold print it's baffling rather than amusing, because it draws its relevance, not only from the Marx Brothers' style of delivery, but from a whole network of references and expectations which appear in the screen setting and action, but not in the mere words. This use of language *reads* negatively, because it is a destruction of language, a demonstration of its falsity, of its conventional functioning, a concealment and alienation. Harpo, who can hardly talk, let alone think, is the least alienated from his *joie de vivre*. They

155

thus anticipate current pessimism about communication, and also go beyond it. Communication is only impossible, implies Harpo (silently, smilingly), if you're fooled by language's habit and lies, and let it trap your heart. For communication is, not explaining yourself to blondes, but wanting them enough to pursue them. Those intellectuals, who, like Godard, affect an anguished feeling that nothing can be communicated except the impossibility of communication, only show that they aren't intellectual enough to challenge the rules of the communications game, to exploit, not serve, its built-in hypocrisies. For the Marx Brothers are intellectuals in that they challenge the habits and the rules. They exploit them, to confuse their opponents, but don't believe them. For them, the rules of language, and of society, are like the railway track in *Go West*. The fun only begins when the train of thought shoots off the rails and starts across the countryside, slicing through houses and bedrooms, while the Marx Brothers chop the coachwork off the carriages to fuel the engine.

Not that language is their only butt. In *A Night in Casablanca* Groucho's date with the vamp is continually disrupted by Chico. This self-appointed bodyguard-cum-spoilsport, in paranoid over-protectiveness (justified, as it turns out), keeps ringing up, or bursting in to ensure that his boss hasn't got a woman in there (like a narrow-minded landlady). To escape his attentions, poor Groucho is reduced to staggering from one room to another under the weight of phonograph, champagne bottle and bucket, roses and all, until he feels less like Don Juan than the Hunchback of Notre Dame. Thus a whole romantic iconography is reduced to its most ludicrous terms, the burden of baggage. Similarly, in *At the Circus*, Harpo cuts the rope mooring a platform to the shore, and an entire symphony orchestra, playing oh, so soulfully, goes drifting away into an audience-less horizon, in a classic image for the pompous, self-enwrapped futility of so much high culture. It's much better, like Harpo, in the intervals of blonde-chasing, to settle down with the clarinet, or the harp, when the whim takes one, with no pretentions at all. He's quite likely to conclude his harp act with a voluminous yawn and drop off to sleep. His music is a refreshment of the spirit, for its own sake, a kind of dreaming, just as during his harp-playing in *The Big Store* his two mirror-images acquire an independent life of their own. This briefly perturbs him until their smiles and nods reassure him that they're friendly.

Similarly the message of the Marx Brothers is not to fear one's inner, unconformist, self, but to let it into one's conscious mind. A film like *The Knack* is, so to speak, applied Marxism–Harpo Marxism.

Because their films have acquired a (well-merited) period charm, it's easy to overlook the virulent callousness of many of their ideas. Thus *Coconuts* (made in full Depression) is set against the background of the Florida real estate boom (the Depression's immediate trigger). Perhaps their most scathing film is *Duck Soup*. The state of Freedonia has been kept from total economic collapse only by huge loans from a gracious American lady, Mrs. Teasdale (Margaret Dumont). She insists that absolute power must be given to a ruthlessly efficient American businessman, Rufus T. Firefly (Groucho), who, on arrival, wastes no time in announcing, in song, the basic principles of Groucho-ism. 'If any form of pleasure is exhibited—it'll straightway be prohibited.' But Groucho's wicked pleasure in wielding absolute power rapidly gives way to his lurking hedonism, for his new marriage laws, it appears, will allow any pretty young wife who's caught in adultery to choose between her mangey old husband and her sprightly young lover (Groucho, of course). Sylvania's attempts to sabotage Freedonia's economy by means of triple agents Pinky and Chikolini almost lead to war, which is not to be averted even by Mrs. Teasdale's peace-making mission. Chikolini's trial for spying is interrupted by the Sylvanian attack, and Freedonia has to radio urgent calls for help. 'Help is on the way!' comes the reply—and we see it on the way —cops on motor-bikes, fire-engines, divers, runners, herds of elephants, baboons scurrying through the treetops, and schools of leaping dolphin.

All this has a kind of permanent relevance to twentieth-century diplomacy. Freedonia's economic difficulties recall the Depression. Mrs. Teasdale's belief in a strong, morally severe, businessman's government recalls the solution offered, in opposition to Roosevelt's New Deal, by the American right-wing (as in La Cava's *Gabriel Over the White House*). The foreign dictatorship theme must also parody Mussolini's régime; and just as *Duck Soup* was being made, Hitler took power in Germany. But even more extraordinary than these contemporary echoes is the film's prophetic quality. The highly irregular trial of Chikolini is like a burlesque preview of the Moscow trials in 1936—while the derisory response to the plea for help forecasts the utter paralysis of the League of Nations. Groucho triggers off the war by his paranoid fear of losing face (he slaps the Sylvanian ambassador's face in case the Sylvanian ambassador means to slap his face, which he doesn't)—and there's a kind of sad truth there about the childish chauvinism and prestige-hunting which, in international politics, can have such disastrous consequences for us all. Even more cutting is the scene where Chikolini's trial is interrupted by a declaration of war, greeted with an enthusiasm which becomes, not only hilariously, but hideously, orgiastic. Everyone in the courtroom, audience, judge, jury, writhe in revivalist-style movements, and chant, of all things, 'All God's chillun got guns.'

The actual war cruelly burlesques all the horrors of 1914–18. For its generals' muddle and incompetence: Firefly is about to award himself the Firefly medal for routing the advancing enemy when his aide tells him, 'But sir, you're firing on our own men,' whereupon Firefly, never at a loss, flings him a couple of coins and says, 'Here, keep it under your hat,' and then, 'On second thoughts, I'll keep it under mine,' which he holds out like a collection plate into which the other automatically places the money. The slaughter of the British volunteer army, and the recourse to conscription, is reflected in Harpo's hopeful attempt to find more recruits by strolling across the battlefield with a sandwich-board proclaiming, 'Join the Army and see the Navy'. When a General radios to say he's resisting a gas attack, Groucho tells him to take a teaspoonful of bicarb (and really it's hardly stranger than the Civil Defence Corps telling us to protect ourselves against fallout with vinegar and brown paper). Looked at from the vantage point of 1965, Groucho's appearing in every scene with a different uniform, from a Davy Crockett hat to a Poilu's tin-helmet, becomes not simply a spoof of history, but a matter of 'The Universal Soldier'.

26 · Hallelujah, I'm a Mouse

During the 30's, the term cartoon becomes all but synonymous with Walt Disney. His cartoons almost oust the two-reel slapstick comedy from cinema programmes, and the genre survives vestigially only in the Three Stooges and Joe Doakes series.

Disney's reputation is embarked on a decline. His popularity, his technical expertise, his charm, exerted a tyrannical effect on cartoon style for twenty years, and the final sclerosis of his imagination is rather sad. From 1928 until 1945 is Disney's artistic heyday, and it is by his triumphs then that he is most happily remembered.

His earlier cartoons have an irresistible freshness, even when bordering on the macabre. *The Mad Doctor* delectably parodies *Frankenstein*: Pluto is carried off by a mad doctor who wears a ghost cloak and has sketched out his pictorial equations on a blackboard: dog + hen ÷ saw = $\dfrac{\text{dog's head}}{\text{hen's body}}$. Mickey, rushing to the rescue, is confronted with a corps of skeletons, who bowl their heads at him and lure him up a trick staircase with coffin-shaped treads. Tight corners and chases galore have a perky, frisky jollity, as when in *Mickey in Arabia*, Mickey, to rescue his abducted Minnie, leaps aboard a camel which is so drunk that it gallops and lollops along on its humps. Violence is hardly lacking, but charmingly devoid of any objective correlative, as when Mickey, in *Steamboat Wil ie*, turns the goat which has swallowed a guitar into a barrel-organ by cranking its tail.

Visually more elaborate, and hardly less delightful, is the 1937 *Lonesome Ghosts*, in which Mickey, Donald and Goofy, as ghost exterminators, constantly fall victim to the pranks of four green phantoms until, drenched in syrup, molasses and flour, they seem to be ghosts themselves and frighten the real ones away. Donald opens a

159

door through which the ghosts have just vanished and is met by a solid wall of water, which engulfs him, and over which the ghosts sail, on surfboards and in 1900 parasols and bathing-costumes.

In more realistic subjects, like *Airmail Pilot* and *Mickey's Trailer*, Mickey survives every kind of onslaught from burly bandits through failed brakes to snow storms, to arrive at his destination, scarcely daunted and unscathed, because his brisk, modest, busy cheerfulness, almost too trusting to be plucky, yet so undeterrable as to be a *tour de force*, is the ideal appeal to a kindly Providence—a Providence which has taken from Christianity its response to childlike faith, from utilitarian puritanism its assent to obsessional single-mindedness as a character ideal, and from a healthy and likeable human mediocrity, the stipulation of suburban domesticity as the ideal framework for happiness. Mickey at his best, incarnates the reconciliation of New Deal euphoria with Republican immobilism. According to Lewis Jacobs, the theme song *Who's Afraid of the Big Bad Wolf*, from *Three Little Pigs*, became a New Deal slogan, a hopeful counter-anthem to *Hallelujah I'm a Bum*. The *Three Little Pigs* set up their chirpy chirrup of American optimism, and, with the huffing and puffing wolf, have become regular motifs in political caricature. Satire, however, is fundamentally alien to Disney humour, and his *Mother Goose Goes Hollywood* spoofs the sophisticated stars rather than the naïve fairy-tales. If the cruellest caricature is of Katherine Hepburn, as a pretentious little Bo-Peep, it is no doubt because her socialite style offended his animal farm idea of culture. While preparing *Fantasia*, he remarked: 'This'll *make* Beethoven.'

In contrast with 30's Disney, Dave Fleischer's *Popeye* series seem both more archaic and more modern. Archaic, in that it always kept something of the outline and ink blob graphics, in that the action had a back-alley simplicity, in that the Popeye–Olive Oil–Bluto–Wimpey family were human, like the Katzenjammer Kids and Betty Boop—and, of course, in Popeye's waterfront style pugilistic prowess. His innocence is that of an adult outsider, rather than that of a child, and he relates, therefore, to immigrant America of the early 20's, rather than to middle-class America of the late 40's. The films are modern in their monomaniac stress on violence, with their tightly repetitive, not to say obsessional, narrative pattern (Popeye is in a tight spot, can he get at his spinach?, Popeye is invincible). Monotony weighs less heavily than might be imagined since many apparently diverse plots relate to equally repetitive patterns anyway and since, even within

160

Feet First: *Harold Lloyd*

It's a great life if you don't weaken

Mad Wednesday: *Harold Lloyd, Jimmy Conlin*

19. **Speak Easily**: *Buster Keaton, Thelma Todd, Jimmy "Schnozzle" Durante*
A Puritan business man with a calculating machine mind meets the big city's flora and fauna. And down below, there's the devil to pay . . .

20. **Hellzapoppin**

that formula, a variety of settings and twists are possible, particularly since Fleischer, in the Krazy Kat tradition, and quite differently from the more literalistic Disney, thought nothing of sending Popeye back in time to participate in, for example, the original Olympic Games.

Popeye found an intriguing feminine stable mate in Betty Boop, a latter-day figure of flapper mischief. Betty was hounded by the Hays Office because, in Ado Kyrou's words, 'Her heart was as sensually shaped as her lips, and at certain crucial moments, it finished up situated at the height of her garter, after having visited both her breasts and all the interesting portions of her maliciously erotic anatomy.' By the late 30's, Fleischer capitulated to the Disney tone and style; 1936 also saw the appearance of Bugs Bunny, whose friendly but laconic inquiry, 'Eh, what's up, Doc?', introduced the cool and cynical violence of the late 40's, and should, perhaps, be looked at again there, alongside *Tom and Jerry*. Meanwhile, what one may call the non-WASP cartoon spirit languished until revived by Tex Avery in the early 40's. But with the cartoon as well as the conventional movie, it's high time we dropped our narrow *politique des auteurs*, for even the more uneven authors have their gems, like Walter Lantz's *Poet and Peasant Overture*.

The enigmatic signature, Ub Iwerks, graces some of the happiest early sound cartoons, whether from the Disney studio (like *Karnival Kid*) or in the subsequent *Willie Whopper* series, of whimsically tall tales ending with the challenge, 'Now you tell one!' *Karnival Kid* has Minnie as a belly dancer and Mickey selling hotdogs which joyously sit in the mustard before leaping happily into the sandwich and wrapping the bread around themselves as snugly as blankets. *Vulcan Entertains* has Willie dream himself at the bottom of a volcano, where Vulcan-Satan entertains Caesar, Napoleon, and other tyrants of history, the last being a mean-faced, gamp-brandishing gent labelled 'Prohibition'. After being hilariously tormented by everybody, he manages to scramble out, only to be dropped back in again by an (American) eagle. It's a rare and charming example of a political entertainment cartoon.

Part Four

KISS THE BOYS GOOD-BYE

27 · The New Sarcasm

With the 40's came prosperity, and, ironically, a new bitterness. The paradox isn't uncommon (more recently, English affluence saw kitchen sink and anger). Often those oppressed use movies to dream, while those who feel less need for escapism can relish the release of their discontents.[1]

It is Preston Sturges who, with *The Great McGinty*, first caught, and revealed, this new mood. It's a mood that runs counter to Hollywood theories, which saw the public as intrinsically and externally naïve and sentimental, and anxious to be shown only as conforming to a middle-class ideal. There was, and still is, unfortunately, more truth to this than many of Hollywood's critics have understood, but there has always been less truth to it than the studio heads (as opposed to so many writers and directors) realized. Sturges's success was so disturbing as to be resented rather than emulated, and not only Hollywood, but many intelligent critics, found Sturges almost too much to take. James Agee welcomed the tonic cynicism of *The Miracle of Morgan's Creek*. He implicitly linked Sturges's vision of America to the streak of black derisiveness in Sennett, and wrote 'in fact, to the degree that this film is disliked by those who see it, whether consciously or passively, I see a measure less of its inadequacies than of the progress of that terrible softening, solemnity and idealization which, increasing over several years, has all but put an end to the output and intake of good moving pictures in this

---

[1] This doesn't mean that affluence in itself always leads to entertainment anger; in any case the causes of discontent are subjective and relative rather than objective and absolute.

country'. But even Agee went on to confess that he too found Sturges's films unpleasant as well as salutary.[1]

Sturges's first film, *The Great McGinty*, might be described as Capra with the gloves off. McGinty (Brian Donlevy) begins by beating up pluckily independent shopkeepers on behalf of a party machine boss, becomes a corrupt politician in his turn, and is broken only when he decides to go straight. A scene contrasting his pro-public spending platform with the class-conscious Senator Honeywell—as well as the contrast of names—leaves little doubt that McGinty is a Democrat. No doubt studio chiefs saw this study in Democrat corruption as useful Republican propaganda. But with that artistic cunning which can triple- or quadruple-cross any censorship, the film, in fact, sweeps the snooty Honeywells contemptuously aside, and poses the real alternatives as either utter cynicism or the Democratic ethos. But since the former is a popular, and respected, American attitude, Sturges has McGinty get away—helped by, appropriately, a disillusioned cop—and end his days, not too uncongenially, as a bartender down South America way.

Sturges's tact matches Capra's, point for point, as is evidenced by a very difficult scene where our hero, as Mister Big's strong-arm man, beats a toughly individualistic bartender to make him pay protection. If the scene is morally explosive as it is, it is because Donlevy retains our human sympathy despite his classic villain behaviour. The reasons are: (a) we've seen Donlevy on his uppers and like him as an underdog, (b) his victim has a bully physiognomy, (c) he's so confident in his own toughness that he starts the fight, which (d) we don't see, instead it is (e) reflected on the face of a comic little man who (f) thinks about joining in with a bottle but can't bring himself to. The (a) to (e) points may be classic examples of entertainment tact, but (f) is more challenging.[2] That little man is, and is felt to be, 'the little man', the American conscience which, in historical fact, has so rarely made up its mind to interfere in cases of political bribery and corruption.

---

[1] Less than a decade has passed before Wilder's black comedies were to be greeted with cries of hatred from critics whose fury would know no bounds if one recalled now what they had said then. No names, no pack drill . . .

[2] To speak of tact is not to accuse Sturges of insincerity, nor to imply that he substitutes mere manipulation for artistry. On the contrary. All concern with communication involves a concern with audience response—and whether this is conscious (as it surely is in Sturges's case) or unconscious is not of the first importance. Far more central is whether this tact is deployed to increase or to decrease the audience's awareness. Shocking is simply a special case of tact.

Cynical, Sturges, explosively, joyously, is, but neither nihilist nor dogmatic. He appeals to no ideology, no perfectionism, no despair, but rather to intuitive decencies and horse-sense (still, Agee's own shock testifies to the extent to which such things rasped against the myths of time). More than almost any other director of the war years, he trusted the audience to possess that mental and moral agility needed to follow his quickfire plots and patterns of sympathy through all their twists and turns. *Christmas in July* begins with the well-tried theme of the young lovers who think they've won a huge prize (in this case, for inventing the winning publicity slogan in a Maxford coffee competition). A 'big scene', where two mean businessmen, Schwindel and Maxford, try to snatch presents back from a crowd of tenement children, is quite as openly anti-Republican as Sturges's quiet puns on the word 'democratic' in *Hail the Conquering Hero*. But Sturges's knack lay in never losing his way through all the subsidiary conflicts which prevented this confrontation scene from being facilely loaded. His likeable characters are full of faults and his dislikeable characters often abound in subtle redeeming qualities. Thus the relationship between the quiet, contented heroine (Ella Raines) and her madly ambitious boyfriend (Dick Powell) is, particularly in the opening scenes, edgy to the point of harshness. The menacing supervisor, who imposes exact timekeeping with the relentlessness that seems to sum up an entire system gives the hero a piece of stern advice about self-respect that liberates him from his overblown anxiety to be a success. He seems to represent an older America, the America of stern, solid, modest inner-direction, as opposed to the more fluid, hectic, anxious, callous values of both the boss and the hero. (*Room Service*, similarly, plays on the Marx Brothers' quick, cunning exploitation of the sentimental side of a stern accountant.) Sturges's picture of success-worship is particularly fair, when, for example, Powell's boss, thinking he's won the prize, enthuses over all his ideas, however bad. But when told that Powell hasn't won the prize after all, he immediately sneers at all his other ideas also. Certainly, he's petty and absurd in that all his enthusiasms are unreal, that he has no mind of his own and is lickspittle to success. But he goes on to admit, frankly, that he's no judge of whether the ideas are good or bad, he's made mistakes before, another man's status is all the guide he has. There's both accuracy and sympathy in this observation, and Sturges prefers this kind of understanding to the too-easy jeer, just as he understands the underlying morality that makes a ruthless businessman keep up an unending stream of pompous, jittery, hypocritical self-justifications. In *Hail The Conquering Hero* he contrives to make one minor character incarnate not only a dogmatic sentimentality about Momism but also a disturbingly callous violence, and, in addition, the hero's bad conscience about pretending to be a tough war hero. By uniting these apparently distinct roles, he spotlights that strange connection, in the American psyche, between apparently contradictory attitudes.

George Seaton remarked that his *Anything Can Happen* was a box-office failure because it referred too openly to the fact that many Americans, being only two or three generations away from immigrants, are bitterly ashamed of any foreign traits, and so cling desperately to the concept of 'Americanism'. Sturges darts that needle in and then withdraws it. It is for no other reason that in *Hail the Conquering Hero* the girl's father suddenly unlooses a German expletive (the krauts being the current enemy), while, in the course of a discussion about families, Franklin Pangborn causes a sudden chill by remarking, 'My grandmother was Lithuanian.' It's just at this period that characterization in American movies generally is most stereotyped, as if audiences were trying to conceal, or, better, obliterate, any tell-tale spontaneities, and renouncing the variety and emotionality arising from their (still faintly foreign) family roots. In fact, the hidden theme of much American comedy is crystallized in Chaplin's title, *The Immigrant*, as carried through to Son of the Immigrant, and, I Was A Teenager Lost In The Conformist Jungle, i.e. *Rebel Without A Cause*, only with Jerry Lewis in the James Dean part. But this is to anticipate.

Sturges's films keep jabbing near the nerves of the American ideal (ambition in *Christmas In July*, puritanism in *The Miracle of Morgan's Creek*, heroism). Their emotional voltage enables them to leap from comedy to pathos, from sentimentality to bitterness, with one line of dialogue, or with one detail—like the disturbingly vivid bruised eye inflicted by the Mom-worshipper on his less reverent buddy. And *The Lady Eve* anticipates Wilder's sadism as on their wedding night, gold-digger Barbara Stanwyck feels obliged to confess to her shy, innocent groom (Henry Foda) that she has lost her innocence with a man . . . and another man . . . and another man . . . and another man. . . .

Nor is Sturges so afraid of anti-anti-Semitism that he shrinks from stressing the Jewishness of a mean Jewish businessman, Schwindel, in *Christmas in July*. It's only at the last moment, after a nice maintenance of ideological tension, that he has him soundly ticked off by a poor Jewish momma (i.e. 'it's not race, it's class'). But then the salt is rubbed in again immediately, when the pressure on Schwindel enables him to yield to his repressed sentimental side—so he can turn on his WASP rival, Maxford, who is less pennypinching, because he's richer, and also less susceptible to sentimentality. Sturges can even allow himself the box-office luxury of (highly implausible) happy endings without weakening his comic sarcasm. This is partly because, contrary to certain theories, the general audience doesn't remember only endings, its memories stress the big scenes, and Sturges's are edgy rather than reassuring. In fact, the happy ending of *Christmas in July* is so zany that it satirizes itself. The slogan-judging jury is finally persuaded, by one incredibly old-fashioned, idiotic and obstinate member, to give the prize to the worst slogan (the hero's, 'If you can't sleep, it's not the coffee, it's the bunk'). This jury theme hilariously prefigures Lumet's solemn *Twelve Angry Men*, and its moral seems to be that it's the ornery old idiots who, by sabotaging business efficiency, make America a happier place for young couples, i.e. the spectator's screen self. Twenty years later, students at Berkeley rebel, fundamentally, against the logical conclusion of efficiency—a computerized existence.

28 · Six Comedians in Search of an Author

Eddie Bracken is the ideal Sturges hero. His fresh, ordinary, awkward face has the odd quality of looking, from different angles, like Danny Kaye's, or Liberace's, or Stan Laurel's, or William Bendix's; physically, he is a link between Eddie Cantor and Bob Hope. Outside Sturges, he rarely had the roles he so richly deserved, and indeed American comedy during the 40's took a stereotyped form. The most popular comedians, Bob Hope, Red Skelton, Danny Kaye and to a lesser extent Abbott and Costello, all seemed preoccupied with 'cowardice' (as if in comic compensation for the anti-emotional toughness which was simultaneously reaching its apotheosis in Alan Ladd and Audie Murphy). Hope seemed at times a wisecrack machine functioning impersonally amidst plots about spies, gangsterism or *Road To* . . . natives, themes which are, in a sense, 'abstract', at least in contrast to the extent to which silent comedians, and Sturges, were deeply rooted in American life. When the villains in *My Favourite Brunette* give Peanuts White the truthdrug, he meanders on, entertainingly but irrelevantly, parodying Cyrano de Bergerac, the Frankenstein Monster, Hamlet and Bing Crosby; one can imagine the confessions a truthdrug might bring forth in a Sturges-spirited movie. It's ironic that the truthdrug should make him behave like everybody except himself, because the truth is that he's so other-directed as to have no personality of his own any longer. . . .

The *Road* series haven't worn too well; *Road to Utopia* has lasted best, perhaps because it tries hardest for those self-spoofing gags which shatter the storyline. To current tastes, the others fall between the two stools of gag comedy and character-comedy; but time may re-endow them with a charm to which the writer, at least, is currently blind.

170

But if one regrets that Hope was so rarely involved with the sharply realistic and satirical slapstick of W. C. Fields and Preston Sturges, enough passages are scattered through the many films of his long career to confirm that Hope's characterization is a rich and relevant one. He has spasms of Harold Lloyd's optimism, Cantor's jitteriness, Fields's disillusionment, and a Dan Duryea desperation, while his bouts of childlike bluff and hopeful cunning expertly transpose into farcical terms the comic vices of salesmanlike opportunism. And, amongst the stylized burlesque of the Old West, Tashlin's *Son of Paleface* abounds in sharp and apposite observations about a salesman's life, with its perpetual humiliations, its fragile morale. In *Thanks For The Memory* Hope's light finesse enables him to bring to romantic scenes something wryly affectionate and meditative which manages to be both ordinary and deep. Of his latest films, perhaps his best are *The Lemon Drop Kid, Military Policemen*, where his personality is splendidly counterpointed by Mickey Rooney's, and the inimitably accurate Eddie Mayehoff, and *That Certain Feeling*, a quietly touching little essay in sophisticated comedy. *The Princess and the Pirate* is perhaps the best, because the most fluid, of his cowardice comedies; and there may well be some sharp realism in his pre-war films.

Danny Kaye, like Cantor and Hope, made many comedies for Goldwyn; he had the widest range of the three, and his career is all the more disappointing. His face is at once handsome, sensitive and infinitely transformable, and he combines a straight romantic appeal with wild plunges into frenetic parody. He showed immense expertise in the most 'sophisticated' medium (cabaret, rather than vaudeville, like Cantor, or radio, like Hope) and he was blessed with an exceptionally ingenious lyric-writer (Sylvia Fine). But his fancy was rarely free, and outside his git-gat-gabble musical numbers, he was hampered, either by the spies-and-gangsters plots of the time, or by a milky goodwill which has since smothered his comic attack. Apart from his sung set pieces, his most consistent film is probably Norman Z. MacLeod's *The Kid From Brooklyn*, because there he plays a milkman and has some slightly realistic scenes.

The same director's *The Secret Life Of Walter Mitty* provides the arch-example of how thematic stereotypes (spies) impoverish the picture of a genuine American reality. Goldwyn set out to enlarge Thurber's short story, so as to span a varied canvas of Americana—horror comics, the matriarchy, psychologists—and he was, to my

171

mind, within 'adaptor's rights' in substituting a more positive attack for Thurber's spare, wry, forlorn tone. The interlinking of daydream and reality could have made a penetrating, funny-sad analysis of optimistic self-delusion and of its basically extremely masochistic desire to be a faultless someone else. But all this required the banishment of the spy story from the 'reality' plot to the status of a daydream, and a talent like Sturges's, first to develop it more realistically, and then to galvanize Kaye into a frantic intensity (which was soon achieved by a younger comedian, Jerry Lewis). One hoped that Tashlin could revitalize Kaye with *The Man From The Diner's Club*, but neither star nor director seemed at his ease. Kaye has long ceased to be a crazy comic, or even, in any real sense, a comedian, and deteriorated into a charmer whose screen heart is as wide as Cinemascope and as sickly sweet as candyfloss. His ostentatious tributes to Harry Lauder are quite embarrassing (especially since Lauder quite calculatingly diluted his stage personality with an eye to the American box-office), while in *Me and the Colonel* Kaye competed for, and easily won, the title of the poor man's Alec Guinness.

Red Skelton, basically a 'salesman', like Hope, but less sly, less rapid, was another comedian of the period who never won the characterization he deserved, despite admirable sequences in Edward Sedgewick's *My Hero*, which recaptured the style and spirit of silent slapstick. In retrospect, S. Sylvan Simon's *The Fuller Brush Man* stays homelier and fresher than any of the *Road* series.

The enormous popularity of Abbott and Costello is a phenomenon of show-business, because they seem totally devoid of any striking characteristic whatsoever, except that one is short and fat and the other tall and thin. J. P. Coursodon describes them as 'null and utterly repugnant', and perhaps this, in a characterless age, is the secret of their appeal. Lou Costello had just the streak of Irish or Italian in him necessary to suggest the immigrant who can hardly keep up with life and has to have everything explained to him by his sharper buddy. In this sense, they were, perhaps, 'earthier' than most comedians of their time, but perhaps the real reason for their popularity was that, with Laurel and Hardy languishing, they maintained the slapstick tradition and pleased the children. Such hits as *In Society* and *Hit The Ice* were built round old slapstick and vaudeville favourites, like crosstalk to the effect that if Lou doesn't have mustard in his sandwich he will be responsible for throwing millions of people out of work (on the 'if everyone followed your example' principle).

29 · Hell is a City

Even more colourless than A. and C. were Ole Olsen and Chic Johnson, who remained deadpan, hardboiled and rather heartless while projecting all their restrained violence into their world. The world of *Hellzapoppin* has always seemed to me the equivalent in fantasy of all the chaotic exasperations of the New York tempo. Indeed, what 'objective correlatives' exist in this amazing film are all 'big city'.

In the projection booth of a Broadway cinema, the projectionist, interrupted by an usherette, spools up and shows a film called *Hellzapoppin*. This film-within-the-film begins with the arrival of O. and J. in Hell, which turns out to be a set in a film studio, where they are shooting a film called *Hellzapoppin*. Dissatisfied with the sequence in which they've just appeared, they run it through, first in quick-motion backwards, then forwards, and quit the set. They then study still photographs from another part of the film, which begin moving and show O. and J. arriving at a country house, to help in preparing the pre-Broadway premiere of a stage show which becomes a stage production of *Hellzapoppin*.

This show despite its name would be utterly conventional if it weren't for O. and J.'s attempts at sabotage. These earn it the contract from a Broadway producer who never laughs once, but finally says, 'They haven't missed a trick.' O. and J.'s sabotage of the show-within-the-film-within-the film-within-the-film is counterpointed by mix-ups in the projection booth and even in our auditorium. This five-dimensional storyline is further confused by space-time cross-ties, e.g. a character who appears in the film studio in the first reel, plaintively calling 'Mrs. Jo-ones' and carrying a small tree, also appears in the final show premiere, still looking for Mrs. Jones but now

173

driving a truck containing a huge tree. (Actually, the show premiere happens *before* the studio scenes, so the tree must have been growing younger and shrinking.) This space-time play makes J. W. Dunne's *An Experiment with Time* look like a five-finger exercise.

And with this fragmentation of the film goes a fragmentation of personality. Thus the frame gets stuck in the projector, and O. and J. in one frame do a nippy bit of teamwork with O. and J. in the next frame, or again O. and J. from the Indian film pick a quarrel with, but then agree to merge into, O. and J. in their own film and later F. Hugh Herbert gets his zip-the-zipper trick all wrong and wipes out Ole's bottom half and Chic's top half, which come together to make one person, proclaims 'Quick March' and promptly sets off in two different directions at once.

In this context, the more familiar gags, like F. Hugh Herbert's face altering disguises as he peekaboos from one side of a post to the other, or Chic shouldering the front end of a ladder so long that he can follow on shouldering the rear end too, become part of a process of shattering personality into a thousand enigmatic pieces, until all that remains of a human being is the (superficial) teamwork and quarrels of O. and J. Similarly, Mischa Auer plays a real Russian Count who pretends to be a phoney because people find that more amusing. After Mischa has been stripped down to his underwear by love-crazy Martha Raye, Chic has only to slap a number on his chest and fire a starting-pistol to send him haring off like a long-distance runner—his 'character' promptly transformed by competitive conditioned reflex.

Disney's jokes about skeletons and ghosts expressed a kind of confidence in the essential harmlessness of evil and goodness of the world. *Hellzapoppin* works the other way round. Hell, by an atmospheric pun, is a combination of the traditional Hell (devils with horns roast blonde angels trussed to spits) and of a modern factory, where devils pedal away at grindstones and produce 'Canned Guy' and 'Canned Gal' (just at this time, of course, America was arming for war, and soon to draft people into munitions factories). Olsen and Johnson turn out to be in charge of Hell, and, while there, strike oil. Hell is a factory and an oilfield, nothing is deeper than raw materials and making money—it can even be reached from New York by taxi-cab, though admittedly the bill is about twelve yards long. In the same way, O. and J., throwing every inhibition aside in order to ruin a show, which they do, only succeed in 'not missing a trick'. However crazy you get, the hectic big city can match you. The 'system' *is* hell, it *is* sabotage, it uses, disintegrates, abuses everybody and everything. There's a splendid irony about the scene where O. and J. automatically change costumes according to the film sets through which they're walking, all the while quarrelling violently with their producer, and insisting, 'We're perfectly happy with things the way they are.' So, in modern life, you hardly notice what's being done to you, everything's so fast and slick. This blend of toughness and victimization by environment is neatly summed up in the final gag, where an irate producer draws a revolver and pumps holes in the scriptwriter (played by Elisha Cook Jnr., a very 'city' character). The victim just shrugs, 'I always wear my bullet-proof vest when I come to the studio' and continues calmly sipping a glass of water until he notices the liquid fountaining out through a dozen holes in his torso.

Though *Hellzapoppin* is tied to slapstick terms, rather than to philosophic ideas of alienation, its sheer frenzy of chaos and depersonalization gives its hilarity a barbed quality which is just sufficient to subsume its *faux-naif* corn and even Universal's fill-in musical items (all, at least, except a dreary, sub-Busby water-ballet). The jitterbugging Negroes contribute a physical, energetic joy and integrity contrasting with the hectic, neurotic frenzy of the storyline.

Alas, in O. and J.'s later films, the proportions of chaos to convention are reversed, and, though the present writer remembers the first reel of *Crazy House*, seen nearly a quarter of a century ago, as vintage, the sense of metaphysical structure disappears, and *Hellzapoppin* remains perhaps the one American film of the war years in the class of *Duck Soup* and Ionesco. If it has dated since it is only because it has been surpassed by the ITMA-Goons tradition which it inspired (it also suffers from TV showing where the continuity with the cinema situation is absent).

Perhaps its principal rival is *The Fifth Chair*, whose guiding spirit seems to have been Fred Allen perpetuating the W. C. Fields tradition with its worried hero (the bags under his eyes were to Allen what his Schnozzle was to Durante), its sardonic tone and its swerves into parody-fantasy. Allen, as a flea-circus proprietor, is caught up in a parodic film noir about a treasure hidden in one of five chairs. Some of the episodes have dated (like Fred Allen's vain attempts to get a seat in a crowded wartime cinema), or now seem laboured (like the 'better mousetrap') but the scene where Jack Benny, though a star, is so incredibly pennypinching that he sells a fan his necktie, and then charges extra for the paper to wrap it up in, smoothly sums up the film's constant harping on greed, coupled with a seedy, anxious meanness of spirit.

30 · Populism Peters Out

Most of these films, often loosely referred to as slapstick comedies, reserve slapstick for their climaxes, and as asides, and are really a continuation of the radio-vaudeville tradition of Joe E. Brown, Mae West and W. C. Fields. The last representatives of pure slapstick, Laurel and Hardy and The Three Stooges, are a sadly tattered rearguard, the former relegated to wretched B features forced on them by MGM and Fox, in one of Hollywood's nastier pieces of business exploitation, the latter to two-reel comedies which do, from time to time, have by their very stupidity a faint interest. Given just a glimmer of originality, the reduction of human nature to something utterly monotonous and grotesque can have an authentically liberating effect.

Sturges has his imitators, among them Damon Runyon. His production of *The Big Street* is a commercially astute confection about a playboy (Henry Fonda) devoted to an ex-singing star (Lucille Ball) who is crippled and dies dreaming of a comeback. So far as the screen is concerned, Runyon tries too calculatingly to merge Sturges's sandpaper rasp and Louis B. Mayer's treacly weepies. One may well prefer George Marshall's *True To Life*, about a TV soap-opera writer who refreshes his flagging inspiration by sponging off a working-class family, though this, too, finally surrenders to the formulae rather than exploiting them as Sturges did. A more sentimental populism is represented by Leo McCarey, the inheritor of Capra's mantle. His vastly popular *Going My Way* and *The Bells of St. Mary's* starred Bing Crosby as a crooning priest scoring a few quick victories over big-city cynicism. He wins over the tough slum kids for art by taking choir practice in baseball kit, but this Father Deeds really goes to town when he turns to his showbiz contacts and makes his choir turn out a pop smash hit. The best one can say of these movies is that a few sad, sour notes about the retirement of a too old-fashioned priest (Barry Fitzgerald) are balm in Gilead.

These populist comedies all but died with the war. Perhaps the last notable example was Leslie Fenton's and King Vidor's *On Our Merry Way*, with Burgess Meredith as a roving radio reporter asking random members of the public what influence a child has had on their life. He hopes it will be inspirational, but by way of reply he gets a clutch of disabused episodes of which the best, written by John O'Hara, features Henry Fonda and James Stewart as a pair of jazz musicians bested by a cool small-town brat.

The war years see the glitter of sophisticated comedy dim. It's not so much that high living seemed unpatriotic, as that war's uncertainties seemed to call for a cosier tone, and a different kind of stylization, represented by the wartime musical. One dreamed not so much of being a person of superior sophistication in frivolous situations, as of being an ordinarily unsophisticated person (like Betty Grable) in a nightclub, i.e. the crowded wartime canteen made sumptuous in Technicolor. If so many wartime musicals and comedies are so graceless and noisy, so gawky and, already, slightly, charmingly, utterly awful, it was not only because much of Hollywood's best talent was preoccupied with the war effort, but because movies were performing this strange shift between reality and dream.

That an internal evolution was involved is established not only by the new sarcasm, but, ironically, by Joe Pasternak's production of *Destry Rides Again* in 1939. James Stewart plays the new sheriff who doesn't believe in guns, Marlene Dietrich the saloon hostess who expiates her tarnished life by stopping the bullet meant for him. The film is a clever marriage of sophisticated comedy and the Western, then out of favour with sophisticated audiences; and though this time the Mae West figure has to expiate her sins by death the vulgar comedy is involved in the fusion too. In other words, previously distinct genres, tones, areas of association, were coming together. With *The Major And The Minor* Billy Wilder, too, made a first try at relating the graceful shamelessness of sophisticated comedy to small-town people. The difficulties of such rendezvous, particularly under the Hays Code, were considerable; and from this point on the sophisticated comedy began to become heavier (and perhaps warmer), and to take heed of doubts as well as manners, while the homely comedy

179

shed the assumptions of innocence which characterized the pre-war genre.

It's fitting therefore that the genre's last blossoming should be tended by two Europeans, whose comedies of manners are set, moreover, in period and fantasy realms. René Clair abandoned the wistful populism, the satirical edge, the sad and witty longshots, of his European style, and took to Hollywood glitter as duck to water. Two light, slight, pastel pieces, *Flame of New Orleans* and *I Married a Witch* evoke the Lubitsch line. But this time it is the Hollywood veteran who endows comedy with the *je ne sais quoi* of wistful poetry. In *Heaven Can Wait*, a late playboy (Don Ameche) explains to Satan (Laird Cregar) that he loved women, champagne, music, life. . . . Satan smiles, for a *bon viveur* is, in his way, a lover of God's creation, and sends him up a Hollywood staircase to heaven. On the way, he spies a pretty girl; and heaven can wait. . . . As Mario Verdone suggests, the playboy is Lubitsch himself, the film an anticipatory last will and testament. The inner contrast between subject and style— exemplified by the opulent staircase linking heaven and hell—a placid rejection of metaphysical depth, a substitution of smooth puppetry for torments of earnestness constitutes a stylistic extremism which is as provocative as it is urbane.

A similar tactic underlay Lubitsch's preceding film, *To Be Or Not To Be*, which is the direct forerunner of bad taste comedy, and has been widely objected to for squeezing comedy out of the Nazi occupation of Warsaw. In 1942 it was, perhaps, less daring than it was subsequently to seem, after the discovery of the camps, and when the English, notably, were priding themselves on meeting horror with humour. Certainly a 1940 British comedy, with The Crazy Gang, *Gasbags*, has some jolly knockabout involving Gestapo brutality and Kapos in what is specifically described as a concentration camp. Lubitsch's movie may not be the masterpiece as which it is claimed by its rediscoverers (and in the generally lazy world of film criticism only exaggeration is contagious; exaggeration leads to controversy, and controversy to compromise, which enables everyone to feel that he has made his point). For all that, *To Be Or Not To Be* uses the mechanics of farce with new terms, half-chilling many jokes by a bad taste context, even while sharpening them into a kind of hysteria.

It opens with a scene, which, an appropriately hectoring commentator explains, shows, stupefyingly, Hitler in full uniform, standing on a Warsaw street corner in 1938. Even more puzzling, he, conspicuously, doesn't quite look like Hitler. Chivvied by the commentator, we wobble between two interpretations: 'This film will have to be really amazing if it's to explain this convincingly,' and 'This is an amazingly bad film.' One's consciousness of the film *qua* film is so sharpened that from then on one is constantly aware of the film as existing within its own frame, as dovetailing it into its theme the paradoxes of artistic illusion and reality. Hitler enters his office, to be greeted by flunkies with 'Heil Hitler', to which he replies, 'Heil myself!' The camera thereupon tracks back to reveal that all this is part of a dress rehearsal and that 'Hitler' is a bit player owing this promotion to a quite fortuitous resemblance to the Fuhrer. He defends this outrage to the play's earnest tone by the forlorn, 'I thought it would get a laugh,' and this egoistic irresponsibility to the play as a whole also relates its heroes' personal preoccupations to the deeper purpose of war, and Lubitsch's comic vision to a tragic one. The play is promptly banned by the Polish Government lest it offend the real Hitler. Thereafter the film, which hinges on the troop of Polish actors helping the Resistance by impersonating Gestapo Officers (and eventually Hitler), switches between reality and appearance. It's logical, but it's also a strange case of *dèjà vu*, that a Polish actor, Joseph Tura, who played a Gestapo officer in a pre-war play, should also play one as part of the real life Resistance—and not only drawing on his stage experience in the role, but also giving himself away by involuntarily importing his actor's narcissism into the playing. It's an even stranger irony that this pseudo-Gestapo officer is played by Jack Benny, American screen incarnation of the smoothly mean Jew. It's logical, but it's also ironic, that the man whom he impersonates should turn out to be Sig Rumann, specialist in Hollywood parody versions of jovial, brutal Prussians. It's ironical that, after Jack Benny has endowed his Gestapo officer with an actor-like delight in fame ('Oh, they call me Concentration Camp Erhardt, do they?'), Sig Rumann should come out with just that line, which, now, oddly, lacks quite any tincture of vanity. It's ironical that the actors should lure the Nazi counterspy into their theatre, stage their 'play' in its offices, chase him through the auditorium, and kill him on the stage. All these—melodramatic—changes are given more intimate roots by Lubitsch's knowing subplots, about the changes between reality and illusion, in art, in everyone's self-image, in one's most intimate relationships (Tura's marital tiffs), and in one's social persona. All these layers are deliriously superposed when Tura's wife (Carole Lombard) regularly receives admirers in her dressing-room while her husband is delivering the 'To be or not to be' soliloquy, and seduces them by putting on a Garbo act, i.e. spoofing a rival Hollywood actress. As these unheroic resisters simultaneously muddle through war's drastic imperatives simultaneously with their messy, petty private lives and their confusions of identity, the film anticipates many of the moves of the tragi-comedy of the absurd, all the more uniquely for relating to the war, for being couched in traditional terms of vanity and panic rather than in the later tones of apathy and gloom. The actors are a bunch of healthily deflatory anti-heroes, and the film comes very near to the anti-heroic tone of *Lucky Toni* and other post-thaw Polish comedies.

Lubitsch was being truer to traditional Polish humour than was realized at the time, and the most delicious irony is that this sophisticated Pirandellian machine works only by relying on the worst conventions of Hollywood war films. If we can even toy with the idea of accepting Jack Benny, with his mean-sensitive gestures, as a Gestapo officer, it is only because Hollywood's seriously meant Gestapo officers are just as unreal, and if we can accept his playing Hamlet in faultless Polish, German, and, to cap it all, English, it is only because all the characters speak American. Thus every convention of the time is revitalized. When the commentary speaks of the Polish planes of the R.A.F., the visuals show American planes with U.S.A.A.F. markings. The effect couldn't be apter—or more nostalgic. . . .

The comedy of bad taste finds another field when Frank Capra returns from Shangri-La and its wise words of universal harmony to *Arsenic and Old Lace*, which not only laughed at murder but incorporated the odd in-joke (the homicidal maniac tying a drama critic to a chair and acting out all the parts of his—atrocious—play). The happily macabre murder mystery has since remained a popular subgenre (*The Trouble With Harry*, *The Gazebo*).

32 · The Drawing-room Jungle

Disney's *Fantasia* was a bold, brave, intermittently successful attempt to push the cartoon into abstraction and expressionism, into philosophy, myth and metaphysics. But the fairies-and-dewdrops attitude to classical music indicates the curious alliance of sentimentality and humour in Disney's thinking, an alliance which increasingly prevented his humour from renewing itself. *Dumbo* is longer, but rather more mechanical, than the early Silly Symphonies, and perhaps Disney's last creative comedy is the *Willie the Whale* episode from the end of *Make Mine Music* (1948) with its grotesque and touching idea of an opera-loving, multi-voiced whale which, slain by the brutal humans, nonetheless sings, at last, at a Heavenly Met.

During the last years of the war, the cartoon, still Disneyfied as to its graphics, caught on to the tougher spirit which was to dominate throughout the 50's. Disney himself seemed aware of that saturnine relish of hostility which propelled Bugs Bunny, Tom and Jerry, Tweety Pie and Sylvester, and the anti-romantic aura of Pepe le Pew, the skunk who speaks with the voice of Charles Boyer in *Casbah*. And back at the by now massively mechanized Disney ranch, bad-tempered Donald Duck increasingly ousted the now spiritually rootless, almost vapid, Mickey. Donald himself became more raucous, mechanical and furious; originally an image for childish bad temper, he was rapidly boringly bragging and petulant. Earlier, the movement flowed as well as bounced; now it became more strident, less rhythmic. The delightful gregariousness of the early Silly Symphonies was lost as Donald, Mickey, Pluto and Goofy were increasingly locked away in their own series. As late as 1942, charming Disney cartoons were still the rule; by 1946 they were the exception, and, increasingly, they made any sort of impact only at those brief moments when they reach, in Disney's own terms, a pitch of violence matching that of the rival series. In Disney the emotional contexts are more sentimental, the violence more varied (as when, Donald, during a picnic, ends up hanging up helplessly by his hands, and is stung, in orderly turn, by every one of a queue of bees).

Even with Donald, the Aesopian atmosphere ('bad temper makes you squawk ridiculously and hurt yourself') is almost as archaic as Disney's increasingly indulged fondness for virtuous countryside animals—mischievous but industrious beavers, chattering and cheery chipmunks, wise old ants and philosophizing crickets. But the newer series limit themselves to pets, and their suburban settings posit a new relationship to society. Mickey Mouse is a householder, but for Jerry Mouse every room in the house is a battlefield, and life is an ever-lasting guerrilla war. The morally seditious atmosphere is only en-hanced by the brief, Macchiavellian alliances which spring up be-tween race enemies (as when the devilishly efficient Ginger threatens to oust poor *Old Rocking Chair Tom*). The archetypal Flagg-and-Quirt formula is reversed; it's not so much that two old pals have regular bouts of fighting as that these natural enemies intermittently become pals. Life's such a jungle that friendship is highly paradoxical, takes on a topsy-turvy air.

More coolly violent is the unending duel between Sylvester and Tweety, the yellow canary whose apparent innocence camouflages his sharp insight into the auto-destructive consequences of Sylvester's raging schemes. In his pseudo-cherubic style, Tweety almost reincar-nates Harry Langdon's—but Harry reborn, with all his wits about him, into the drawing-room jungle. Bugs Bunny (born 1936), simi-larly, seems to be a hick, while actually talking and thinking like a wise guy out of Damon Runyon. Sentimental Grandma proves a redoubtable enemy of Sylvester's schemes, but she has little more idea of the true ferocity of the combat raging around her than the later Mr. Magoo. These films lyricize a world of cat-eat-mouse (and vice versa), and the forces of order exist aloof from and exterior to the conflict (like the adult world to childish feelings, or Washington to Earthquake McGoonery). They follow (though not invariably) the rule that the peace-loving defeat the aggressive, the cool defeat the angry, and the amiably shrewd the malicious on the one hand and the suckers on the other. There's plenty of scope for amorality in all this, and the cartoons function as a tearaway's riposte against such con-formism-inculcating children's tales as *Tootle the Engine* (described by David Reisman in *The Lonely Crowd*). Similarly, fairytales aren't so much burlesqued as transformed into brilliantly curdled tales, like Tex Avery's extraordinary *Swing Shift Cinderella* or Friz Freleng's *Red Riding Hoodwinked*.

Tex Avery's *The Cat That Hated People* is a *Just-So Story* set, not in the jungle, but in our overcrowded cities. Disintegrated by ringing blows from frying-pans, tormented by 'sweet' little children, drenched while courting, Puss soliloquizes, in a Schnozzle voice, that 'there's only one thing that's wrong with the world today, and that's people'. Since, in cartoonland, the wish is father to the thought, he rapidly finds himself enjoying a blissful catnap on the surface of the moon. But abruptly his peace is shattered by a Surrealistic procession of objects gone mad. A pencil-sharpener sharpens his tail, a nappy and safety-pin treat him like a baby, a garden spade buries him deep, a bulb and a watering-can brings him sprouting up like a daffodil. Objects-gone-mad, processes-run-amok, all following their own autonomous logic, devoid of any human discrimination, inflict upon him every sort of indignity, and finally we see him back on earth, wrapping the pavement round him like cosy bedclothes, kissing it and crying 'I love people . . .' as hurrying crowds walk on him, tread on him, walk on him, tread on him. . . .

This modern equivalent of *The Cat That Walked By Himself* responds to many of the emotional stresses marked as particularly significant by David Reisman in *The Lonely Crowd*. The once inner-directed, individualistic, competitive American ethos, caught in an age of conformism and teamwork, constantly hesitates (more vehemently than the more staid and cynical European) between aggression and goodwill.[1] Similarly, Loopy-de-Loop, the *Do-Good Wolf*, con-

[1] Democratic thought tends to admit, and discuss, the tensions in American society, since admitting them leads to attempts to manipulate and reform the social system. The Republicans tend to see problems in terms, not of social malfunction, so much as of individual moral flaws, e.g. 'moral decay', or of non-social-class networks, such as Communist agents and their intellectual sympathizers. Republican sociology tends to an anti-urban view of American society. It sees the small town as the stronghold of traditional neighbourliness and idealism, the city as the melting-pot of corrupt, cynical, imperfectly assimilated un-Americans. The Democrats tend to share this myth, but, to the Republican 'fantasy of goodwill' (and attendant paranoias), the typical Democrat film will tend to insist that, under its placid surface, the small town also seethes with self-interest and prejudice. Thus Democratic thinking tends to be more cynical, and more tolerant of cynicism, than Republican thinking, which is more idealistic, but paranoiad about any absence of idealism (so the Republican film will have it that it's a failure of morale, or the one rotten apple in the barrel, which is

stantly comes a cropper because he tries to de-nature himself into a good little lamb, a complete reversal of the 'fantasy of goodwill'.

Other cartoons are more conventional in morality, but no less drastic in tone, like Tex Avery's orgiastic *Slap Happy Lion*, which proves that not even lions should throw their weight about in the jungle, because everyone's neurotic about something. It is given astonishing virulence by Avery's visual ideas. These, and a handful of other cartoons, surely number among the classics of cinema, with their startling crystallizations of the spirit of our times.

---

responsible for any falling away from America's traditional state of freedom and goodwill).

If these general trends exist, it's obvious that the film-maker, like the rhetorician, can soon become expert at working on interior contradictions to create seductive and intriguing conflicts.

Part Five

AND THEREFORE TAKE THE PRESENT TIME

33 · High, High, So High, So-Ci

Post-war America remains prosperous, and gracefully carefree sophistication hasn't the appeal it possessed in the 30's. Just as dramas tend to be slower, more broodingly realistic about moral, personal and social problems, so the comedy tends to be warmer, more thoughtful. It decreasingly concerns itself with playboys and heiresses at the Ritz and Savoy, and increasingly with the pleasant, but recognizable, problems of journalists, advertising executives, cartoonists and upper-middle-class couples living in a sumptuous but recognizable version of the workaday world. The carefree personal grace ceases to be sufficient, to feel empty rather than liberating, and the comedy of manners is replaced by the comedy of behaviour.

The highlife comedy remains, but loses its champagne style. The evolution may be summed up by two comedies in which initially cynical journalists confront highlife innocence. In William Wyler's *Roman Holiday* newspaperman Gregory Peck pursues a modern princess (Audrey Hepburn), and Lubitschian artifice is eschewed for a visually documentary Rome. Charles Walter's *High Society* is a remake of *The Philadelphia Story*. With its rainbow-coloured, barn-size sets, it is less a comedy of manners than a comedy of highlife spectacle. In both films the personal style is slower, quieter and more brooding in sentimentality and bitterness alike. Perhaps the most interesting aspect of Laurence Olivier's *The Prince and The Showgirl* is the almost grinding contrast of personal styles and rhythms between Olivier and Marilyn Monroe.

The genre can still produce some extremely popular hits (like Wyler's and Walters's), but apparently very similar films are barely saved from disaster by their star-studded cast: a sure sign that some other criterion is operating, that a new genre is due to emerge. And

50's Hollywood, wedded, by tradition and habit, to a belief that escapism must involve highlife, twists this way and that, trying to revive or readapt the genre. Stanley Donen renounces such brilliant musicals as *Give a Girl a Break* and *The Pyjama Game* to perform more or less anachronistic exercises in ponderous levity (*Indiscreet, Once More With Feeling, Surprise Package*). Michael Curtiz's *A Breath of Scandal* is an experimental throwback to mid-30's Lubitsch, flying a kite, perhaps for the theory that it was high time for the tide to turn from realism back to escapism, and that Technicolored sets, the monumentally sumptuous Sophia Loren, and period charm (*à la Around the World in Eighty Days*) would tickle modern taste. In 1956 the same studio had entrusted to the same veteran's hands an experiment at reviving the operetta, with Oreste as *The Vagabond King*. But as so often, theories that popular taste is cyclical prove misleading. If they contain a grain of truth, the real cause of the public's preferences in entertainment, including its preference for certain kinds of escapism, depends on the relationship between its daydreams and its real experiences. The latter certainly, and eventually also the former, depend on what's happening in society, which changes quite fast enough to accommodate any desire for change for its own sake.

Henry Levin's *Come Fly With Me* is more inventive: a vulgar but sincere Texas oil millionaire (Karl Malden) hires a jumbojet airline indefinitely so as to court its hostess. The film is memorable only as a comedy of conspicuous consumption and its wide screen displays of lavish buffets seem to cover up a kind of spiritual desperation, echoed in Charles Walters's *The Unsinkable Molly Brown*, a faintly self-critical, but, alas, too dated, comedy about the self-made *nouveaux riches* who blossomed on the American scene around the turn of the century and are the subjects also of *Ruggles of Red Gap*.

34 · Old Wine in New Bottles

The cosy comedy maintains some sort of position, not without difficulty. *Bringing Up Father*, in 1951, is the last evocation of a secure period childhood to be really successful. In its less extreme form, the genre is, of course, a hardy perennial, and must exist, wherever families do. But through the 50's it shows some difficulty in finding a new compromise between the family audience (which increasingly stays away from the cinemas to watch TV) and the new preponderance in cinemas, of teenagers who are actively fleeing the family hearth, or who have a taste, not so much for more realism, as for more violence, and for the more bitter tone which that brings with it.

Thus, a drier, heavier, more deliberate style presides over *The Private War Of Major Benson*, with Charlton Heston as a military martinet being softened by the Sisters and kids of a military-orientated junior school run by nuns(!). The comparison with *Going My Way* is telling; the film can no longer glide slickly, quickly, friskily, between laughter, tears and reassurance. We are no longer asked to identify with a kindly man softening a rough, tough, big-city world; but with an insensitive, too-masculine, man, whose gospel of ferocity renders him gawky and nervous in a middle-class, feminine environment. The film never really solves the problems of presenting this softening without making it feel like emasculation, and one may well blame the new climate, rather than any individuals within it. Perhaps, indeed, the new climate is an improvement. For the missionary daydreams of *Going My Way* it substitutes a tentative awareness of tensions within the WASP ethos—though still too tentative to make an interesting conflict. What it's concealing is suggested if one profits from hindsight and makes a mental transposition, imagining roughly

191

the same story, taking place, not in an American convent school, but in a Vietnam orphanage.

Cross-currents between family sentimentality and rat-race bitterness appear disturbingly, and interestingly, in *The Seven Little Foys*, directed by Melville Shavelson, a gag-writer turned sentimentalist. Bob Hope is cast, tartly, against type, as a misogynist comedian whose act is none too good but who desperately milks popularity by trading on the appeal of his seven motherless children—until his ill-used children's loyalty converts him to a real fondness for them. Another Technicolor flirtation with the sadder aspects of reality appears in Panama-Frank's *The Facts of Life*, with Bob Hope (again) and Lucille Ball as two middle-aged suburbanites who become better acquainted during a Miami holiday and have a wistful affair which is a curious, not unengaging, mixture of *Brief Encounter*, *Mad Wednesday* and rainbow-coloured slapstick. It dabbles, at least, in the shallows of that dull resignation which it's hard for Hollywood to handle except with all sorts of defence mechanisms. Another essay on the same lines, *The Pleasure Of His Company* stars Fred Astaire, in an interesting variation on his type, as an ageing playboy whose egocentricity gives his daughter in-law trouble and his ex-wife's current intended old flame trouble. This touch of sourness ends with a note of voluntary resignation; the playboy goes off on his own with only his Chinese manservant for company. This is a (well-heeled) image for celibate loneliness, for being past it, and the film does at least touch on the fears which it's a (blatant) denial of; those of growing old, boring, embarrassing and violently unwanted in a society dedicated to youth and fun. To this vein one may also relate Morton da Costa's *Auntie Mame*, with Rosalind Russell (the spinster of *Picnic*) in rip-roaring form, in a colourful and jovial riposte to—and paraphrase of—those militantly managing married bachelor girls whose women's club ethos has been, if not exactly the iron fist in the velvet glove, but the iron heel in the tennis-shoes—from Prohibition to Goldwater.

If circumspection at this end of the age scale is understandable, people's idea of entertainment being what it is, Hollywood's hesitations at the other end are less so. By the 1950's, Hollywood was a city of old men. Nowhere was their innate conservatism more evident than in their absolute blank-mindedness about the younger generation. Not, of course, that America has had the New Morality in the way that Britain and France have had it. None the less, the success of British and French movies in America is a pointer to Hollywood's

1. **Show People:** *Marion Davies, Dell Henderson*
   From puritanism to Momism
2. **Roxie Hart:** *Ginger Rogers, Adolphe Menjou*

23
My Man Godfrey:
William Powell, Carole Lombard

Personal people solve the class struggle

24
The Philadelphia Story:
Katharine Hepburn, James Stewart

limitations. France produced Bardot, England Julie Christie and Hollywood *Tammy* and *Gidget*. Elvis Presley was rapidly relegated to flaccid suburban-hillbilly musicals—despite the success of *Jailhouse Rock*, which, influenced by Brando-Deanery, indulged, promisingly, a certain paranoia about society, and despite the fact that, on stage, his outrageous and weird sexuality put him in the class of such sacred monsters as Joan Crawford, Robert Strauss or Andy Griffith (his encounter with Jane Fonda was surely a spiritual necessity). So witty and civilized—and relatively young-minded—a film as *Love In A Goldfish Bowl* implies that teenage sexuality is a figment of parental imagination, and that all the kids want is privacy. Because teenagers live in families, teenage comedy is brought too firmly within the cosiness of family comedy.[1]

These new gropings between family themes and something more realistic tend to be cautious, erratic, artistically dissatisfying, and to strike many critics as queasy and unpleasant. Yet their queasiness results from an awkward, but real, growth in artistic range, a confrontation between sentimentality and disillusionment. The genre coincides with the progress of The Method; its switches of tone and attitude may be seen as another attempt to confront the complexities of psychology and morality.

In the end it is Walt Disney who restores self-confidence to the cosy comedy, simply by turning aside from any sort of complexity and basing his films frankly on children-parent-pet appeal. Cats and dolphins apart, the queenpins of the genre are Hayley Mills, the ideal suburban brat, and Julie Andrews, the sparkling governess. The former stars in Disney's remake of *Pollyanna*, and in *The Parent Trap*, with lovable children cheerfully sabotaging their parents' remarriage, the latter in *Mary Poppins*. Disney's audience's image of happiness is based on a dream of nicely balancing modern freedom and old-fashioned innocence, good neighbourliness and self-advancement, within families which are as happily stable as small towns—while maintaining a cosily, yet genuinely, romantic escape through a quite unmalicious sense of topsy-turvydom. This WASP middle-class dream, though more archaic now, can still masquerade as a non-controversial innocence. A Disney secret is neatly exemplified by *The Absent-Minded Professor*, with Fred MacMurray's real, solid presence, a rather tart Nancy Olsen, and big close-ups of sheds, lathes

---

[1] Alternatively, of course, the teenager becomes a delinquent and a problem, the 'orgy' merely a prelude to violence.

and other homely things, giving a good sober everyday feel to a comedy-fantasy about a 'flubberized' (gravity-resistant) Ford Model T. The choice of this nostalgic old jalopy is no more accidental than the Dickensian London of *Mary Poppins*. Both these over-the-rooftop fantasies can touch the heart, and at least one hard-core Surrealist looks on the former film as one of Disney's honourably long canon of masterpieces. Without Hayley and Julie, Disney generally seems less happy, and one may happily leave to the toddlers of the Middle West such tedious trifles as *Darby O'Gill and the Little People*, *Moon Pilot* and *Blackbeard's Ghost*.

A subsequent twist to the rosy comedy is given by Melville Shavelson's *Yours, Mine And Ours*, based, like *The Seven Little Foys*, on a real story, unrecognizably transformed. A widowed naval officer (Henry Fonda), father of ten, meets, courts and marries a navy nurse (Lucille Ball), mother of eight. Breaking its story expertly into situation comedy *à la* Lucille and gags *à la* Hope, it crams every *temps mort* with kids and bright colours and is clearly Hollywood firing on all cylinders, eupeptically cramming in zooms, freeze-frames, split-screens and every kind of daydream—romantic, domestic, financial, philoprogenitive—while maintaining some kind of zany echo of reality. Yet, underneath it all, a *je ne sais quoi* of style suggests that somehow the spirit in the film is running scared.

Right at the beginning the camera goes into ecstatic movements around the aircraft carrier *Enterprise*, which doesn't have too much to do with Fonda's family ways. Of course, one thought, it might be just a piece of stylistic bravoura. And then again the Christmas scene had an unusual emphasis on carol-singing and gift-giving, as if positively asserting a combination of traditionalism and commercialism. But then, why not, it's a style of living. But then again, the eldest daughter's boyfriend, who sports long hair and invites her to a love-in, makes a suggestion about which she consults her father; and though he's preoccupied with his wife's labour pangs at the time he goes into a long reply about the new morality being as old as the hills. When she interjects that maybe the pill has changed matters, he replies, 'Well, maybe having eighteen children is taking things a bit far, but if we had to live all over again, who should we miss out, you?' A splendid line, exalting old-fashioned fecundity and faith in the future as against modern pleasure and caution. Fair enough, but the shift in moral gear between the inconsequential contact and so sharply etched a riposte is startling. And it's curious, too, that given

1967–8 current controversies about the draft, a non-controversial film should go out of its narrative way to show the chip off the old block receiving his calling-up papers with placid gladness. Consistently, too, it glorifies the relationship between family and navy. Thus, he is ready to give up the sea for her, but when a special job comes up she insists he go off on it, the whole sequence of altruistic *quid pro quos* being continued by the navy, which flies him home when her child-birth looms. Almost the film's last shot is of the son going off to do his bit while a solid block of family waves him good-bye ('Don't all write at once,' he says cheerfully). There are also quite a few lines about large families as democracies, and about father's serious moral authority. No 'Bringing Up Father' nonsense here. A naval father is a good strong father, yessir.

In 1967–8 it was impossible to prepare this without having the Vietnam war in mind. Even the politically unconscious can sense a call to rally round America's traditional moral values (family, optimism, Christianity, material possessions) in this, America's hour of moral crisis. One may even suspect a call to hurl Malthusian prudence aside and match Asia's population explosion. But at least there's no positive ill-will towards the immoral characters—the long-haired boy and the nymphomaniac—and the unmalicious reaction against fun morality isn't without its charm; in fact it has a great deal of truth on its side. At least it leaves no doubt that Melville Shavelson, on the strength of his aggressive optimism, qualifies as an authentic *auteur*. The Vietnam-era intensification of America's moral tensions would, of itself, tend to have a twofold effect on the cosy comedy—inspiring, on the one hand, a sentimental backlash, ranging from Disney's films to Shavelson's, to, on the other, new attempts to face, and cope with, prickly reality. Stanley Kramer's *Guess Who's Coming To Dinner* is not only a sophisticated comedy, with civil rights relevance, but a cosy comedy progressed from *Quality Street* as far as *Liberal Street*.

The rustic comedy, if we leave aside excursions into the long grass by Elia Kazan (the opening of *A Face In The Crowd*), and Joshua Logan (*Bus Stop*), to be returned to later, scrapes the bottom of the plastic imitation cracker barrel. The representatives of rural America are Francis, the talking mule, and Ma and Pa Kettle. It's no accident that their stories soon take them off Waikiki or the WRACS, etc., and that their titles are interchangeable with one another and with the Abbott and Costello series concurrently coming from Universal; one can permutate *Abbott and Costello In The Ozarks, Francis Meets The*

Keystone Kops, Ma and Pa Kettle In Society (the last title does in fact lead one to the TV Beverly Hillbillies formula).

As rural America rapidly vanishes from the screen, so the Wild West sprawls ever more boisterously across it. Another, more nostalgic, genre might be described as the rugged comedy, and the longing for the bold brawling days of the Old Wild West spills over to World War II, to the South Seas, or any arena in which the restraints of cold calculation and humdrum protocol can be lifted, and masculine exuberance be allowed free play. Just as, during the Depression, Mae West revived the plummy splendours of bordello days, so, in the grey flannel suit 50's, cinema spectators, male and female alike, fondly contemplate the truculent muscularity and masculine camaraderie of John Wayne and a host of he-men. Among such films one may name John Sturges's *Sergeants Three*, Henry Hathaway's *North To Alaska*, John Ford's remake of *What Price Glory*, his *Donovan's Reef*, and even his *When Willie Comes Marching Home*, which, involving disquietingly massive crashes of heavy bombers, is imbued with tincture of the old Sturges acid. The genre easily blends with sex comedy, like the Wayne–McLaglen–Maureen O'Hara tag-match in Ford's *The Quiet Man*. Later, Elliott Silverstein's *Cat Ballou*, with Jane Fonda, parallels *Johnny Guitar* as a comedy of pistol-packing Momism (though a French film, Malle's *Viva Maria!*, was doubtless an additional stimulus to its inspiration).

The genre has long existed, though previously only John Ford's exercises in it had found eager critical indulgence. But from the early 60's, however, this is extended to almost any sort of he-man brawl. No doubt many intellectuals also find the tough and summary conflicts of the Old West are a soul-restoring change from modern complexities, from modern middle-class society's reduction of the male role to a passive correctness. But it's also true that the Western is often used to vindicate simple-minded views of might and right. It's certainly curious, as Lee Russell has pointed out, how Ford, increasingly, sees the Indian-massacring U.S. cavalry as the natural framework for male camaraderie; as if military service is the only situation in which loyalty is a natural condition of man.

Rarer and preciously iconoclastic is the comedy of sensible self-preservation, some would say, an absence of heroism, and it's in these few but agreeable films that one finds the most realistic touches of character. Thus, a cavalry trooper in George Marshall's *Company Of Cowards* is coyly anxious about the fact that horses like his smell and follow him around (the man who crushes the spines of those whom he hugs affectionately is too easy a loan from *Of Mice and Men* imagery). A pity, too, that the climax settles for a pitched battle won by *infra dig* means (braces for catapults, etc.), rather than for the more tigerish send-up of the cavalry ethos which is really overdue. The process whereby the historical West was transmuted, by journalists, into a myth, even while it was going on, should offer rich opportunities for satire. Meanwhile one can console oneself with episodes: Ford's sketch of white cowardice and hysteria in *Cheyenne Autumn*; the frenzied confusion of Sturges's *The Hallelujah Trail*; the 'ghost town' of sadly tamed bad men in *Cat Ballou*, and its dance-hall punch-up where a long-haired Indian, surrounded by young white toughs, cheerfully declares, 'It's Custer's Last Stand all over again— only this time I'm in the middle!' The impenitent reminder of the time the Indians slaughtered the cavalry has just a faintest little tinge of, if not Black Power, exactly, but—Red Power. And high time.

35 · Cold War, Cold Feet

The bitterness and fear spread by McCarthyism rather queers the pitch for socio-political comedy. Inspired by the hopes and fears of the Depression, the genre weathers with difficulty this new, subtler and more devious demoralization. H. C. Potter's *The Farmer's Daughter* (*Katie For Congress*) had resumed political comedy in the Democrats' favour, and was shortly countered by Frank Capra's *State of the Union* (in England, *The World and His Wife*), on behalf of the Republicans. This time an innocent aeroplane manufacturer (Spencer Tracy) runs for the Republican nomination, is disillusioned by that party's intrigue, corruption and selfishness, and appeals directly to the voters on an 'absolute honesty' ticket. He goes up, where McGinty went down. One or two anti-Communist asides imply a wholehearted acquiescence, by the erstwhile fantasist of goodwill, in the current witch-hunts.

Probably the smoothest of the post-war comedies of internal politics is George Cukor's *Born Yesterday*. Judy Holliday plays a politician's not-so-dumb broad who learns too much too fast about the facts of politics for Washington's comfort. Ford's *The Last Hurrah* is a nostalgically brawling farewell to the corrupt old Tamany-type boss (Spencer Tracy), who, though as anachronistic, now, as the gun-fighter, had a rough and ready moral grandeur to him. Just as *When Willie Comes Marching Home* can be paired with *Hail The Conquering Hero*, so *The Last Hurrah* can be paired with *Down Went McGinty*; the Ford–Sturges comparison is intriguing, both for the sake of the similarities (Ford is less of a reverent traditionalist than his left-wing admirers, of all people, love to present him), and for the sake of the differences (Ford blurs Sturges's healthy clarity).

A few years after McCarthy's fall, international politics return to

American screens. Carl Foreman, a liberal refugee from McCarthyism, living in exile in England, ventures *The Mouse That Roared*, with a Ruritanian statesman (Peter Sellers) leading his comic opera army on an invasion of New York, to qualify for aid as a defeated nation. In asking us to approve the machinations of an uncommitted nation, it offers a delightfully non-Manichean view of global politics, and is whimsically 'third world' in its orientation. Its American success doubtless encouraged Universal-International to commission another Ruritanian comedy, *Romanoff and Juliet*. Peter Ustinov's amiable, charming and often surprisingly sharp verbal thrusts, are often openly neutralist in direction. A pity, though, that they are muffled, rather than matched, by rather sentimental visuals and juvenile leads. Billy Wilder's *One, Two, Three*, with its soft-drink salesman—played by James Cagney, erstwhile Prohibition bootlegger!—is a mischievous comedy which might almost be subtitled 'Coca-Colonization Meets The Iron Curtain'. As eupeptic as one would expect from a comedy about irresistible salesmen meeting immovable front doors, the confrontation is so direct that the film can do scant justice to its interesting transposition of *The Emperor Waltz*; a Ruritanian setting might have allowed more elbow room. And Stanley Kubrick has to stay in England to make *Dr. Strangelove, or How I Learned To Stop Worrying And Love The Bomb*, a very black satire on right-wing paranoia which it is disturbingly impossible to dismiss as left-wing paranoia, particularly when one remembers how only a desperate and last-minute English intervention stopped the French and American governments from together using the atomic bomb to save the day at Dien Bien Phu. Between Cuba and Detroit there is a brief, mild thaw in political tension, of which Norman Jewison cleverly takes advantage for his charming *The Russians Are Coming The Russians Are Coming*, which brings a little of the Sturges spirit to its satire of American invasion hysterias when a damaged Russian submarine slips into a New England cove for repairs. In view of the sudden near-seriousness at its climax, it was unbelievably naïve of the Americans to expect the Russians not to resent the film, but it's almost the only Hollywood cold-war movie to allow that Communists can ever be anything but coldly monstrous.

From time to time, post-war Hollywood essays a comedy which, without being political, focuses less on the individual than on society's networks and systems. Oddly enough, these are almost entirely musicals, and so fall outside our scope. Thus, Stanley Donen's *The Pyjama*

Game can deal overtly with garment trade unions, in their convivial aspect. Vincente Minnelli's *The Bells Are Ringing* so develops its story about a lonely but friendly answering service operator (Judy Holliday) who cares about her subscribers as people rather than dismissing them as numbers, as to make it a charming little study in the 57 varieties of big-city alienation. Perhaps music, and its associations with *joie de vivre*, makes things easier.

The same precaution seems to underlie David Swift's lively *How To Succeed In Business Without Really Trying*. For a country as concerned with business as America is, business comedy is surprisingly timid in venturing beyond such agreeable stereotypes as the irate executive played by Fred Clark. Certainly, Billy Wilder's, and other, comedies, of which more later, often criticize the extent to which one's screen identification figures let ambition, and its dark twin, desperation, corrupt their humanity. A few comedies dip, albeit tentatively, into the storehouse of absurdities catalogued by such serious, yet popular, writers as Vance Packard and Ernest Dichter. Perhaps the liveliest are Arthur Hiller's *The Wheeler Dealers* (in G.B. *Separate Beds*), and Irvin Kershner's *The Flim-Flam Man* (in G.B. *One Born Every Minute*). The first ventures into the areas where business confidence becomes a confidence racket; James Garner, raising funds for three oilmen, meets Lee Remick, doing a PR job on 'Universal Widgets'. Unfortunately, the film, Capra-style, half-shifts its satire from business to art (action paintings made with tricycles), and adopts the conservative ('homespun') conclusion that would-be career girls are happiest when big strong men put them in their Texan kitchen to get on with their 'home cookin' '. Kershner's film centres on a small-league hometown con man (George C. Scott), who's resigned to never growing rich but enjoys the game for its own sake; his blend of fanatic zest and sensible resignation is a very interesting one. The films' changes of title are indicative; not only the abundance of purely American references, but the admiration for sprightly dishonesty, mitigate the films' appeal abroad, and there's certainly been nothing from Hollywood to match the tragic radicalism of Alexander Mackendrick's *The Man In The White Suit*.

For the comedy of business relationships (which involve, in the end, all relationships), Hollywood substitutes the comedy of communications. Possibly the most interesting non-musical communication comedies are George Cukor's *It Should Happen To You* and Robert Mulligan's *The Rat Race*.

In Cukor's film, Judy Holliday plays Gladys Glover, a small-time girdle model who, furious at her New York anonymity, splashes all her savings to hire a hoarding across which she plasters her name. A rich advertising agent (Peter Lawford) covets the site; the teaser effect intrigues the public; and she becomes a starlet until, sickened by the hypocrisy of it all, and the discomforts of not being particularly talented, she gives up and goes back to her down-to-earth Central Park pick-up (Jack Lemmon). In a beautifully tailored script, as self-effacing as ingenious, the themes of image and identity inspire almost every line of dialogue, every detail. Lemmon manages the opening pick-up by training a ciné-camera on her: 'I saw a guy do this in a French movie last week, I've been meaning to try it ever since.' When he shows her his 'documentary', her cautious murmurs become a commentary on his commentary (and on the truthfulness of documentaries!). Gladys, though pretty enough, isn't so gifted at delivering her speeches, and when asked by a U.S.A.A.F. unit to christen a plane 'Gladys Glover' she messes her lines, breaks down and bursts out, 'Why not call your plane "One of the Crowd"?' She finds a little happiness from fame, but, like so many girls with such dreams, she is at once too nervous and too genuine to make a success of it. Wistfully she observes: 'I could have been on the cover of matchboxes, pencils, everything. . . .' Her naïve pleasure over dancing in a place where 'everybody's somebody. . . . That makes the seventh big name I've seen here! What a night!' gives a deeper meaning to such throw-away metaphysics as 'Who are you?'—'Nobody, that's who!', or a complacent quizmaster's declaration that 'the average American girl *is* unusual!' Gladys's boyfriend asks what's happened to turn her mind against fame, and she replies, 'I've not changed in myself, I'm exactly the same as before, but in a different way.' A visit to the zoo gives us a glimpse of the faces in the crowd as they look to the animals, in a neat reversal of the theme of being looked at as a sign of success. The theme of image as behavioural trap recurs ('It's a fake, and not only that, it's dishonest. And it's undignified.' The crescendo is interesting.). Eventually, Gladys, reformed, sees an interesting hoarding, and briefly falls back into the mass communications era Narcissism of fame; she is brought round by her boyfriend's question, 'What are you looking at?' and replies, 'Nothing, absolutely nothing,' which is what an image is.

In contrast, *The Rat Race* takes the theme of good neighbourliness to a logical conclusion. Two strangers, a jazzplayer (Tony Curtis) and a dance-hall hostess (Debbie Reynolds) are forced to share a cramped and uncomfortable New York apartment. The temperamental exasperations are nicely counterpointed by others—the scowling neighbours, the scathing indifference of the New York cops when Curtis reports the theft of his instrument (shades of *Bicycle Thieves*!), the dance-hall owner's use of the trucking system to blackmail Debbie into prostitution. It's easy to forgive the film its final, agreeably done, cascade into goodwill all around for one classic scene. The erstwhile flat-mates, having nowhere else to find privacy, sit talking in a stationary taxi, which goes no place—with its meter ticking infuriatingly away. The film always gains from what might at first sight seem miscasting, Tony Curtis as the country boy; for the speed with which his personal tone fits in with the city's refutes the Middle West WASP myths about small town and big city as moral opposites. It's interesting too to think of his role as it might be played by Van Johnson—an initially small-town, cleancut hero who has interestingly made the transition to a tougher, more troubled style.

Usually social comment is made, tacitly and obliquely, through individual experiences like this. If a spectator can identify with a hero's experience, he will usually admit that this experience is typical, or at least significant (conversely, even people who claim to be indifferent to 'significance' will attack a movie which angers them by protesting that it's not 'typical', or that it's 'an extreme case'). These comedies, blending something of the old sophistication with a new, intimate ordinariness, may be divided into the 'rosy comedy' and the 'black comedy'—the former typified by the films of Cukor, Minnelli, Blake Edwards and Richard Quine, the latter by those of Billy Wilder, Howard Hawks and Stanley Kubrick. There is of course no hard and fast line between the two genres, and each category has traits from the other as its undercurrent. One can classify them another way. Such films as Cukor's *The Marrying Kind*, Blake Edwards's *Breakfast At Tiffany's*, and Billy Wilder's *The Apartment*, follow the ordinary rhythm and logic of dramatic relationships, exaggerating and stylizing the tone a little; it's often a moot point whether they should be described as dramatic comedies or light dramas. On the other hand, Cukor's *It Should Happen To You*, Richard Quine's *How To Murder Your Wife* and Blake Edwards's *What Did You Do In The War, Daddy?*, take a more or less implausible central idea and fill it out with a certain amount of dramatic detail.

Immediately after the war, the way of rosy comedy was straight-forward. The heroes of *The Jackpot, The Bachelor and the Bobby-Soxer* (*Bachelor Knight*), *Mr. Blandings Builds His Dream House, The Egg And I* and *Sitting Pretty* take rather more prosperous and assured representatives of the ordinary persons in situations which are climactic but not essentially unreal. A middle-class couple (James Stewart, Maureen O'Hara) are snowed under by snags when they win a TV prize; a teenager (Shirley Temple) gets a crush on a middle-aged bachelor (Cary Grant); an advertising copywriter (Cary Grant) has trouble dreaming up the slogan which is spontaneously produced by his coloured maid; city sophisticated Fred MacMurray and Claudette Colbert find themselves down on the chicken farm; an ordinary young couple (Roland Young, Maureen O'Hara) are afflicted with a mastermind babysitter (Clifton Webb) who's not only pompous and authoritarian but breathtakingly uninhibited by the customary code of compromise and goodwill.

Of the rosy comedies of plausibility, pride of place must go to George Cukor's, for their director's consistent power to stimulate, and respond to, the warmth and inventiveness of such players as Katherine Hepburn, Spencer Tracy and Judy Holliday. Cukor's description of his methods of work throws more light on his qualities than critical analysis, which, faced with nuances of gesture, is always cumbersome or approximative:

'When I was preparing *Born Yesterday*, I went back to Washington, which I knew well, and saw it through different eyes, on behalf of the film. I studied the tourists; they don't behave like cinema extras, who always look at things . . . like children at school. You have to study the real thing. It's always fascinating to see what really goes on.'

'Jack Lemmon, in *It Should Happen To You*, had to play a quarrel scene. I told him: "I don't believe you, you're not angry at all! What do you do when you're really angry?" "What do I do? Oh, it's no good, you'll never be able to use it; when I'm angry I get stomach-ache." "All right, have a stomach ache!" So in the middle of the argument he sits down and holds his stomach. It's so much truer. . . .'

In another scene from the same film, 'Judy . . . was very nervous. She said, "I'm going to giggle." I said, "If you giggle, I'll kill you." But the more nervous she was, the worse she had the giggles. You might have thought she'd ruin everything. In fact, that sort of reaction was excellent, because when you're nervous, you behave like an idiot, and in a comedy that's what you need. So I let her go on. . . .'

'Similarly with Jean Simmons. Spencer Tracy played her father in *The Actress*. In a particularly dramatic scene, he was scolding her, for squandering a fortune. . . . He was really terrifying. Moreover, Jean Simmons is a stunning actress, but a curious thing happens to her; during rehearsals, she sniggers. Faced with this snigger, Spencer Tracy began to improvise: "I know I'm ugly, I know I'm old. But why the devil do you have to laugh at me?" "Perfect," I said, "we'll use it." It was just right. . . .'

In such comedies as *Pat and Mike* and *Adam's Rib*, Katherine Hepburn and Spencer Tracy incarnate a perfect American couple; he, ruggedly classless and cynical, but responsive to her idealism, each the other's ideal foil. And, in Cukor's hands particularly, Judy Holliday becomes a fascinating counterpart to Katherine Hepburn. Where the heroine of *The Philadelphia Story* is patrician, intellectual, alertly aloof, morally proud, yet with a beautiful, because conscious, submissiveness shining through, the heroine of *Born Yesterday* is forlornly convinced of her own ordinariness, is a dumb blonde, is impulsively involved, is morally unselfconscious, and yet an obstinate sense of fairness gives her scattiest whims, notions and reflexes a sinewy, democratic logic. Even as her voice slides into a demotically nasal wail of alarm or self-pity, thins out into an affectation of pre-cision, or opens out into an ear-splitting bawl, a keenness of gaze and a warmth of attack assert a robust generosity which divests her optimism of that mechanical quality which so often vitiates it.

If Cukor has never made the masterpiece which one has never ceased to expect from him, it is, perhaps, because he has all the responsiveness of a great artist without the bloody-mindedness. More sensitive to nuances, more devoid of prejudices, over a wider range of subjects, than almost any Hollywood director, he has always been content to 'do it without making it seem gritty, or vulgar, or disagreeable', to make of it 'rather a romp'. As he remarks, 'I am, for better or worse, an interpretative director, and the text always determines the way I shoot a picture. . . . I don't think that I have an axe to grind. . . .' The limits of Cukor's style lie in the smooth, flowing movement round or even through any clash, and this is most easily seen in terms of drama. *A Star Is Born* remains within the limits of the very best woman's film, rather than a tragedy, while *A Double Life*, about an actor who plays Othello so hard he becomes him, is a contrivance. It's not cynicism if, as Jean Domarchi remarks, 'Whenever I talk about a film with Cukor, the response is immediate: "Was it a popular success?" If my reply is evasive, he contemplates me ironically. . . .' Domarchi defends Cukor from any charge of inverted aesthetic snobbery, citing his literary culture which, as one would expect from his way with dialogue, and from his smoothly unaffected recreation of Dickensian gesture in *David Copperfield*, is extensive. If this lively interest in popularity is perhaps a gentle rejoinder to that hermetic intellectual intensity to which French critics are sometimes prone, it may, more profoundly, arise from Cukor's sensitive preoccupation with those personal responses which are a cultural common denominator. One may still wish that he had brought his good taste and his delicacy to subjects which, without grinding any axe, still shot off all the sparks one finds in Wilder. It may seem strange to compare the two directors, but, if so, it is because Wilder's willingness to rub people up the wrong way is a precondition of thought as serious as Cukor's sensitivity pushing out beyond that Hollywood decorum within which Cukor feels at ease, as, one feels, he could feel at ease anywhere. In its combination of dynamism and obscurantism, upperclass America is still very nineteenth-century, and Cukor is, at heart, perhaps, the last Victorian novelist, the Thackeray of twentieth-century intimacies. And when *auteur* theory has resettled itself, when such test-cases as Hawks have been returned to their appropriate niches, and when criticism has lost its preoccupation with the hardboiled tone in favour of an intimate sensitivity whose secret is shared by women and artists, then the films of Cukor, particularly the underrated *The Marrying Kind*, will rank alongside Wilder's and Chayefsky's intimate glimpses of American realities.

Cukor is, essentially, an intimist, for whom the black-and-white small screen is as spacious as the rainbow-coloured panoramas which came with Cinemascope. Jean Negulesco's *How To Marry A Millionaire* and Vincente Minnelli's *Designing Woman* were notable examples of essentially slight comedies set in apartments whose sumptuous décor rolled towards the far walls like the prairies rolling towards the horizon. In general, Minnelli's comedies are the minor items in an *oeuvre* as distinguished in drama as in the musical. Frank Capra, who retires in the early 50's, re-emerges to offer another message of hope to this sarcasm-ravaged world. *A Hole in the Head* picks out another favourite American theme, the palhood of father and son, and various paradoxes of worldliness and innocence, of mellow immaturity and brash common sense. Here, Frank Sinatra plays a nightclub operator who prefers to play about with broads (notably Carolyn Jones) rather than find a mother for his son, the pair making 'a child of 41 and a son of 11'. Finding himself in financial trouble, the father has to turn for help to *his* father-figure, his elder brother (Edward G. Robinson) who clings to older-generation ideas about arranged marriages, about entertainment business not being real work, and nonchalance about large sums of money being sinful irresponsibility rather than a precondition of success. Sinatra plays along with his brother's plans to marry him to a rich, homely Mrs. Rogers, until he meets her, and since she's as attractive and sophisticated as Eleanor Parker he renounces her, confesses his complicated deception, lets her change his mind, marries her and lives happily ever after. As Peter John Dyer remarks in the *Monthly Film Bulletin*, 'Only Capra could repeat a gag as unoriginal as the discomfort of a large man falling into a small, low chair, and by timing and subtle variation go on repeating it six or seven times with no loss of impact.' Far from being unoriginal, the gag is dramatically fitting: a low chair is of course an informal-styled, outer-directed furnishing, and the feudalist's discomfort in it is astutely sensed. Similarly, Mrs. Rogers's wry confession that she feels lonely while buying one lamb chop is an almost too clever example of how to evoke loneliness without depressing anyone.

The film's sketch of American business troubles is neatly compressed. From *Little Caesar* in 1930 to *All My Sons* in 1948, Edward G. Robinson had incarnated the ruthless, self-made man, hardly assimilated to the WASP image, and who has to be repudiated by his all-American son or kid brother (Anthony Quinn continues the role in several Hal Wallis dramas of the 50's). As several critics pointed out, Capra seemed somewhat confused as to whether he was dealing with an Italian or a Jewish milieu, but perhaps he thought he was creating an 'ideal type'. Frank Sinatra represents the modern, egalitarian, *Playboy*-era, but home-loving, individualist trying to retain, on the one hand, his Americanism against the older immigrant-peasant notion of family, and, on the other, his ambitious individualism against the smiling, shark-sharp tycoon represented by another older buddy, Keenan Wynn. Caught between the two, Sinatra is something of a lost figure, and it's a pity that the film smooths over all his difficulties, psychological and financial, with the moral that for a happy life you need (*a*) 'high hopes, high in the sky, apple-pie hopes', and (*b*) the hole in the head, the irrationality that makes life worth living. Only Hollywood would dream of taking a nightclub owner as the type of the little man, just as only Hollywood could have passed in complete silence for so long over the startlingly high proportion (estimates range from 20 to 40 per cent) of Americans who live on or below the poverty line.

In two comedies mating Doris Day and Rock Hudson, and directed by Michael Gordon, the intimate spectacular crosses itself with sex-war comedy. *Pillow Talk* and *Move Over Darling*, both intriguingly, if dissatisfyingly, walk a tightrope between sentimentality and a sex comedy, which, in straining to be as suggestive as its titles without actually offending anybody, attains a curious quality of derisoriness; an acreage of cosily sumptuous gadgetry oddly implies some Technicolored desert of the soul, a sort of Death Valley of luxury. Tensions are covertly entertained also in the comedies of Richard Quine, whose *Full of Life*, with Judy Holliday, bids fair to continue the Cukor line. Since then, Quine's comedies have been intelligent enough, but brittle. The best, *Bell, Book and Candle*, a gravely romantic comedy, has Kim Novak as a modern Manhattan witch who realizes love has made her human when a tear wells up in her eye. *Paris When It Sizzles*, though, suggests Quine's curious hesitations between illusion and awareness of illusion. Its hard-drinking scriptwriter (William Holden) dictates to his temporary secretary (Audrey Hepburn) a script which is shown to us in 'flashback' and constitutes a burlesque of Hollywood cliché. But the film-within-the-film is so cliché-ridden that it's not even half-believable, while reality is too obviously dream-shaped, so that we're left soothed but half-bored, rather than wrung and revivified, by the clash and merger of reality and dream. In *How To Murder Your Wife* Quine comes near hitting on something which Hollywood, for all its many flirtations with psychoanalysis, has rarely managed: asserting the rebellious and restorative aspects of inner worlds. Jack Lemmon plays a strip-cartoonist-cum-bachelor-about-town who falls for an Italian blonde (Virna Lisi) and is progressively smothered by her chintz-and-pizza domesticity. The interaction of real nightmares and the comic-strip daydreams which he laboriously acts out *in situ* to ensure that they're realistic is promising, but a blend of sumptuousness and facetiousness combine to edulcorate the comic barbs.

Quine's unidentical twin is Blake Edwards, whose dramas, promisingly, link the rosy world and the black one. Even in its mutilated release version, *Days of Wine and Roses* is a haunting middle term between Cukor's *A Star Is Born* and Wilder's *The Lost Weekend*, while *Breakfast at Tiffany's* evokes the *Sunset Boulevard* theme of writer-gigolo (George Peppard) and sugar-mummy (Patricia Neal). And the charming-sad kookery of Holly Golightly (Audrey Hepburn) cleverly transposes the beatnik ethos into the upper-income-brackets. But this is apparent comedy progressively revealing itself as drama, and when Blake Edwards turns to comedy, in our sense (whereby a certain stylization, robustness or hopefulness underlines even the solidest moments of the action), he has increasingly come to rely on a blend of luxury, ingenuity, speed and slapstick. *The Pink Panther* and *A Shot in the Dark* are almost photographed strip-cartoons. Their keystone is Peter Sellers's bumbling Inspector Clouseau, bravely trying, despite his bumbling, his cackhandedness, his regularly misplaced bouts of trustfulness and suspicion, generosity and megalomania, to keep up with this ever-more-sophisticated, fluid and complex world. Peter Sellers's variations on his Everyman figure make him one of the cinema's classic comic icons. Since these two films, Blake Edwards has directed a comic spectacular, *The Great Race*, with a certain galumphing charm, and *What Did You Do In The War, Daddy?*, about G.I.s liberating happy-go-lucky Italian villagers. Though not uncritical of the Americans, it is boringly dependant on Hollywood's stranger assumptions, e.g. that G.I.s are everywhere beloved by the local yokels, that the Italian poor are lazy, peace-loving, harmless and contented, and that foreign countries exist mainly to provide an unending supply of nymphomaniac damsels for the use of their American ally. Although Edwards does supply an obscure hint that those hot foreign dishes are really girls bewildered into something like prostitution by the dual impact of devastation and the dollar, the general attitude still seems to be, 'We Americans

5. **Mr. Smith Goes To Washington:** *Claude Rains, James Stewart*
   Administrative problems

6. **Nothing Sacred:** *Frederick March, Carole Lombard*

27. **The Miracle of Morgan's Creek:** *Betty Hutton, William Demarest, Eddie Bracken, Diana Lynn*
Off to the cleaners

28. **Where There's Life:** *Bob Hope*

liberated you, and therefore deserve all your women.' But a study of the Technicolor daydreams with which Americans so desperately screen the resentments such attitudes arouse in poorer peoples would be a chapter in itself, and a very depressing one, since it involves even such sensitive films as Minnelli's *An American In Paris* and Ford's *The Quiet Man.*

Artistically more encouraging is the acute eye shown by some young directors, often from TV, towards niceties of gesture. Sometimes they rival the speed of 30's comedy (though rarely the rhythm), but with a keener sense of doubt, remorse and frailty. A brief gesture of Janet Leigh sagging wearily at the kitchen sink in John Rich's *Wives and Lovers* effectively reminds us of the other, the *Marty*-like, film for which the first part of this one so interestingly prepares us. Fred Coe's *One Thousand Clowns,* a New York film aspiring to Hollywood markets, begins promisingly, with Jason Robards Jnr. as a feckless Bohemian defending his truant son from the priggish prying of two social workers. But its search for surprising dramatic development takes it no further than a double back to conformism, i.e. our hero admits that he's an arrested adolescent, and that's that. Moral: 'Who do you think you are, to rebel?' Gene Sak's *Barefoot in the Park* begins with Jane Fonda, honeymooning in a stiff-necked hotel, posing in the corridors as her husband's whore, but once again the promise trails away into tediously traditional jokes about defective heating and marital tiffs. Stanley Donen's *Two For The Road* reveals an older director experimenting in the same vein. Audrey Hepburn and Albert Finney, married, rich and bored, drive down the same European roads along which they had hitchhiked and courted ten years before. The intercutting between past and present imperfectly camouflages a thin and static story, and little effort is made to exploit or explore the fascinating discrepancies between Finney's down-to-earth style and Audrey Hepburn's elegance, which comes to seem aristocratic and archaic. Many incidentals (the American family) are happily observed, and, as often, one has the feeling that it would take very little more for Hollywood comedies to take up a stronger realistic charge, to become a natural, and understood, channel for entertainment realism. Jules Dassin's *Never On Sunday* sets a precedent which Hollywood hardly dares bring home. True, in *Bachelor Girl Apartment* (*Any Wednesday*), the married hero keeps an absolutely unequivocal mistress (played by the irreplaceable Jane Fonda). The situation is controlled, however, by a sophisticatedly

o   209

punitive conclusion, and by the mistress's inability to make love if the room isn't filled with balloons (charmingly kooky, and childlike, but unstable, tyrannical . . .).

Meanwhile the Hollywood comedy teeters on the brink of sexual realism, the storylines consistently betraying some first-rate openings and actors. Francis-Ford Coppola's *You're A Big Boy Now* is a rainbow-hued curate's egg about a contemporary Mickey Rooney-type lad (Peter Kastner) trying hard to shuck off his virginity. Under cover of being about a very real type (the lively but shy boy whose success with the ladies is less than mediocre), it settles for the traditional tease whereby the one girl who yields to him is his true love and wife to be, so that, in old morality style, a little anticipation is retrospectively put right. Whether its wishing away of the social barriers is escapist in effect, or a good example, is another ambiguity which stops short of Kinsey-era realism. It abounds in alert notations (e.g. in establishing that bush telegraph of matrons and spinsters which helps wreck the youth's struggles for independence). Its canny use of comic exaggeration enables it to introduce some splendidly decadent touches (notably the actress's boarding-school seduction by a wooden-legged hypnotherapist). True to form, the sharpest characterization is the vamp's (Elizabeth Hartmann), and the scene in which she simultaneously seduces and humiliates the hero into a condition of yearning impotence is a setpiece of saturnine comedy. At this point, indeed, the rosy comedy shows signs of merging with its alter ego, the black comedy of which Billy Wilder is the Hollywood doyen.

37 · Wilder Still and Wilder

Chaplin's humour could shift from black to rosy and back again without self-consciousness. His America was less assimilated, less respectable, less complacent. Those in his audience who might have been offended by his bitterness could fail to register it, amidst the humour and tears; his choreographed, and, in a sense, stylized tramp, could seem as much a philosophic clown as a social rebel; in fact, the idea of a rebel could seem agreeably romantic: 'all artists are rebels because they are so pure; because they are so pure, they are not dangerous; they are children, their art mere nostalgia, the clown cries for the moon'. Meanwhile, others could understand the pain, the bitterness, the rage, leading to retaliatory murders of *M. Verdoux*.

Cruze, Wellman and Sturges have to contend with an audience which, only recently assimilated, is over-sensitive about any divergence from the norm. It may have modified the soot-and-whitewash morality with which silent earlier movies united their culturally more diverse audience. But when a partial sophistication is combined with increasing realism, the cinema moves into an awkward transition stage where bitterness is apt to be recognized for what it is, but resented, rather than accepted as part and parcel of human feelings. From these limitations the American cinema seems within striking distance of emerging.[1]

[1] A parallel process appears in the very names of film stars. Foreign names abound in the 20's (Valentino, Navarro, Nazimova, Negri, Garbo), became rarer through the 30's, almost disappear in the 40's, and reappear with Marlon Brando and Kim Novak. It is as if, in the 50's, a certain breakthrough point had been attained. It's not so much that the middle-class ethos relaxed, as that alternative attitudes acquired confidence. The pattern is paralleled by the way with emotions: romantic-rhapsodic-exotic in the 20's, quietening through the 30's, deadpan in the 40's, Method acting in the 50's,

Cruze, Wellman and Sturges could make tensions work for them, rather than having to deny them, but they're living increasingly dangerously. Cruze turned from satires to Westerns, and thence declined to B Westerns. By 1945 Wellman had ceased grappling with the socio-moral complexities of *Public Enemy* and *Roxie Hart*, and reverted to rural inspirationalism (*Gallant Journey*), to Sunday School moralities (*The Next Voice You Hear*, on your radio set, is God's!), and to anti-Commie-spy movies of some crudity (*The Iron Curtain*). Sturges made five brilliant social comedies in four years; after a two-year pause came *Mad Wednesday*; then two satires on genres (*Unfaithfully Yours, The Beautiful Blonde From Bashful Bend*); and then the McCarthyites chased him into exile. Satirists, in Hollywood, don't grow old gracefully. In fact they rarely grow old at all. They only fade away.

Even the hectic, cynical, vulgar, proletarian comedies, and those which drew on vaudeville-style talent, were at a low ebb by the 40's. United Artists released a scattering of low-budget movies which harked back to immigrant folklore—*Abie's Irish Rose*—or to city sex-farce—*Up In Mabel's Room, Getting Gertie's Garter*, whose titles, at least, are rich in Feydeauvian possibilities. But race problems, now, had to be dealt with solemnly, seriously, as moral problems, rather than in the sentimental, but rougher and readier, terms of tenement folklore. *Abie's Irish Rose* is a proletarian title; *Gentleman's Agreement* is a middle-class one.

The odd 40's comedy sets out to bring a critical tone to middle-class life. Richard Fleischer's *So This Is New York* strikes a Sturges note, taking as its theme the impact of New York on a small-town family visiting it during the 20's. Though agreeably caustic, it never quite defines a purpose for itself, and comes to seem a little too brittle, a little too remote in spirit, a little too negative all round. Joseph L. Mankiewicz becomes the white hope of caustic comedy with his *Letter To Three Wives*, which goes just that little further than Cukor's *The Women* and combines a high degree of verisimilitude with an almost radical criticism of middle-class America. Three wives, going on their annual picnic, find a letter from one Adele Ross, saying that she's run off with one of their husbands—but which? Soap-opera writer Anne Sothern is married to an idealist teacher (Kirk Douglas), who resents his wife's trucking to her sponsor's tastelessness and lies. The country girl (Jeanne Crain) dreads the effect of her social gaucherie on her socialite husband. And the gold-digger (Linda Darnell) and self-made man (Paul Douglas) have long pursued a conjugal duel as to whether she wants only a meal-ticket, he only a playmate. The other woman, never seen, has, in each wife's eyes, all the qualities which she herself lacks—a pity, perhaps, that the film doesn't make overt her function as the perfectionist ideal, as a nightmare generated by American optimism.

At any rate, Adele the ideal, the invisible, the ubiquitous, is perfectly contrasted with that earthier archetype, mother-in-law—in this case, Linda Darnell's, whose life is all beer, bingo and a rickety refrigerator, in a small shack which is not only on the wrong side of the tracks, but so near them that passing trains shake everybody off their chairs.[1] Brittle commentary and wisecracks—a girl hands another a drink with the words, 'Here, darling, a new inner tube'—are counterpointed by linking devices which give life a curiously mechanical texture (drips from a washbasin, knockings from steamboat machinery, the passing train). If the film suggests that all that's needed for general domestic happiness to reign is for the individual to break through one or two moral blocks, it does at least relate those blocks to social issues (culture, class-gaps, money) and it does give a relatively realistic picture of society as, necessarily, a criss-cross of jostling tensions, exclusions and uncertainties. Mankiewicz follows it with *All About Eve*, which is even more cutting. But, apart from the fact that, despite its wisecracks, it is more drama than comedy, it marks a retreat from society as such to that old scapegoat, rich artists; and Mankiewicz increasingly retreats from comedy and everyday reality alike, until the cosmopolitan mondanities of *The Honeypot* (1967).

Letter To Three Wives was made for Fox which made one or two efforts to repeat the formula. Edmund Goulding's *We're Not Married* has diverse couples discovering their marriages are invalid; and its army of experienced and expert players (Ginger Rogers, Fred Allen, Paul Douglas, Eve Arden, Victor Moore, Marilyn Monroe, David Wayne, Louis Calhern, Zsa Zsa Gabor, Eddie Bracken, James Gleason, Jane Darwell and Paul Stewart) often catch a gruff, rude,

---

[1] During the 50's, many critics felt that any reference to class bitterness, even in such covert forms as references to 'the wrong side of the tracks', were dated clichés, mere excuses for immoral self-indulgence, and perhaps they were, since Hollywood, or its middle-class audience, seemed to have lost all consciousness of the fact that American prosperity included enormous enclaves of poverty —in the South, in the city centres—and that money- and status-tensions aren't at all absent from the everyday behaviour of most people of all levels and kinds.

hectic vernacular style. The 'compendium' format allows for a certain sharpness—the audience is not required to identify so consistently with any one character, and so can be more detached, and therefore ironic, than the one-story movie tends to allow. Its successor, *O. Henry's Full House*, has its moments, though generally in a more sentimental key. Charles Brackett produces two gently abrasive comedies, *Miss Tatlock's Millions*, and *The Model and The Marriage Broker*; in the latter, an agreeably rasping performance by Thelma Ritter as the marriage broker brings a weary, plain, disillusioned woman's unwelcome wisdom to the processes of romance. Too cynical for English critics of the time, Thelma Ritter's screen character makes her almost the last incarnation of W. C. Fields-type waspishness.

Simultaneously, Howard Hawks alternates his little epics with comedies which express an uneasy fascination with the grotesqueries of pleasure. *I Was A Male War Bride* (*You Can't Sleep Here*) put Cary Grant in drag, anticipating a later obsession. *Monkey Business* mocked the American assumption of eternal youth by having a monkey concoct a youth serum, as a result of which Cary Grant acquires the mind of a two-year-old child. *Gentlemen Prefer Blondes* contrasts two glittering and vivacious gold-diggers (Marilyn Monroe, Jane Russell) with a collection of mere males so helpless, hapless and gormless that the only one with any common sense is an under-age child. Hawks's stoic 'man's world' has as its counterpart the world of pleasure-love, where man is fearful, stunted and clumsy. Hard-boiled as his films are, they reveal a fascinatingly uneasy ambivalence as between puritanism and fun morality.[1] Their happy endings are so odd and ironic that they never really sell out to an optimistic complacency. The 'gymnasium' number of *Gentlemen Prefer Blondes* is a little classic; as the bulging-muscled athletes puff and pant in their poker-faced exercises, Jane Russell vainly asks, in dance and song, 'Is there anyone here for love?' It turns the film into an agreeable example of double-edged moral criticism. If the men aren't stuffed shirts pursuing the ruthless girl with diamonds, they're narcissistic self-perfectionists. The lyrics, too, have a nasty wisdom: 'Square-cut or pear-shaped, These rocks won't lose their shape. . . .'

---

[1] 'Fun morality': the post-puritan attitude whereby it's your duty to have fun, and if you fail you feel not only sad, but positively guilty. It's the puritan conscience devoted to post-puritan goals, and as preoccupied with one's own salvation. Hence it's far from generous either (which is probably why it's so unrewarding).

These comedies, too, came from Fox, who seemed on the point of reviving the vaudeville-populist tradition. At the same time, the Judy Holliday movies offered a promising compromise between the sophisticated comedy, an intimist cosiness, and a renewed urge to realism. Sadly, the revival never quite appeared. Fox preferred to dedicate itself to Cinemascope spectacle and acreages of high-life décor, while the stylized pseudo-intimacies of TV situation comedy queered the big screen's small-scale pitch. The fullest achievements of populist intimacy are dramatic—like *Marty*, *The Middle Of The Night*, *Let No Man Write My Epitaph*, *Two For The Seesaw*, *Studs Lonigan*—and, apart from the very special case of *Marty*, which was helped by its Oscars, the genre was not conspicuous for its box-office successes.[1]

For a few years the flame of caustic comedy is kept burning, almost alone, by Billy Wilder, who arraigns, like Hawks, the same misogyny, the same unfitness for love, in the ambitious (or desperate) American male. It is as if he were constantly returning to the opening quarrels in *Christmas In July*, each time developing the same theme in a new setting and in a new way. It's a sign of the increasing self-consciousness of the time that his comedies are visually just as gloomy as his dramas. In his case it's especially dissatisfying to consider the two genres apart. After all, his gruelling *The Lost Week End* takes in twice as many wisecracks as nine out of ten comedies. Two Lubitsch films whose scripts bear Wilder's name, *Bluebeard's Eighth Wife*, had introduced the Wilder touch into the hitherto more-sweet-than-bitter films of his old master and fellow-Berliner. The representative of capitalism for whom Ninotchka falls is an ex-gigolo, who has been kept by a White Russian Countess. Though Wilder occasionally hankers after Lubitsch frivolity (in *The Emperor Waltz*, *Sabrina Fair* and *Love In The Afternoon*), the best parts of these films, like his best films, have all been in the Sturges tradition, and sometimes more

---

[1] The awareness of tensions as sharp, irreconcilable and real, which has such difficulty in appearing clearly on the Hollywood screen, emerges, deviously, in the grim pitilessness of physical violence—punchings, burnings—and in the embittered Western. Violence and Westerns become increasingly popular throughout the 50's, and functioned as a valuable index of covert tensions. To deplore *screen* violence, in the way so many critics did, was to miss the point altogether—it was, in fact, to ally oneself with the Hays Code mentality. As subsequent effects make clear, Hollywood was again proving itself a better index to American moods than those critics who deplore its lack of 'good taste'. Indeed it's always worth asking oneself, when a critic seems very concerned with good taste, whether he isn't more concerned with preventing the appearance of people's actual attitudes in art, in favour of some moral elitism of his own. Many a critic is a censor manqué!

virulent. And Wilder has described his own style as a cross between Lubitsch and Stroheim, the cynical realist.

The Emperor Waltz was reputedly exacted by Paramount as the price for *Sunset Boulevard*. It matches the love-hate affair of two dogs with their owners' love-hate affair. One is a scruffy but high-spirited mongrel belonging to a cynical but democratic American salesman (Bing Crosby), the other a pedigree bitch belonging to an aristocratic Countess (Joan Fontaine).

Wilder gets banter about doggie-love to refer to human matings in a way which is sweet, or cynical, or both, whichever is preferred. More lightly than other Wilder movies, it sketches his recurrent plot-pattern: the ambitious man deceives the decent girl, and then repents —in time in the comedies, too late in the dramas.

Sometimes the comic heroine is a prig too (like Jean Arthur's Congresswoman in *A Foreign Affair*), sometimes she's amoral in a generous way (as in *Sabrina Fair* and in *Some Like It Hot*). But either way her attitude to love is a humane norm in comparison with which the man, though not devoid of decent qualms, is ruthless or mean. If Wilder's constant theme is that of the male exploiting the female (whether as salesman, as seducer, as gigolo or pimp) it is because it permits the sharpest, least comfortable conflict between the profit motive and human decency.

A Foreign Affair is something of an all-American variation on *Ninotchka*. Cupid eventually engineers a moral compromise between a rigidly upright Congresswoman (Jean Arthur) and a cynical American soldier (William Holden). She is driven by love to drink and to frivolous clothes, bought in the black market; while he realizes that he's a heel. Though Marlene Dietrich, Queen of the kraut rackets, ends being driven off to prison, her military escort keep tripping over steps, i.e. they are so dazzled and confused by her charms that life generally is clearly a stalemate between justice and corruption.

But Wilder's most rasping comedy (and, apparently, one of his biggest commercial successes) is *Stalag 17*. Here William Holden, capitalistic to the last, grimly hoards the little stock of watches and cameras which he trades with the guards against small concessions, which, in turn, he uses to screw every last *Pfennig* out of his fellow-P.O.W.'s. Topically, this tale of a G.I. trading with the German Nazis was released at the outset of America's campaign to stop her allies trading with Communist countries. Other hilarious, and hideous, gags include American servicemen queueing to watch the nakedness

of Polish women who are being deloused; the repeated disappoint-
ments of mail-starved men; and the explosive lewdness of a character
called 'Animal' (Robert Strauss). The one apparently heroic character
is last seen whining for mercy in the Commandant's office, while a
kindly old guard is mercilessly ribbed and abused (never give a
sucker . . .). The only relief the men enjoy from mud, bugs, boredom
and bullying is via the hero's money-grubbing enterprises—his Peep-
ing Tom telescope, his hooch distillery, his tote on cockroach races.
But, at last, he goes too far. His comrades beat him up, and he sees
the light of human decency. The film is almost as unbearable as it's
funny; 'excruciating' is the word; but it's sustained by its incredible
energy. In its picture of nastiness and squalor, though, it's not unlike
The Pawnshop—it's Chaplin's bitter world as it would more obviously
appear were it not for the redemptive power of love and for the charm
of age.

Sabrina Fair is a neat comic exploration of American meanness in
relation to love. Sabrina (Audrey Hepburn), the chauffeur's daughter,
loves David (William Holden), an idle thirty-year-old. ('The last pair
of legs you looked at cost the family 20,000 dollars.') He fancies her
too, but his dutiful elder brother Linus (Humphrey Bogart) keeps
reminding him that he must, for the good of the family business,
marry a millionaire heiress. David's seductive tactics seem as grubby
as his motives beside Sabrina's sweet, sophisticated generosity, and
it's no accident that, bringing champagne to the tennis-court where
she waits to be seduced, he sits on the glasses and is incapacitated (his
frustration inspires him to poetry: 'What rhymes with glass?'). A last
twist makes it a Cinderella story, but the cynicism in it sticks, whether
expressed by a remark of Sabrina's deferentially class-conscious
father ('No one ever called a poor girl democratic for marrying a rich
man'), or in David's phoney tussle of conscience over whether to
marry a poor girl *or* to see that poor boys in Puerto Rico get shoes.
The happy end, incidentally, means that they won't get them. If the
film occasionally seems heavy, it's because the climate then hardly
allowed Wilder to give full rein to Sabrina's Lubitschian attitude to
love.

Some Like It Hot uses the Prohibition era as an almost expressionistic setting for everything that's harsh and hectic in American life.
With its hearse piled high with hooch-filled coffins, its bullet-hole-
riddled double-bass, its two heroes turned into grotesque women by
juddering fear, its senile but incurably adolescent millionaire (Joe E.

Brown), and its ludicrous scene of a genuinely motherly gold-digger trying to 'cure' a fake millionaire's fake impotence, it becomes a comic *danse macabre* of personal maladjustments. Transvestism is a comic perennial, but to double it, and then have Lemmon constantly slipping into a genuine conviction that he really is a woman, is to put an altogether sharper edge on things. And when Joe E. Brown, on being told that the woman he loves is really a man, replies, unabashed, 'Well, nobody's perfect,' then it really is a Mad, Mad, Mad, Mad Sex-Life, to adapt the title of Stanley Kramer's equally black comedy on American avarice.

When, in Wilder's *The Apartment*, Jack Lemmon finds himself the lucky possessor of an apartment which senior executives want to use for their amorous escapades, we're very near a comedy of pimping. The oppressively open plan office is a reference to its forerunner in King Vidor's *The Crowd*; and Wilder takes his harshest, most accomplished comedy as near as makes no matter to a tragic climax in Shirley MacLaine's near-suicide. The pimping theme recurs when, in *Kiss Me Stupid*, a middle-class music teacher (Ray Walston), anxious to quit this small town for the Hollywood bigtime, tries to push his alleged wife (Kim Novak), actually the town whore, into bed with a visiting film star (Dean Martin). The imputation of such base motives to a music teacher, a veritable symbol of the schoolmarm culture, is cutting, and the whole thing so well schemed, that the film remains first-rate despite a central and pervasive flaw. The part of the music teacher was conceived for the unique personality of Peter Sellers. When illness forced him to withdraw from shooting it was impossible to adapt it ideally for a very clever, but a very different comic actor.

An acerbity not unlike Wilder's seems progressively to have invaded, and improved, the work of George Axelrod, usually adapted for the screen by the author. The title of *Phfft!* (1954) uses the sound of an expiring match as a metaphor for an expiring marriage. The overtone, of marriage as equally trivial, is too firmly soft-pedalled by Mark Robson in what becomes another variation on the Holliday–Lemmon menage. *The Seven-Year Itch* offered Marilyn Monroe as a blonde so tactile she keeps her undies in the fridge in hot weather, and provided Billy Wilder with his commercially most successful movie. Its innovation in its time was the benignly longing eye which it cast on the opportunity for extra-marital frolics, even if Axelrod's too-professional plotting sneaks neatly around any real crunch. Frank Tashlin's whimsical embroidery of *Will Success Spoil Rock Hunter?*

(*Oh, For A Man*) frequently hits happily gruesome notes, as in the bad-taste gags about the heroine sweating away with breast expanders to gratify her suburban boyfriend's fetishistic appreciation of mammary hypertrophies. *Goodbye Charlie* is below par, but in *Lord Love A Duck* Axelrod produces, directs and adapts another novelist's work into a strange Pygmalion–Eliza piece about a college student (Roddy MacDowall) who by hypnotism clarifies the mind of a classmate (Tuesday Weld) about just what she wants and just what she's ready to do to get it. She ends as a film star, an image of American wholesomeness, he, as a psychiatrist's punchball in a clinic. But the 'hypnosis' gimmick only draws attention to the real moral. This manipulating young man, whose operations may recall Ray Walston's in *Kiss Me Stupid*, is not the heroine's Higgins, nor even her Svengali, but her Mr. Hyde. He is a covert norm, in this 'hidden persuasion' society. And after all, aren't the advertising men, employing provocative models to sell everything from soap-suds to boot-polish, engaged in a refined, but real, variety of pimping? reducing every purchase to a matter of sexuality?

A similar moral underlines Bud Yorkin's *Divorce—American Style*, an adaptation, as its title implies, of a European genre of social criticism. Dick Van Dyke is pauperized by alimony to his ex-wife, Debbie Reynolds. When he falls in love with the ex-wife (Jean Simmons) of an equally pauperized friend (Jason Robards), the disparity in their fortunes makes marriage unthinkable until they've found his ex-wife a rich husband, which will minimize his payments. (Again, the sex-money nexus leads to what one might call a neo-pimping situation.) Other-direction is invoked with a vengeance by the couple's home, so open-plan and intercom-riddled that when they quarrel their son scores off points for each side like a boxing referee. Dick Van Dyke and Debbie Reynolds, icons of unspoiled American enthusiasm, play with a ravaged sharpness which is something of a demystification in itself. Again, a hypnosis gimmick is used, to manœuvre a transparently happy end—but only after it has exposed an entire vocabulary of human relationships as futile or exploitative, beneath its optimistic veneer.

Elia Kazan's *A Face In The Crowd* is a formidable attempt to blend black comedy with an almost 'straight' treatment of a social issue. Could a pop singer be built up into a demagogue by a ruthless group of extreme right-wing politicians and businessmen? Kazan doesn't miss a trick in his gallant attempt to make the idea of America accepting 'Elvis for Pres' plausible. His hero, Lonesome Rhodes (Andy Griffith) is not simply a sex-energy symbol; but a hillbilly with a sufficient store of coarse wisdom to qualify as a symbol of cracker-barrel horse sense (which another entertainer, Will Rogers, had been, during the 20's). But Kazan's film never quite solves the, to my mind, insoluble problems involved when one appeals to that very same common sense in one's audience which one is denying to the typical audience on the screen. A lighter treatment might have made of the film a neater aesthetic entity; but one may still prefer it imperfect, with Andy Griffith's incredible animal verve giving a kick like a mule's to a movie which is not so much satirical as sarcastic, in the fullest sense of flesh-tearing, and quite as tigerish as Kubrick's *Lolita*, which, like *Dr. Strangelove*, had to be made in England. Meanwhile, an Englishman in Hollywood, Tony Richardson, takes the black comedy to the pitch of necrophilia, and attains an almost Stroheimian footage, with the imperfect, but rivetingly gruesome, *The Loved One*.

The black comedy takes on a protective glitter, while remaining true to itself, in Arthur Heller's *The Americanization Of Emily*, written by Paddy Chayefsky. Its title suggests that Julie Andrews, playing a beautiful but duty-bound and prim English widow, will be triumphantly converted to the aggressive hedonism of fun morality. But its picture of the Normandy landings is pointedly sardonic in detail (seasick Marines . . .). And with the Top Brass's resolve that the first man to die on Omaha Beach must be a Marine, it contrasts the determination of its Yossarian-like hero (James Coburn) that that honour won't be his. Since the world is mad, the sane man can stay alive only by a policy of systematic cowardice. Robert Benayoun's translation of the film's moral in French terms is illuminating:

'Imagine a light comedy on the battle of Verdun, which explains that the men in detention, the deserters and the defeatists were the only heroes worthy of admiration, and that the victory parade was one of the publicity gimmicks of French militarism. And try to imagine its Parisian première, under the patronage of *Anciens Combatants* and War Widows. . . .'

Any suspicion that the picture of the Marines' Top Brass is, in essentials, exaggerated, must be checked by the frequent reports that American Marines in Vietnam suffered far higher casualties than necessary, because Marine officers thought that the Marine tradition of attack forbade proper preparations for defence. This could hardly be said in a 'serious' American film about warfare. And, as so often, a comic tone comes to the rescue of America's traditional anarchism, an anarchism as subversive, now, as the American constitution (public opinion surveys have shown that its ideals as to individual liberty have, since the McCarthy era, become dead letters in most American minds).

The difficulty Hollywood is only slowly making up its mind to face is that modern society is such as to make us all more conscious than ever before of social problems as human problems and human problems as social problems. Hence America, like any rapidly evolving society, abounds in unresolved issues for which black comedy is the natural entertainment style. If a comparatively thin play like *The Owl and the Pussycat* can be the Broadway success it is, it can only be because it provokes, even if it doesn't explore, certain desperate feelings about race, about sexuality, about intellectuals, about class, about loneliness. Changing America needs new players, new stories, new styles, and it is only by following, rather than fleeing, the questions looming large in people's minds that Hollywood can provoke the fullest responses and renew its inspiration. Oddly, its 'runaway' productions, such as *The Knack* and *Bedazzled*, seem to be following this policy more systematically than the domestic product. It may be that the exotic effect of English settings helps to distance the issues a little, make their resonance to the American scene seem less pointed. None the less they posit a much sharper and closer approach to the nerve-points of experience than Hollywood as a whole has ventured, and it's hard to see how their example can fail to reinforce that of Hollywood's own black comedians, to spark off a new audacity and depth in productorial strategies.

So fondly remembered is 30's sophisticated comedy that its grace and lightness, enhanced rather than dimmed by thirty intervening years, are often evoked as a standard which current Hollywood comedy constantly fails to reach. But such comparisons are misplaced, since much contemporary comedy is deeply concerned with confusions of behaviour and identity. The comedy of manners has given place to the comedy of character, necessarily less stylish, more probing, at once introverted and explosive. Hollywood's crazy casebook may not be the revolutionary manifesto one might relish, but from the marriage of the sophisticated sons of slapstick with the vulgarized ghosts of Freud there arises an interesting genre; the comedy of personal grotesquerie.

On such a theme, sex comedy looms large. The most obvious route to introverted comedy is traced through Otto Preminger's *The Moon Is Blue*, which, after twenty years, first breached the Hays Code. It allowed its young heroine (Maggie McNamara) to breathe the word 'virgin', and to contemplate, with not merely complacency, but actual enthusiasm, the extramarital loss of that condition. Preminger had directed Lubitsch's last production, *That Lady In Ermine*, a few years previously, and if *The Moon Is Blue* hasn't, after all, that Lubitsch touch, and is too cautious for Kinsey, at least it's sub-Kinsey *à la pastiche* Lubitsch.

In so far as films in this stream (*The Tender Trap, Ask Any Girl, Come Blow Your Horn, Boys' Night Out, Move Over Darling*) involve some romantic interest, they tend to run into the snags posed by the American combination of puritanism ('nothing is allowable'), romanticism ('everything is possible') and fun morality ('to get nothing is shameful'). Even playboy bachelors, Frank Sinatra or Dean Martin style, still tend to be other than virginal by implication only, or before the movie began, or in so far as that saucy girl who keeps popping in and out of their apartment might be considered to be a naughty girl, or a single symbol for all their casual affairs, a girl, in fact, whose name is Legion. And if that true love, which should keep hubby, be he Tom Ewell or Jack Lemmon, from straying, is momentarily below par, then coincidence intervenes, just as it intervenes to save the too-eager heroine from seducing the man she wants, until such time as he has discovered he loves her, when there's no need to anticipate their marriage, is there? Quarrels still tend to originate from wives' refusals to so much as listen to their helpless husbands' explanations of the suspicious circumstances he seems to be in, because any actual adulterous act would bring us into the mood of tragic expiations and soulful sufferings. One might suspect that any film which faithfully rendered the boyish ungraciousness of which the American male is capable, in matters of sexual conquest, would endear itself to hardly anybody. The matter of heavy petting has hardly been noted on Hollywood screens, outside a splendidly bad-taste verse sung by Dean Martin in *The Silencers*: 'She took her coat and took her hat—but left her brassiere on the doormat.' The reversal of conventional active-passive roles is one answer to the puritan problem: the playboy hero is so cool (or satiated, even?), that he doesn't even want to seduce the heroine, and only responds to her real love. One way or another the male is frequently pushed into the passive position *vis-à-vis* the American female; only partly a contrivance, this turnabout might be related to the transvestite theme touched on elsewhere, to such titles as *Cinderella* and *Father Goose*, as well as to the Playboy Club syndrome touched on in *Boys' Night Out*. One formulation is that for most American boys the mother is a nearer, and more imposing, authority figure than 'Pop'; and since the child is father to the man, a man's wife takes on the redoubtable quality of 'Mom'. 'Pop' is felt to be more of a pal, a brother, a sibling (and conversely, pals, brothers and siblings quickly arouse the Oedipal fear of 'Pop' . . .). A complementary reason might be that, in a competitive world, domesticity, and the yielding morality which it implies, create, in the already anxious male, a bewilderment, a guilt, which stimulate a switch to passivity. To possess is taken for granted, and mutual possession is felt as being possessed; the male feels captured by the woman, rather than capturing. No doubt the female partner makes a complementary switch, vehemently making sentimentally idealist assumptions, or assuming a moral authority, or a tough cynicism, or a manipulative style —all these attitudes being, in a sense, smothering, castratory and unrealistic. No doubt, too, any culture's emotional arrangements must fail to resolve all possible tensions and maladjustments, and Europe seems to be evolving from its traditional kinds of unhappiness towards the American ones.

Another type of comic development, less obvious, more fruitful, was begun by, perhaps, Howard Hawks, when, in *Monkey Business*, he paired the suavest of 30's comedy stars, Cary Grant, and the most earthily commonsensical, Ginger Rogers, and made something rather sillier than monkeys out of the pair of them. If this film typifies the devolution of sophisticated comedy towards a more undignified style, something broader and more slapsticky, Jerry Lewis, at about the same time, comes, like Danny Kaye, to slapstick from cabaret, and begins bestowing on it an unprecedentedly introverted quality, reconciling it with sophisticated milieux.

There is also a new trend towards thoughtful comedy, exemplified by Joshua Logan's *Bus Stop*, whose critical reception illustrates the misunderstandings to which the most interesting new genres are so often subject. Its theme is yet another variation on the country-city contrast. Bo (Don Murray), a young Montana cowboy, triumphs in a rodeo, and goes, for the first time, to a cabaret. There, with some gallantry, he thumps the rowdies who have been heckling a rather dispirited 'chantoose', Cherie (Marilyn Monroe). Innocent of the world's ways, and very attracted by her, he makes an arrogantly unilateral decision to marry her, and won't take no for an answer—in fact he's so arrogant he doesn't realize she's trying to say no. In the course of a cross-country bus-ride, she appeals, surreptitiously, to Bo's friend Vergil (Arthur O'Connell), to another passenger (Hope Lange), to the bus-driver (Robert Bray), and to his girlfriend Grace (Betty Field), who all take Cherie's part. Bo comes to blows with the bus-driver, and, for the first time in his young life, and in public, and before the girl he'd hoped to champion, Bo eats dirt. Shamed by defeat, he matures, apologizes, relinquishes Cherie. He understands, at last, just what humiliation is, what her life has been, what life is, and respects her still. At the last moment, they realize that his inexperience and her over-experience balance out nicely (a thought which, incidentally, recurs in *Jules Et Jim*). Off they go in the bus together, and though it's clear that he'll be unconsciously conceited and domineering until his dying day, he drapes his sheepskin pro-

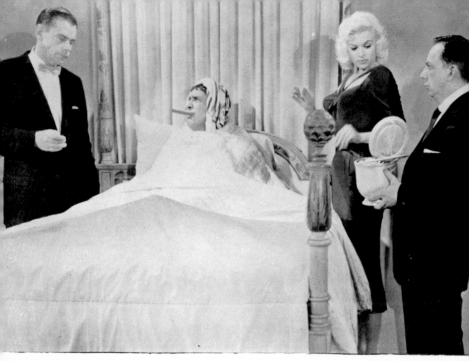

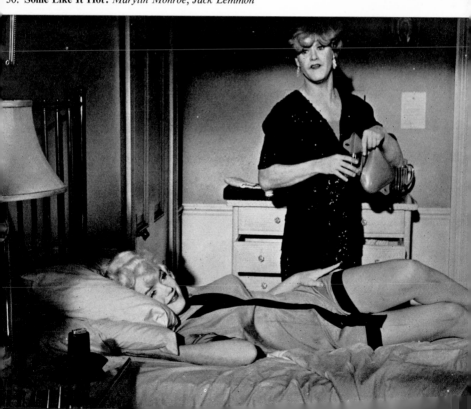

31
That's My Boy:
*Jerry Lewis, Eddie
Mayehoff*

Anti-heroes and
outsiders

32
Visit To A Small Planet:
*Joan Blackman, Jerry
Lewis*

tectively over the timid girl. The film can conclude in a bitterness-tinged happiness.

Directed by Joshua Logan, and with Marilyn Monroe and Susan Strasberg, the acting owes a great deal to The Method, and opposes a systematic grittiness to 30's flow. It tells its story in very physical terms, and its joyous, but also troubled, emphasis on flesh, on energy, on muscular strength, is supported by a great deal of physical detail—the dousing of a stove sending clouds of steam drifting about the room, the falling snow, a sunset's blue and gold.

Such a style, though, was offensive to many. Resigned as one is to the obsessive old-maidishness of the *Sight and Sound* circle, one still raises one's eyebrows at the interpretation of *Bus Stop*. Logan's film, apparently, 'reduces life to terms of animal sexuality. . . . The fight between the two men becomes a torrid orgasmic ecstasy for Grace while Cherie averts the children's eyes as if from a spectacle of copulation. Bawdy and sexuality can provide good literary and dramatic material of course, but they must be eked out with fun or wit or humour. There is little comedy here that does not wear the wry sly smiles of lust. . . . In general . . . the film demands of its principle performers a purely physical display of their bodies viewed as sexual machinery. *Bus Stop* would be of little importance if it were not that so many audiences will find it not just something sticky, sexy and exciting, but a perfectly acceptable farcical romp.'

But that exaggeration, that super-sensuality, far from being wry and sly, provides a gusto which, in the fights as in the sex-play, reminds one of the bar-room brawls of John Ford or Raoul Walsh. Ironically, it is just those gestures which most upset our critic which decrease the tension by providing comic distance. When the film's idioms are put in this popular perspective, then a phrase like 'torrid orgasmic ecstasy' becomes a ludicrous misdescription of Grace's reaction—she just likes watching fights, and her relish helps reassure the audience that this is to be a bar-room brawl in the John Ford tradition. But a second distance is involved: moral distance. Bo represents that American ideal, the rustic, virgin, knight-errant hercules; he is L'il Abner, or one of the seven brothers who stole the sobbin' women, seen sympathetically, but also very critically, that is, with his Earthquake McGoon streak showing. Since the critic didn't like the picture, and, so to speak, de-emotionalized it, he saw only physicality, without its emotional meaning, and therefore missed its critical attitude, and expresses his dislike of the attitudes which he thinks it approves of by

P 225

recourse to ideas of sexual perversion. It certainly never occurred to the present writer that the fight between the two men resembled copulation—any more than wrestling resembles copulation, though it might to sexually obsessed or to excessively detached minds. If Cherie averts the children's eyes, it's to show what a gentle, motherly soul she is—she doesn't want them to see a fight. A wife who shields children from violence is just the wife Bo needs, to balance his brashness. It's astonishing that the reviewer, instead of applauding her gesture, seems to consider it obscene!

The left-wing French critic, Louis Seguin, raised no objection to the violence or the heterosexuality, but criticized the film on rather different grounds: '. . . the principal victim of the enterprise is a certain Marilyn Monroe, delighted, it is said, with her experience, a delight easily explained by a pin-up girl's rejoicing in her first real acting role. Everyone can make a mistake, and we are always ready to forgive Marilyn anything, but we can't forgive Joshua, whose misogyny is replenished by the only too clear, and Broadwayish, fountain head of sexual indecisiveness. The process has four stages.

'(1) choose as hero a "beautiful animal", a muscled and leaping male, a "child-man" just as there are "child-women";

'(2) contrast with him the "unhealthy" flesh of a woman smeared with powder and garnished with gawdy, moth-eaten rags (cf. Vivien Leigh in *A Streetcar Named Desire*);

'(3) in the reverse-angles, give the cowboy the best of the bargain; (ten seconds for Don Murray, three for Marilyn);

'(4) in order to dispel any equivocation . . . insert a long scene in which two men lie sprawling, grappling and embracing in the snow.

'Since there are those who appreciate such amusements, I should be reluctant, so little taste have I for moralizing, to invite them to other sports. No doubt Logan and Inge are preparing other subjects for their delectation.

'But what the devil was Marilyn doing on their 'bus?'

Clearly, this criticism is altogether more sophisticated than and less earnest than the English one. However, the general public, for whom the film was, after all, designed, approaches it in a rather different way. As Louis Seguin remarks, Marilyn is faded and Don Murray gets the lion's share. This helps the film to be emotionally more complex than it would be were she allowed to be as radiant as in, say, *Gentlemen Prefer Blondes*. If Bo had simply won the most gorgeous girl for miles around, the essential quality of expiation and human tenderness in his eventual attitude would be lost. The shift of balance towards the male is a necessary counterbalance to the fact that, despite the greasepaint, Marilyn's sex appeal is still likely to mesmerize audiences. In any case (and this is a point which critics of mass media erotica constantly forget) half the general public just happens to be female, and would feel a special sympathy for a faded but loving Marilyn. They may also enjoy a little male sex appeal. And in any case, both sexes can appreciate beefcake just as both sexes can enjoy cheesecake. John Francis Lane reported how, 'On the Italian front, surprising as it may seem, the greatest stakes are on the male rather than on the female figure . . . in Travestere, the popular quarter of Rome, the local boys can be seen leaving their girlfriends to see Queen Gina of Sheba, while they themselves crowd into a smaller cinema to see Steve Reeves alone against the Persian fleet.' In England, the fear of homosexuality is particularly strong among intellectuals of middle-class origin, whereas working-class lads are the audience *par excellence* of stripped-to-the-buff action films, as the *Tarzan* series makes obvious. The better educated, and more status-conscious, not caring too much about physical fitness, not feeling much in physical terms, don't make the happy identification with strength which working-class lads do. Hence they feel the male body must be something which even the male audience is looking at rather than feeling with. Yet, after all, it's difficult to see why a film where the male is more attractive and magnificent than the female must be any more aberrant than a film where the female is more attractive and magnificent than the male. Or perhaps any human relationship other than a perfect match is unhealthy? Whether or not *Bus Stop* is particularly congenial to homosexuals and misogynists is another question, but in any case such art is freely enjoyed by the general public, at all levels of sophistication, because it expresses some of the normal person's repressions and undertows.[1]

Marilyn's Cherie is not Marilyn, but of all her films, *Bus Stop*, with *The Misfits*, is psychologically the most exploratory. The comedies of Kim Novak, her spiritual sister in alienation, have been disappointing, after *Jeanne Eagels* and *Vertigo, Boys' Night Out* is fairly typical.

---

[1] This point is worth stressing, because the psychological hypochondria underlying such attitudes is almost all-pervasive in serious criticism of the mass media. It arises, not so much from a residual puritanism, as from a kind of emotional inhibition which is more English than American and more middle-class than upper-class. Emotion lacking, a fifth-former's Freudianism is wheeled in for a desultory attempt at explanation.

The boys' night out is a weekly get-together, run rather on the *Marty* principle: 'What do you wanna do?', 'I dunno, what do you wanna do?' They're all firmly trussed to their womenfolks' apron-strings, until a glimpse of their hitherto respected boss's expense-account floozie gives them the idea of clubbing together, renting a luxurious love-nest, and a blonde to match, to visit on a rota system. Their catch (Kim) is really a sociology student researching into the sexual fantasies of the adult American male. She finds it very easy to defend her honour without offending her protectors, since they, though desperate to impress their buddies as insatiable Romeos, are touchingly happy to sit quietly by their sybaritic icon. One tells her his life-story, another does handy jobs, a third savours her home-from-home cooking. Finally she weds the one eligible bachelor (James Garner), the rest are rounded up, and forgiven, by their wives. The film's admirable central idea verges on several intriguing aspects of the American scene. Not only might it have sported as subtitles *The Apartment, Bachelor Party* and *Never On Sunday* (or rather *Never, Period*), but, like the Playboy clubs, it relates to that vast area in which the American love of exploiting everything commercially veers away, under puritan, idealistic and very human pressures, from its logical conclusion, to what might be described as the purchase of friendly human contact. It matches the apparently provocative, but manipulating and intellectualizing, female with that sad, and common, male, for whom sexuality is merely a means of proving himself to himself, and to rival males, who might laugh at him, and for whom the act itself is, when it comes to it, rather more frightening than the fantasy of it is appealing. It's a pity that the development of this idea suggests that the only sexual fantasy of the American adult male is his belief that he has any fantasies, and that the story eschews its more logical development, including the girl getting caught in her own trap and realizing that her research was only a substitute form of living a courtesan's life anyway.

Perhaps the neatest idea of the cycle so far was Charles Walters's *Ask Any Girl*. A secretary (Shirley MacLaine) in a motivational research agency persuades her boss (David Niven) to carry out consumer research on the playboy she thinks she loves—who happens to be his brother. To ascertain his subject's tastes, Niven, overcoming his natural fastidiousness, romances all his girlfriends, eventually enabling his client to transform herself into a one-girl pantechnicon of all her prey's favourite feminine features. But just as she wins him, she realizes that she's lost herself and that it's her boss that she loves anyway. Ruthlessly done, this study in masks and fantasies, in hidden persuasion and image-building, in pseudo-identity and all the fetishisms of 'false personalization', in all the paradoxes of role-playing and the merchandizing of intimacies, could have been a little classic of our image-ridden era. After all, it's an anagram of *Vertigo*, where James Stewart heartlessly converts a shopgirl into the exact replica of the dead rich woman whom he loved. One can imagine, for example, a more realistic approach, with a lonely New York girl desperately adopting the techniques on which she eavesdrops at conferences; a subplot involving the new capitalist habit of vetting (i.e. conscripting) wives; and fraternal tensions expressing some of the more complex tensions between the puritan ethos and fun morality. Alas, the film plods along in the Louis B. Mayer tradition in which its producer, Joe Pasternak, was formed, and to which he has remained faithful. The film remains worth seeing, not only for the *other* film shining, blackly, through, but for the playing of Shirley MacLaine, who can run the gamut from the tragi-comic grotesquerie of *The Apartment* to the animated cartoon expressions of the cigarette-tasting sequence here. As the nearest feminine counterpart of Jerry Lewis, she continues the line of profound comediennes which includes Mabel Normand, Clara Bow, Mae West, Katherine Hepburn, Judy Holliday, and, potentially, at least, Jane Fonda. Similarly, as Bob Hope and Eddie Bracken did for the 40's, Tony Curtis, Jack Lemmon and Tony Randall typify the sharp, sensitive, ruthless, anxious style of the 60's —with the advantage of vastly better scripts.

Minnelli's *Goodbye Charlie* is a more narrowly missed opportunity. A deceased Casanova is reborn as a girl (Debbie Reynolds) and, finally, reappears as the heroine's dog. It takes one stage further the vein of sophisticated (as opposed to farcical) transvestite comedy which is currently obsessional in screen and TV comedy. The tendency of our routinizing, intellectualizing, push-button civilization, to soften, and, in a sense, feminize men, while maintaining them in a state of anxious passivity and frustration, is fairly obviously responsible, and probably it's not so much a sign of homosexuality as an expression of despair; it becomes easier to mentally change one's sex into the naturally passive one than to live out one's own fully. But where Wilder has Jack Lemmon forced to keep repeating 'I'm a boy', *Goodbye Charlie*, after a promising opening with Charlie discovering his/her new 'equipment' (an interestingly technological view of one's own body), a more or less conventional intrigue takes over, and the psychological energy which is kept out of the story by the various tabus is limited to the stunning orchestration of the title-song. Its normal hero is a writer, a reminder of the changed status of intellectuals since the pre-war years, when if they weren't played by Leslie Howard (for the ladies) or Humphrey Bogart (for the men) they were either cissy snobs who required socking by Christmas card versifiers, or strayed into unnatural behaviour like Doctors Jekyll and Clitterhouse. A few liberal movies had defended Pasteur, Ehrlich, Zola and anti-Nazi Jewish professors, but it was not until the late 40's that *Sitting Pretty* established, as David Reisman noted, a new attitude towards the intellectual, as a 'social deviant' who establishes the individual's 'right to explore and elaborate his own personality and sensitivity with a work-leisure competence that goes beyond the requirements of the peers'. In other words, the mastermind, hitherto menacing, snobbish and associated with schoolmarm requirements, suddenly seems more friendly (and probably is, given the general extension of more sophisticated education). He dares to be a Daniel, to stand alone, although, as Reisman observes, 'he attains his range of skill and competence only in situations where society permits a high degree of individualism; and he is allowed to create his breath-taking personal style only because of his astonishing dexterity'. But from there it takes only one further turn of fashion's wheel to turn the intellectual into the 'lone wolf', the outcast, the individualist who is not so much rugged as prickly. The 50's trend is revealed by a series of Minnelli films which centre on, or feature, the artist or the intellectual as outsider-hero (*The Bad and the Beautiful, The Band Wagon, The Cobweb, Lust for Life, Designing Woman, Some Came Running, The Bells Are Ringing*).

By 1966 cries of protest against required conformity as spiritual death have reached a point at which the poet's fate can stand for every man's. In Irving Kershner's *A Fine Madness* Sean Connery plays a frustrated poet who cleans carpets for a living, shocks a woman's club by giving a drunken lecture, seduces his psychiatrist's wife (Jean Seberg), and magically survives the pre-frontal lobotomy which society deems the kindest cure for that disabling disease, a mind of one's own.

39 · I dreamed I Flew through the Air on a Custard Pie; What Could That Mean, Doctor?

But it is Frank Tashlin and Jerry Lewis who deepen the merger of the sophisticated and the slapstick genre, and continue where Sturges left off. If their slapstick hasn't the poetic purity of the silent years, it has taken on a new dimension. Coalesced with the comedy of personal maladjustment and grotesquerie, it becomes itself psychological, expressing inner conflicts.

Frank Tashlin came to features from cartoons. He had worked for Dave Fleischer, Hal Roach and Walt Disney, on Bugs Bunny and also on the Marx Brothers' *Love Happy* (hindsight may detect his touch in the brilliantly conceived chase around rooftop advertising signs). But it is with *Susan Slept Here* (1954) that he first emerges as an *auteur*. A weary and disillusioned Hollywood scriptwriter (Dick Powell) is badly short of inspiration, until a friendly cop brings him a juvenile delinquent (Debbie Reynolds), who first reinvigorates him and then hustles him into a happy marriage. The film's apt blend of sophisticated settings and teenage appeal is agreeably garnished with danced dream sequences whose frank eroticism underlines the wryly Freudian air of much of the dialogue, e.g. the hero telling the girl, 'I'm old enough to be your mother.' The film anticipates (by two whole years) many aspects of the B.B. ethos (a sexually emancipated tomboy feminist), while Tashlin takes up Sturges's wry sense of chaos, not so much in the plot (which is sentimental enough), as in a tone indicated by Dick Powell's response to the girl's proposal: 'I'm a hypersensitive hypochondriac with hypertension, I take pills till I rattle, pills to send me to sleep, pills to wake me up, pills to remind me to take pills, and anyway I come from a long line of bachelors.' This plea for peace she counters with a charmingly peremptory street-car conductor's cry: 'End of the line, ding ding, all get off!' With its terse switch from despair ('end of the line') to rebirth, from solitude-upon-solitude to gregariousness, this is one of those movie phrases that's much richer than it seems. It's a minor film, but a swallow prefiguring a summer.

Susan Slept Here was followed by *Artists and Models*. It matches Shirley MacLaine with Jerry Lewis as a young neurotic who dreams industriously so as to keep the publisher of horror comics supplied with new story-ideas. Again, the film moves in the area of insomnia, neurosis and high-pressure fantasies. *The Girl Can't Help It* works sixteen rock-and-roll numbers into the tale of another disillusioned Hollywood character. This time it's an agent (Tom Ewell) who is forced by an old-time gangster (Edmond O'Brien) to try and make a pop star out of his old buddy's daughter (Jayne Mansfield). These wholly successful films are followed by another Hollywood fable, *Oh, For A Man* (in America, *Will Success Spoil Rock Hunter?*).

This engaging trio inaugurate the delectable Tashlin mish-mash of anatomical jokes (Jayne Mansfield clasps a pint milk bottle over each breast, Jerry Lewis gets himself inextricably tangled with his masseur and several too-helpful nurses), Freudian undertones (zany structures of father-and-mother-figures), dream sequences, parodies of other movies, burlesqued historical vignettes, jokes about the medium (the 'Scope screen shrinks to tiny black-and-white so that TV-addicts will feel at home), gruesome ideas in the way of drink and food (pickles and strawberries for breakfast), deeply disturbing sensual jokes (in *Rock-A-Bye-Baby* Jerry bottle-feeds quins by piercing a hole in each finger-tip of a huge rubber glove down whose wrist he then empties a milk bottle), female drunk scenes, an irreverence which approaches satire (heavenly music sounding as Tom Ewell is given the key to the Executive Washroom) together with some splendidly gruesome moments (ex-con Edmond O'Brien sings 'There's no lights on the Christmas Tree, mother, They're using the Electric Chair tonight').

The Girl Can't Help It is a classic crystallization of the spirit of rock-and-roll, and of teenage hedonism bubbling up and overwhelming the violence-and-ulcers world of their elders. This trio of imperfect but fascinating comedies is completed by *Artists and Models*, which also has a hypochondriac hero, a figure who enables Tashlin to play off, in comedy, a kind of hysteric exhaustion, against a sardonic

232

enjoyment of all the plumage of Americana—rock-'n'-roll, hard liquor, sumptuous automobiles, movie fans, consumer goods, breasts, comic-strips, comic-strip sentiments. Much of today's 'pop art' is concerned with just that mixture of despair and acquiescence, that inspires Tashlin. And it's quite arguable that Tashlin puts it all very much better than most. Yet Tashlin's predicament, as an artist, parallels the defeatism implied in Andy Warhol's 'I think everyone should think alike. I think everyone should be a machine and think like everyone else'. Tashlin's attitude to his gags, and to his characters, parallels Warhol's paintings of soup-cans, in that cartoonization implies a kind of heartlessness, allowing him to reduce 'flesh-and-blood' situation to physical and caricatural mechanisms. And side by side with it, there is a rather schematic kind of sentimentality, an anticlimatic acceptance of the notions he has been spoofing. The interplay of sympathetic and satiric attitudes, of dryness and of sentimentality is quite as alive and interesting, although it exists within the 'high culture' angle, whereby one looks at the artist's vision for its own sake rather than for the story. The films themselves often have a dissatisfying thinness, as throughout much of *Hollywood Or Bust*, *Oh, For a Man* and *The Disorderly Orderly*. Tashlin's evokes Fields's hollowness, but without Fields's corrective astringency to Fields himself. Still, one would like to see a Tashlin comedy about 'beats' and 'pop' painters, in the hope that a vehemently nonconformist way of life would reactivate the voltage of his three 'hypochondriac' films.

Not that Tashlin is, basically, a satirical moralist, like Sturges or Wilder. He resembles them in some ways, but in others his outlook, like Laurel and Hardy's, is that of ideological innocence, and is all the better for it, emphasizing, as they do, the trials and tribulations of everyday living and feeling. What sometimes seems defective is that dramatic tension, as a result of which the best comedies would be very sad indeed if they weren't very funny instead. For all that, he has given us three sustainedly first-rate films, as well as innumerable splendid sequences, ideas and anthology-pieces—'half-reelers' that amply justify the films in which they appear.

It's impossible to separate the work of Tashlin from that of Jerry Lewis. Lewis emerged in the late 40's as the Bowery Boys 'died', and all their imbecilities, however contradictory, were united in one idiot. In the midst of the 'deadpan', tough, era, out burst this frenzied weakling, bringing male emotion and weakness back to the screen, a good ten years before James Dean in *Rebel Without A Cause*.

Any idiot can play the fool but only Jerry Lewis can play so many idiots simultaneously. He is imbecility sunk to the height of genius. He appears to have the mentality of a child of six, but a six-year-old primed to explode into every emotion which he has been suppressing since he was one. He doesn't so much emote, as disintegrate into an emotional gamut ranging through Donald Duck, the Frankenstein Monster, Pluto, Cheetah, Alfred E. Neumann, Phlebus, Stan Laurel, Michel Simon in *La Chienne*, and, in *The Nutty Professor*, Humphrey Bogart pretending to be the kind of dirty old man who buys expensive pornography in *The Big Sleep*. Any appearance of tranquillity is actually a catatonic spasm before he reverts to his normal state of fizzily incoherent benevolence. Like all the great expressionists, he thinks with his body, and translates the soul's impulses into a sema-phor of spastic acrobacy; he stutters with his feet, trips over his tongue, squints with his kneecaps and turns the simple act of crossing his legs into a bout of cat's cradle. His strabismus, quite devoid of the peaceful blankness of Ben Turpin's of yore, startles the spectator like a klaxon; I wasn't surprised when a friend complained that watching our hero in *Artists and Models* made him feel seasick.

Spectator-empathy can be pretty gruelling. Props take second place to, are mere pretexts for, a purely spiritual slapstick. He is most lovable when most repulsive and most wistful when in convulsions. He offers neither quick quips like Bob Hope nor the caustic anti-logic of Marxism; for our contemporary verbal saturation can be by-passed only by incoherence. A farewell line like 'My life is out of yours!' isn't just a satire on the clichés it recalls; its inarticulacy articulates a lingering dizziness of longing, just as 'ooh, the heat of the hot heat' re-creates by its frenzy of verbal primitivism the timidly broken silence of Stan Laurel.

Though he's basically a 'city' comedian, Jerry's character is as complex as any product of Method principles. In *That's My Boy* he plays a small-town boy as earnest as Harold Lloyd as *The Freshman*. He also continues the Stan Laurel tradition (as underlined by a charming in-joke-tribute in *The Bellboy*). It's true that his hectic, fissile and every-which-away style, so suitable to the Tranquillizer Age, seems the exact opposite of Stan's humbly artisanal, classically quiet simplicity. Thus, Stan, passionately kissed by the fiery artist's flirtatious wife in *The Fixer-Uppers*, blinks as blissfully as a baby, where Jerry would more likely feel inspired to run round the room on top of the furniture, cry ecstatically 'Make more with the lip', and so on. But his frenzies arise from the interaction of Stan's hopeful passivity with the urgent, up-and-at-'em of eager-beaver Harold, convinced that success is for those who believe in the goodness of the world. For Jerry, though, the only 'success' is: love and happiness.

But where Stan so mutely and simply accepts his own paralysis, Jerry's frenetic cadenzas express a different kind of confusion. In common with most of us in this more sophisticated world, he is more aware of emotional complexities and conflicts and of all the possible (but mutually exclusive) ways of reaction to them. . . . His emotional gears crash and freewheel from one response to the other. His innocence is a rapturously hopeful-desperate sensitivity to *everything*, and is usually played off against either the relaxed cunning of Dean Martin, or of the self-aware world which Jerry disrupts, whether by his well-meaning destructiveness or by his sincerity.

His first 'period' can be described as his 'Hal Wallis' period, where he made a kind of Mutt-and-Jeff duo with Dean Martin. Perhaps the zaniest film of this more conventional period is Tashlin's *Artists and Models*, his most delicate, *That's My Boy*, with sensitive characterization by Jerry as a sickly college-boy and Eddie Mayehoff as his sports-loving father, a brashly manly hearty trying to be liberal, sensitive and reasonable, but still getting his way. Subsequently Wallis, Jerry and Dean Martin went their separate ways and Jerry became his own producer-director. *The Bellboy* ushers in his experimental period, where the storyline lapses, or disappears, to liberate the gag, which, in turn, becomes rococo, in the sense of a fanciful lingering over offbeat detail. *The Ladies' Man* is probably the most successful from this era.

Throughout both periods, two themes interweave: Jerry's desperate attempts to live up to his own ideals of 'benevolent toughness', and his equally desperate search to find, be worthy of, and be accepted by a loving world. In the earlier films, his buddy is Dean Martin, whom he never recognizes as the heel he really is. In the later films, a slight but obstinate emotional block makes Jerry see the world as loving when it's cynical and cynical when it's loving, or else prevents him from coming to terms with it in one way or another.

Both *The Ladies' Man* and *The Disorderly Orderly* present Jerry as a very lovable misfit in a world of people who love him really (not that there aren't disquieting elements, quite apart from the usual villainous character or two. Even the kindly women tend to look like either momistic battleaxes, or *femmes fatales*). But this softer view of the world is consistent with a current trend in comedy. In Gerald

Thomas's *Carry on Sergeant* (from Britain) and Mervyn Leroy's rumbustious *No Time for Sergeants* (from the U.S.A.) we find a friendlier view of the 'old sweat' N.C.O.—probably due to the fact that authority, like people generally, has been softening its style, from the obviously arbitrary to something more reasonable and manipulative. There is a characteristic contrast between Will Hay's reception by the station staff of Buggleskelly in *Oh Mr. Porter*, and the loving care with which Kathleen Freeman surrounds her new handyman in *The Ladies' Man*. The Lewis film perfectly catches this mood, a general desire to be friendly and reasonable, and evokes the more subtle but pervasive misunderstandings, failures of contact, expressions of indifference and lonelinesses which, since we're all more sensitive as well as more thoughtful, hurt us just as much as the grosser, more robust hostilities of early days. The style of the human contacts—for example, Jerry's mail-delivery—is so astutely observed that it rivals any social study in exploring the nuances and tensions of the well-meaning middle-class liberal, lost in lonely hypersensitivity, though only temporarily, of course.

Since gagology, despite all our efforts, is still the most anaesthetized aspect of aesthetic theory, this study of this film's *avant-garde* gags will have to content itself with three main principles:

1. The lapses in, or disappearance of, storyline, create a strange osmosis between gag and build-up, unprecedented even in its own predecessor, Tati's *Mon Oncle*. The whole film is a *temps-mort*, since the story, even when suggested, is all but unstated. The shift of emotion from dramatic thread to the trivial or absurd events which are the topics of its gags is very cool, and in this respect parallels Godard's eye for environmental minutiae. But also the absence of continuous dramatic thread piles a special intensity of audience attention on to a gag, and on to its build-up, which permit more sophisticated forms.

2. Part of a gag is a *non sequitur* from the previous gag and *non sequiturs* are indispensable links in the casual chain within each gag. Many gags are shaggy dog gags, or partly shaggy dog gags, or shaggy dogs in sheep's clothing. Or they are played down to become incredulous titters rather than belly-laughs, that is, to create a mood of liberation and alienation rather than of howling hilarity. Excellent examples are provided by the still photographs accompanying the credits and by the film's 101 décor jokes. What's very funny is that we catch ourselves unsure whether or not they're funny . . . there's a kind

of 'Tickle me or am I dreaming?' vacillation, enhanced, in the case of the décor gags, by the fact that much of the décor is as absurd as it is largely by being extremely beautiful. The all-white room of Miss Cartilage is a masterpiece, not only of how to construct a gag on *non sequiturs* and foxed expectation, but of lyrical feeling. Similarly, an astonishing 'aubade', with fifty or sixty beautiful girls in their various rooms, past which the camera roams in cross-section, hovers tantalizingly on the edge of being a Busby Berkeley dance-number without *quite* becoming one.

3. The illusion never prevails over the fact that : this is a film. When Herbert's fiancée kisses The Other Man, both their faces are conspicuously cut off by the top of the screen. Thus the frame *as such* is part of the picture. This is the opposite of *Hellzapoppin*, which was a film about inner films. This is a film about itself. This gag is completely meaningless but it feels right (the kiss is a fact too awesome to show—'off screen', like a repressed memory?).

It's all the more disappointing that since *The Ladies' Man* Jerry has been increasingly unsuccessful in avoiding the danger of sentimentality. It's paradoxical, no doubt, that one of his more moving films is the most openly sentimental, *Cinderfella*. But its story depends on Jerry constantly persuading himself that his stepmother and his ugly brothers love him, whereas they're deliberately exploiting him. Thus the film indulges sentimentality only to criticize it, at least, until the last reel. *The Patsy*, however, is potentially an extremely bitter film, with Jerry as a Hollywood nobody who's built into the double of a dead comedian, and exploited by his retinue, who despise him as much as they despise the public. But story and gags alike seem uninspired, almost as if the theme were too near Jerry's heart for him to bear to work it out with the necessary gusto-in-ruthlessness. *The Nutty Professor*, brilliantly funny in its first half, inventively develops its Jekyll-and-Hyde theme into a contradiction of Stephenson's pessimism. Creaky old hopfrog Kelp turns himself into a handsome, boorish crooner called Buddy Love (alias Dean Martin?). What he unleashes in himself is not hidden cruelty, but its opposite—self-love, and with it, he loses his crippling inhibitions. Certainly, he becomes vulgar, poised, arrogant. But he can 'liberate' other people too. In our self-critical era, this insight is perhaps as important as Stevenson's was in relation to Victorian hypocrisy. The storyline has some admirable touches. Thus, as the potion wears off, Buddy has to quit his date, as abruptly as Cinderfella. And there's a final sharp touch, whereby Stella Stevens takes some of the magic tonic off on their honeymoon, revealing that she does prefer the slick and unreal Buddy to the pathetic but real Kelp.

If the storyline flounders in the second half, it's because Jerry seems unwilling to work into it the disconcerting or disturbing aspects which the theme naturally calls forth. It's comic convention, rather than sentimentality, if Kelp is loved by the sexiest girl in the college. But the plot meanders on instead of exploring the theme. For example, Kelp might have realized that, by seducing Stella as Buddy, he's stealing her from himself (and she could say as much to him: 'I loved Kelp until you came along . . .'). Then Kelp tries various ways of competing with, or getting rid of, Love—when the problem of being reconciled to what one is becomes much sharper than it appears from Jerry's little sermon. Similarly, *The Disorderly Orderly* has a classic finale, and a rousing Sturges-like denunciation of the profit-motive in American medicine, and it has some superb fragments, but it loses sight of what might have been a strong serio-comic theme, Jerry's devotion to embittered Susan Oliver. It hints at, but hardly explores, its ironic patterns: Jerry, meaning well, persecuting her with his devotions, to which she retaliates by persecuting him with rejection, and finally driving him into berserk rage with her, and only when all his own sadism has been lengthily thought through is he liberated from his 'negative identification empathy'.

Thus Jerry's experiments with plotlessness sometimes become pretexts for sloppiness. It's not that sentimentality is in itself inimical to comedy, simply that Jerry allows it to weaken the comic tension. He even goes in for 'straight' moral homilies, a solemnity which Chaplin's Little Man allowed himself only in the very special case of *The Great Dictator*. In a way, Jerry wants to make *Limelight*—but to leave out its harshness and sadness; and the result must be sentimental. Jerry's weakness is that he wants to be loved for his lovability, Danny Kaye-style, as well as for his comedy.

Yet his failures are not failures of mediocrity, or slickness, but of inventiveness and sincerity. He is constantly trying new things—notably in *The Bellboy*, a plotless succession of shaggy dog, crazy, cartoon and off-beat gags. With Tashlin he has made crazy comedy relevant to the preoccupations of a cool, Kinsey-and-Reisman age. His emotional subtlety in slapstick rivals Chaplin's—as when in *The Disorderly Orderly* he 'tastes' Susan Oliver's kiss and finds it extremely agreeable but still lacking in Roman candle effects on his metabolism, or when he begs Alice Pearce to detail all her gruesome symptoms so as to see whether he has overcome his crippling empathy. It's when he's acting a collision between two or three violently opposed emotions that his genius—not too strong a word—can be given full rein.

If Tashlin's and Jerry's inspiration has lost its original impetus, it's possibly because this period of quick social change and crisis needs a slightly keener and more wicked sense of crisis points, or a slightly stronger dramatic sense, than either has yet adopted.

But a wicked glee inspires Clive Donner's *What's New Pussycat?*, where Peter Sellers and Peter O'Toole are on the verge of becoming a Lewis-and-Martin duo (though their *not* cohering so intensely is also part of the new, cool, attitude to human relationships). For the old monogamies—even the Flagg-and-Quirk fidelity—seem to have dissolved along with a few class-barriers, hierarchies and certainties. Amidst affluence, a new theme emerges—How To Be A Person—how to feel more than two feet tall (Sellers in *A Shot in the Dark*), how to live up to one's ideal (like Jerry Lewis), how to be the sort of girl that men love (like Shirley MacLaine in *Ask Any Girl*), how to be undaunted by the impersonality of modern life (like Judy Holliday bringing old-fashioned good neighbourliness into the communications system of *The Bells Are Ringing*), how to make stable relationships in an unstable world (*Susan Slept Here*), whether, indeed, one wants to (*What's New Pussycat?*), how to be reconciled to others (*The Ladies' Man*) or to oneself (*The Nutty Professor*). It is basically introverted, exploring and re-exploring, in its uninhibited way, the constant doubts and hesitancies of Henry James, and fears of 'inauthenticity' and of lack of real contact or being. Not that this mood is particularly existentialist; there is no philosophical questioning of commonly accepted aims of life, love or being. Yet the questions round which these comedies pivot are among those posed by Pirandello, by Freud and Reisman, and many others, and they pose them more clearly than many high culture works which seem *avant-garde* only because they're as muddled as they're hermetic.

40 · That's All, Folks

The cartoon has shown a parallel evolution.

Although Disney made many adult cartoons for the U.S. forces, it was a younger outfit, U.P.A., which had the idea of bringing a more adult wit and an appropriately sophisticated graphic style to more adult topics. First, U.P.A. brought a Steinberg-era line to the cartoon saga of *Gerald McBoing-Boing*, a youthful prodigy who, as his name implies, speaks in sound effects, and invented Mr. Magoo, a benevolent fuddy-duddy so short-sighted that he strolls through perils galore (and even gets to Mars) reinterpreting everything into utter security as he goes. *Christopher Crumpet* takes the childhood topic traditional to the cartoon but gives it an adult treatment, contriving to transcend its textbook Freudianism by inventive charm. *Mr. Fudget's Budget* is thoroughly adult in topic (a householder's money worries), while *Rooty-Toot-Toot* is an affectionate take-off of the Frankie and Johnny theme. Mr. Magoo was, perhaps, a pointed rejoinder to the McCarthy-era paranoia; but a variety of factors combined to limit his appeal. In himself he was never a very interesting person, while U.P.A.'s graphics created a world so abstract that the jokes were often theoretical, rather than actual, their timing being further confused by one's eyes roving over the images. U.P.A.'s enormous importance is, perhaps, to the history of screen graphics rather than to Hollywood comedy, and subsequent comedies produced under that label, though by a different team, including one or two features, are distinctly mechanical in conception.

Similarly Tom and Jerry's other new series, visually renovated, more sadly lacked their predecessor's verve. The TV market and its partial animation have slowed the cartoon's pace. Yet when this calmer, more verbose style accords with new personal styles the results are artistically not unhappy. The feudin' and fightin' of Tom and Jerry is hot, but, though Yogi Bear and the game-warden, or Deputy Dawg and the wild animals, still duel doggedly, the stress is less on paroxysms of destruction than on coexistence. Thus Snagglepuss the Lion, after trying to barbecue Yacky, is so struck by his complete innocence that he explains self-preservation to him—not only out of pity for his childish defencelessness, but in a desperate attempt to make the game fair, to keep his own virility alive. He pulls down a recognition chart from the wall, and points to a diagram: 'This is a duck. You are one. This is a duck hunter. If he enters stage left, you exit stage right. And vice versa.' Here, the lion and duck are both denatured, like Loopy-de-Loop, or like a character of Ionesco's. Yet the tone is less destructive, there is a kind of semi-withdrawal from the earnestness of the hunt. Everything is a *role* one *plays*, one identifies less completely with one's status, job or role. Again, a dog unwisely attempting to fly plummets down a chimney and hops yelping about on the blazing logs. The puppy bulldog within the room asks his dad, 'Is that Santa Claus?' Father bulldog says, 'No son, that's a dog,' and continues reading his paper. What's bizarre about modern life is that nothing's bizarre enough to arouse strong feelings or to disturb routine. In a routinized, alienating world, the routine or the alien are one. Boredom has repudiated, not only the romantic, but the real: only the boring is real. The mechanical has devoured the living. The soul has at last become a reticulation of habits. 'Next July we collide with Mars—well, did you ever?'

41 · Pizzicato Pussycats

The causes of this apathy are not only technological. Once, wide-spread poverty gave many lives a common dream. People might compete against each other but they were all competing for one thing. Thus the Hollywood film could postulate simple goals, of a romantic kiss, security and success. But with affluence, and more sophisticated forms of bitterness, the simple, common dream dissolves. With more leisure, and education, people can look further, and think further, and become more aware of the diversity of conflicting social, cultural, moral and spiritual groups. As separate groups become less different, and try harder to get along, the frictions become more surprising, subtler and more painful. There is a disturbing sense that one's every belief, aim and emotion is undermined by the possibilities of some other culture. While tradition-directed societies offer unanalysed, viable, obvious, attitudes and rules, which, being stable compromises between divergent goals, feel firm and secure, our more fluid society offers a variety of inconsistent, or conflicting, positions, from which every individual has painfully to find his own balance. Even the old certainties inspiring the traditionalist lashback tend to find it harder to conceal their cynicism. A sense of common purpose is lost. It's not surprising if meaning is sought more intensely than ever in the only form of personal human meaning and contact which has gained, rather than lost, cultural ground during the twentieth century: that of erotic experience.

It's under the dazzle-camouflage of crazy sophistication that the New Morality achieves, in America, its first unabashed screen manifesto. Clive Donner's *What's New Pussycat?* makes an apt pair with Tony Richardson's *The Loved One*; the one lifting fun morality to the status of a Quest, the other defying the concurrent *bourgeois* tabu-sentimentality about death. Both are American films, directed by British directors (the British, being both less sentimental and less cynical than the Americans, have a head-start in developing Anglo-Saxon morality), both were condemned by American critics for their bad taste (but not by British critics), and both were enthusiastically welcomed by the American public. In both, the crazy comedy enters its post-Christian phase.

What's New Pussycat? is Lubitsch on roller-skates. It's novel not just because it's the Kinsey Report as presented by Mack Sennett, but because it's a festive escape from the current hypochondria about being, or at least appearing to be, normal and well adjusted. Since nuttiness is inevitable we might as well all relax and enjoy it. The hunt for pleasure can be also an ebullition of the soul, at least it can be when it's as devoid of dross as the Don Juanism of Peter O'Toole, who has all but shed the egoisms, malices, competitiveness and pride which encumber and poison *la ronde*. The film says, 'Why should we bother to conceal our whims, obsessions, irresponsibilities, spats, woes and humiliations? Why not display them as brashly as peacocks, and tolerate or relish them in others? Then we can become as good-natured and obliging as we are colourful ourselves.' Accordingly, it shows us a madly maladjusted psychiatrist (Peter Sellers), makes fun of its Don Juan with less affection than it extends a loving fellow-feeling to the perpetually frustrated (Woody Allen).

The film is a *chassée-croisée* between three gentlemen and five ladies. Peter Sellers plays a psychiatrist who pursues his female patients with an invariably frustrated obsessiveness (which they scarcely criticize or resent), and wears, like a cry of longing for eternal youth, a P. J. Proby haircut over suits of red velvet. His performance, in its blend of caricature and intensity, is of the calibre of Groucho's. His amorous misadventures intertwine with the scarcely less un-successful career of Woody Allen (intellectual 'Chico' to his Groucho) and with the very successful career of the (aptly named) O'Toole, who delightedly finds a thousand excuses for not yet marrying his steady (Romy Schneider). If his comedy style isn't a great advance on Zeppo's, at least the Marxist comparison springs to mind. An almost equally predatory team of ladies is headed by Romy Schneider, who spiritedly gives the film what little it possesses in the way of normal domesticity. Capucine displays her gift for haughty-faced knockabout, as if to prove that the aloof and expensive models of *Vogue* are pleasantly equipped with feet of clay ('you, spectator, need never

243

despair'). Paula Prentiss and Ursula Andress exemplify the ready, able and willing goddesses who so pleasantly devastate Peter O'Toole. The former plays a stripper-cum-beat-poetess (a natural combination of alienated occupations) whose voice swings down from amorous wail to gutbucket tenor as wildly as she wavers between, on the one hand, nymphomania laced with frigidity and sapphism and, on the other, suicidal mania (all the sex acts she schemes become suicide attempts). The latter appears as an outdoor Amazon who goes parachuting in a cobra-skin cat-suit and remains an awe-inspiring exotic even in our unromantic times. Each character is built on a paradox (frustrated psychiatrist, exotic outdoor girl, knockabout model) as if to celebrate the dazzling transformation of being in our melting-pot culture. Whatever the film's shortcomings may be (not all the actors have the Grouchian mix of absurd and intense, nor has the script the precise resonances of *The Knack*, so that it periodically and lengthily collapses into facetiousness), its claim to a little aesthetic fame (apart from its nice visual tutti-frutti of *art nouveau*) are, notably, its combination of:

1. Neo-Marxism.

2. Spasmodicism. It is the first American adaptation of the British 'spasmodic school' (*A Hard Day's Night, The Knack, Help*). Rather charmingly, the American film was directed by an English *émigré*, and all the English films by an American *émigré*.

3. Social Atomicism. The characters' relationships have a fragmentary quality, a contemporary mixture of the cool and the superficial.

4. Molecularism, or, more precisely, 'Introverted disintegrationism'. The characters rush about hithering-and-dithering, helter-skeltering, hardly knowing their own minds for two seconds together, like corpuscles in a rainbow-coloured bloodstream. It all concludes in runaway Go-Karts—Named Desire. Its layabouts are runabouts.

5. Hyperessentialism. Its characters are conceived with what may at first seem an expressionist excess, but in fact they are conceived on the cartoon-and-comic-strip principle of the simple-but-paradoxical bunch of traits (like L'il Abner).

6. Dadaism. In its incessant pursuits it rivals the early films of René Clair (though it hasn't their melancholy and is deliberately non-precise in its gesticulations). It all but calls for two notable Clair titles: *A Nous Le Libertinisme* and *Entr'acte*. Clair's *Entr'acte* was a Dadaist film (and, some allege, actually directed by Picabia).

7. Mack Sennettism. To venture a *Private Eye*-ism, it's about the Keystone Kocks.

8. Fauvism. In the bold strokes with which it depicts fugitive, and essentially volatile, states of mind, in the characters' response to the superficial and decorative aspects of human nature, its sense of soul is fauve.

9. Bouduism. It is an irresponsible, libertarian, Priapic film.

42 · The New Frontiers

Steadily through the 50's Hollywood lost its home family audience to TV; except in the matter of violence, for teenagers and others, its innate conservatism, its habit of thinking big, or not at all, has a special difficulty in going for any of the minority audiences and in renewing itself. The response, reluctant at first, was inevitable. Hollywood movie production became a rump activity, to TV, agency or other interests; or it became cosmopolitan. The spice, the imagination, the novelty, the cynicism, the realism, which Hollywood had all but forgotten how to provide, or which the suburban American ethos would accept only if the themes carried the exoticism, the prestige, the escapism, of foreign-ness, were provided by characters, settings and talents which were wholly or partially French (Bardot), Italian (various Sophia Loren movies), Greek (*Never On Sunday*) or 'swinging London'. It's curious, too, how often Wilder (like Lubitsch before him) draws his themes from European plays transposed (notably *Some Like It Hot* and *Kiss Me Stupid*).

This isn't a matter, as some Americans urge, of American 'innocence' versus European 'corruption'. One can easily imagine a version of *Susan Slept Here*, which, rescripted *à la* Vadim–Bardot, or *à la* Vadim–Fonda, would be even truer of American realities than Tashlin's admirable piece. Or a version of *Rally Round The Flag Boys*, where the menace to property values comes not from the American army but from a gaggle of *Supremes*-style coloured girls. Or topical updatings of tenement comedy. Or regional comedies as real and critical as *Bus Stop*. Or a *Peyton Place* setting of *Here We Go Round The Mulberry Bush*. Or something which, set in a military prison, comes between *Stalag 17* and *The Brig*. What's so peculiarly tantalizing is how much better than most European movies Hollywood movies might be if they allied their own qualities with a European depth.

Stylistically, the domestic American comedy seems not far from a new merger of styles—a merger between, on the one hand, the comedy of personal grotesquerie, which could shed all its slapstick camouflage, and on the other, the critical realism of *Letter To Three Wives*. Wilder, Kramer, Blake Edwards and others have all come right up to this point; Jerry Lewis's latter-day sentimentality can be seen as another venture into the same area. Essentially, the process is one of taking those topics which have been usually relegated to the safe absurdity of comedy or farce, and handling them as critical comedy. Maybe *The Loved One* went too far too fast. None the less, it's only by turning aside from the limitations of middle-class assumptions, and by a sharper mixture of comic realism, that Hollywood could revivify its inspiration. It's certainly what it needs to tickle European palates, which need richer, less bland flavours, in movie entertainment as in food, than unvaried steak and ice-cream. And it's the clue to the international art-house circuit, which Hollywood has never understood, and which, to judge from its sour-grapes parodies in *Valley of the Dolls* and *Yours, Mine and Ours*, it misunderstands as completely as ever.

The 'new American cinema', and certain fringe productions, have sensed this, although their tentatives have suffered, artistically, and often commercially, from *either* excessive compromise with show-business formula (thus falling between two stools), or with a pre-occupation with one's 'vision' which is only the flip side of Hollywood's disdain of reality. *Goldstein* exemplifies the second trait. This intelligent, sensitive film is, alas, centred on an aged prophet-type figure who emerges from the waters to trail two young artist disciples after him, through an immense variety of American locations, from slaughterhouses to bunny clubs, all beautifully photographed, but null and void, because straightforward human interaction within, and between, its heroes, the other characters and social pressures are obliterated by the 'poetic' gloss.

Infinitely more poetic is the trajectory of another innocent picaro— Harry Langdon in *Tramp Tramp Tramp*; infinitely more touching is the battered wryness of W. C. Fields, stung by every silent sneer as by a hornet; infinitely more resilient, yet sinister, the drastically rapid way with dignity-destroying grotesqueries, of Phyllis Diller (that intriguing mixture of Zasu Pitts, Lucille Ball and Thelma Ritter . . .).

It's futile to wish away the easy, comforting, sentimental comedies

247

which must loom large in any entertainment system—and loom larger in art systems than their advocates like to admit. There's certainly an opportunity for greater boldness in a newer kind of movie. The time is ripe for Hollywood, five hundred years after Christopher Columbus, to discover America; to explore it, rather than land briefly from daydream cloudbanks.

References

ABEGG, Lily, *The Mind of East Asia*, Thames & Hudson, 1952.

AGEE, James, *Agee on Films: Vol. I, Reviews and Comments*, Beacon Press, 1964.

B., *Never On Sunday*, in *Annunciation*, Jan. 1961.

BELL, Daniel, *The End of Ideology*, The Free Press, 1960.

BENAYOUN, Robert, *Le Regard de Buster Keaton*, in *Positif*, No. 77–8, Summer 1966.

BENAYOUN, Robert, *Le Dessin Animé Depuis Walt Disney*, J. J. Pauvert, 1961.

BERGSON, Henri, *Laughter*, in SYPHER, Wylie, ed., *Comedy*, Doubleday, 1956.

BILLINGS, Josh, *Your Films*, in *Kinematograph Weekly*, 19th Feb. 1961.

BORDE, Raymond, *Chaplin Une Fois de Plus*, in *Positif*, No. 32, Feb. 1962.

BORDE, Raymond, *Le Film Retrouvé: Le Mystere Bricolo*, in *Midi-Minuit Fantastique*, No. 17, June 1967.

CANCER, *Comedy of Manners (American)*, in *Kulchur*, No. 5, Spring 1962.

COURSODON, Jean-Pierre, *La Tradition de l'Absurde et le Cinema Americain*, in *Cinema 60*, No. 49, Aug.–Sept. 1960.

COURSODON, Jean-Pierre, *Les Comiques Americains*, in *Cinema 60*, No. 50, Oct. 1960.

CUKOR, George, cited in DOMARCHI, Jean and ROHMER, Eric, *Entretien Avec George Cukor*, in *Cahiers du Cinema*, No. 115, Jan. 1961.

CUKOR, George, cited in GILLETT, John and ROBINSON, David, *Conversation with George Cukor*, in *Sight and Sound*, Autumn 1964.

DAVIDSON, Bernard, *Un Certain Monsieur Jerry . . .*, in *Cinema 60*, No. 49, Aug.–Sept. 1960.

DOMARCHI, Jean, *George Cukor*, Editions Seghers, 1965.

DURGNAT, Raymond, *Films and Feelings*, Faber & Faber, 1967.

GORER, Geoffrey, *The Americans*, Arrow Books, 1959.

GRIFFITH, Richard, in ROTHA, Paul and GRIFFITH, Richard, *The Film Till Now*, Vision Press, 1951.

HERRIMAN, George, *Krazy Kat*, cited in SELDES, Gilbert, *The Krazy Kat That Walks By Himself*, in WHITE, David Manning, and ABEL,

249

Robert H., eds., *The Funnies: An American Idiom*, Free Press of Glencoe, 1963.

HOBBES, Thomas, *Leviathan* (1651), Dent-Dutton-Everyman's Library.

JACOBS, Lewis, *The Rise of the American Film*, Harcourt Brace, 1939.

KEATON, Buster, cited in LEUWEN, Marc, *Buster Keaton*, in *Cinema 60*, No. 49, Aug.–Sept. 1960.

KEEN, Jeff, *Amazing Rayday*, No. 2, 1965.

KYROU, Ado, *L'Amour-Erotisme Au Cinema*, 2nd ed., Le Terrain Vague, 1967.

LANE, John Francis, *Money in Muscles*, in *Films and Filming*, July 1960.

LEITES, Nathan and WOLFENSTEIN, Martha, *Movies: A Psychological Study*, The Free Press, 1950.

MAYER, Arthur and GRIFFITH, Richard, *The Movies*, Bonanza Books, 1957.

MAYER, J. P., *British Cinemas and Their Audiences*, Dennis Dobson, 1948.

MCCABE, John, *Mr. Laurel and Mr. Hardy*, Doubleday, 1961.

MCLEAN, Albert F., Jnr., *American Vaudeville as Ritual*, University of Kentucky Press, 1965.

MONKHOUSE, Bob, *False Teeth*, in *Films and Filming*, Dec. 1965.

RAYNOR, Henry, *Chaplin as Pierrot*, in *Sequence*, No. 7, Spring 1949.

REIK, Theodore, *Masochism in Modern Man*, Grove Press, 1960.

REISMAN, David, GLAZER, Nathan and DENNEY, Reuel, *The Lonely Crowd*, Yale University Press, 1950.

RIPLEY, Arthur, cited in GOODMAN, Ezra F., *The 50-Year Decline and Fall of Hollywood*, MacFadden Books, 1962.

ROACH, Hal, *Living with Laughter*, in *Films and Filming*, Oct. 1964.

ROSSITER, A. P., *English Drama from Early Times to the Elizabethans*, Hutchinson's University Library, 1950.

SARRIS, Andrew, *Directorial Chronology 1915–1962*, in *Film Culture*, No. 28, Spring 1963.

SCHWOB, Marcel, *Laughter* (1890), in *Evergreen Review*, No. 13, May–June 1960.

SEATON, George, *Getting Out On A Limb*, in *Films and Filming*, April 1961.

SELDES, Gilbert, see HERRIMAN, George, op. cit.

SENNETT, Mack, cited in JACOBS, op. cit.

SICLIER, Jacques, *Le Mythe de la Femme dans le Cinema Americain*, Editions du Cerf, 1956.

STORA, Bernard, FRANCHINI, Claude and DEMUN, Philippe, in *Buster Keaton Est de Retour*, in *Contre-Champ*, No. 3, May 1962.

TAYLOR, Deems, PETERSON, Marcelene and HALE, Bryant, *A Pictorial History of the Movies*, Simon & Schuster, 1949.

TYNAN, Ken, in *The Observer*, 1967.

VEDRES, Nicole, *Images du Cinema Francais*, Les Editions du Chene, 1945.

VERDONE, Mario, *Ernst Lubitsch*, Premier Plan No. 32, 1965.

Some Further Reading

For various obvious reasons this bibliography can offer only a few entries into the labyrinth of relevant movie criticism. But these additional recommendations may well be useful to those who have enjoyed this book, but for their further details, diverse approaches and contradictions. Of theories of humour, the nearest to this is Ralph Piddington, *The Psychology of Laughter*, Figurehead, 1933.

On American comedy generally, useful guides and surveys include Jacques Chavellier's *Le Cinema Burlesque Americain Au Temps du Muet* (Institut Pedagogique National, 1965); two special issues of *Cinema 60*, Nos. 49 and 50; an article by Ado Kyrou, with the comprehensive title of *Slapstick, Burlesque, Goona-Goona, Non-Sense and Crazy-Show* in *Positif* 32, and a *Positif* Special Issue on *Le Rire* (Nos. 77–8). Francois Mars's *Le Gag* (Editions du Cerf) is also interesting.

Mack Sennett's *King of Comedy* was published by Peter Davies in 1965, and Hal Roach gave a brief but useful interview to *Films and Filming* in October 1964.

Probably the most analytical of the various long studies of Chaplin are Jean Mitry's *Charlot et la Fabulation Chaplinesque* (Editions Universitaires 1955) and Premier Plan's No. 28 (1965). Chaplin's autobiography is essential, while Peter Cotes's *The Little Fellow* and Robert Payne's *The Great Charlie* are well worth consulting, as is an evocative article by Douglas McVay in *Films and Filming*, November 1964.

The current cascade of Keaton volumes could fill a bookshelf; we have had Rudi Blesh's *Keaton* (Secker, 1967), J. P. Lebel's *Buster Keaton* (Zwemmer-Barnes, 1967), *Premier Plan* No. 31, and a hommage and dossier in *Cinema 66*, Nos. 104 and 105. Keaton's *My Wonderful World of Slapstick*, with Charles Samuels, is an obvious

251

reference, and there is a challenging comparison between Keaton and Chaplin in *Cinema 62*, No. 69. Lorca's Buster Keaton play is usefully reprinted in *Sight and Sound*, Winter 1965.

William Cahn's *Harold Lloyd's World of Comedy* (Allen & Unwin) is invaluable for Lloyd's own comments; there is a good interview with Lloyd also in *Films and Filming*, January 1964. *Cinema 68* featured a valuable three-part dossier on Harold Lloyd's films, by Roland Lacombe (Nos. 124–6).

Perhaps the first recent reassertion of Laurel and Hardy as major figures was by Peter Barnes in an article entitled 'Cuckoo' in *Films and Filming*, August 1960. Since then they have been the subject of three excellent critical studies: *Premier Plan* No. 38, a volume by J. P. Coursodon in the Seghers series, and now Charles Barr's Movie paperback (1967). I'm also grateful to Charles Barr for pointing out three errors in the magazine draft of this section—my only regret is that he doesn't seem to enjoy *Saps at Sea* as much as I do!

The French Surrealists were almost the only critics to vividly recall Harry Langdon throughout the 40's and 50's, and it's worth referring, not only to the Kyrou book cited in the references, but to Jean-George Auriol's article in *La Revue du Cinema*, April 1930. This magazine's writing, if poetic rather than analytical, is astonishingly vivid and modern, and well worth consulting on all comedies, or indeed, films, up to and including its period (as also are the post-war series directly preceding *Cahiers*).

Some sort of glimpse into the obscure field of American cartoons is provided by Ralph Stephenson's *Animation in the Cinema* (Zwemmer-Barnes) and in the special issue on Animation in *Cinema 57*. There are also some useful data in J. L. Gasca's *Los Comics En La Pantalla* (Festival Internacional Del Cine de San Sebastian, Seccion de Activi-dades Culturales, 1965).

A useful summary of Clara Bow's career is given in *Films in Review*, October 1963. This magazine is exceptionally useful on Hollywood history, although its opinions are summary, politically outside-right, and culturally Legion-of-Decencyish. Lewis Jacobs's biblio-graphy is valuably extensive, and it's a great pity that this and the Mayer-Griffith volume haven't become standard over here, instead of the very partial line laid down by the documentarists (who were bonny fighters, but narrow), or by the *Sequence* line (which began so promisingly but so sadly ossified so soon).

The general climate of cosy comedy is well evoked in Ray Hagen's

The Day of the Runaway Heiress in *Films and Filming* (April 1966), while the same magazine printed usefully detailed studies of *Ninotchka* and *The Philadelphia Story*, by John Cutts, in March and July 1962.

Mae West's autobiography, *Goodness Had Nothing To Do With It* (Prentice-Hall, 1959), is highly agreeable; Kyrou summarizes her career usefully and the invaluable second issue of *L'Ecran* (1958) includes Jean Boullet's *Je Vous Salue, Mae West, Plein de Diams*. The fullest references for W. C. Fields are in Robert Lewis Taylor's *W. C. Fields; His Follies and Fortunes*, wittily reviewed by Ken Tynan in his *Curtains!* (Longmans, 1961). Robert Benayoun is excellent on *Le Dernier Excentrique* in *Cinema 60* No. 42 and the Citadel Press issued a large illustrated book, *The Films of W. C. Fields*, in 1966. Those with any interest in *avant-garde* literature will thoroughly enjoy A. Hansen's *Incomplete Requiem for W. C. Fields* (Great Bear Pamphlets, 1966).

The Marx Brothers have been the subject of several autobiographies, notably Groucho's *Groucho and Me* (Gollancz, 1959) and Harpo's *Harpo Speaks!* (with Rowland Barber, Random House, 1961). Longer critical studies include Allen Eyles's *The Marx Brothers; Their World of Comedy* (Zwemmer-Barnes), while the German translation of the relevant chapters here are amplified by further critical biographical material in the present writer's brochure for the Austrian Film Museum at Vienna.

An influential piece was Richard Rowland's *American Classic; The Marx Brothers*, which appeared in *Hollywood Quarterly* and then in *Penguin Film Review* No. 7 (1948).

Walt Disney has been the subject of several heavy, and heavily adulatory, volumes. *Sequence* is mildly critical in its tenth issue (1950) but the first trenchant attack is by Robert Benayoun in *Citizen Walt, ou le Dernier Tycoon* (*Positif* 34, 1960). André Martin is entertaining on his affectionate disappointment on briefly meeting *Betty Boop Disparue* in the second issue of *L'Ecran*, now, alas, equally 'disparu'. A defence of Frank Capra's sentimentality, in terms which interestingly criss-cross with the criticisms made here, is persuasively put forth by William S. Pechter in an article entitled *American Madness* in *Kulchur* No. 12 (1963).

Preston Sturges's films appeared during the 40's, when the war cut criticism down to pithy brevities of which Richard Winnington was the master. Few comedians of the 40's have had much criticism in depth, and usually under the Tashlin heading. The chapter on *To Be*

Or Not To Be in Gilles Jacobs's *Le Cinema Moderne* (Serdoc, 1964) is entertaining to compare with the account given here, for the piquant and slightly comical contradictions within a generally similar approach.

On Tex Avery, and the post-Disney cartoons generally, almost the only exegeses are by the 'Positifists', especially in Nos. 12 (1954), 18 (1966), 21 (1957), 54–5 (1963) and 57 (1963). Ken Tynan wrote a vivid short piece in *Sight and Sound*, *circa* 1951, before its iron curtain came down. David Rider's Animation Column in *Films and Filming* is indispensable, particularly the pieces on Warner Brothers cartoons (March 1963), M.G.M. (July 1963), Walter Lantz (July 1965) and on Hollywood's unhappy attempts at revamping (May 1966).

Billy Wilder is fascinating in an interview published in the Autumn 1967 issue of *Sight and Sound*. *Positif* devoted its twenty-ninth issue to Frank Tashlin (in 1958), and the next long study was by Ian Cameron in *Oxford Opinion* No. 39 in 1960. *Premier Plan* No. 36 was devoted to Jerry Lewis on whom there are good articles, in No. 29 again, by Robert Benayoun, and by André S. Labarthe in *Cahiers du Cinema* No. 132, June 1962. The script of *The Nutty Professor* was published in the *Avant-Scene* (*Cinema*) series in 1965.

The present writer is restricted to English and French, but there is a great deal of imposing-looking material in German, Italian and Swedish magazines, which might well reward inspection by those linguistically qualified.

Index

2. Film Names

Note: This list does not include names listed only in the Filmography

S

3. General References

Note: This list excludes the *Some Further Reading* chapter

DATE D